Aiki Secrets

Six Precepts and the Dynamic COB

William Dockery

aikisecrets.com

ISBN: 0615479987
ISBN-13: 9780615479989
LCCN: 2011906356

Note to the Reader

The information in this book is distributed without warranty and is only presented as a means of preserving a unique aspect of the heritage of the martial arts. All information and techniques are to be used at the reader's sole discretion. While every precaution has been taken in preparation of this book, neither the author nor publisher shall have any liability to any person or entity with respect to liability, loss, or damage caused or alleged to be caused directly or indirectly by the contents contained in this book or by the procedures or processes described herein. There is no guarantee that the techniques described or shown in this book will be safe or effective in any self-defense or medical situation, or otherwise. The activities, physical and otherwise, may be too strenuous or dangerous for some people. You may be injured if you apply or train in the techniques described in this book. Consult a physician regarding whether or not to attempt any technique described in this book. We therefore suggest you use restraint when practicing all techniques contained within this book, and practice only under the supervision of a qualified instructor. Specific self-defense responses illustrated in this book may not be justified in any particular situation in view of all the circumstances or under the applicable federal, state, or local laws.

Dedicated to the four angels that let Daddy go play with his friends

Spiral out

Contents

Preface

This is not your typical book about Aiki.

It was written by an intermediate level student for other intermediate students.

What started out as notes eventually grew into a dictionary, then into curriculum, and it continues to snowball.

I tried to keep the original notes intact, but there were sections that were simply too "raw." The rough sections received an update, but the most necessary change was to reorder the content. I did not learn the Precepts in order, and the notes were all over the place.

At its core, this book is a study of the body in motion. It is a layman's view of kinesiology applied to Aikido. Expect to find the "mechanics" of Aiki (in lieu of "principles").

Do not expect that this book will make you into another Ueshiba, but do look forward to making it to black belt much faster than simply following "do as I do" instruction.

For all of the content that went into this book, there is at least twice as much that did not make it. It was taking too long and I had to draw the line.

Lastly, good luck as you apply an understanding of the COB to Aikido or whichever sport, dance, or martial arts practice you enjoy.

WHY WRITE THIS BOOK?

Moe Stevens and Chris Parkerson make a chance contact and a once-in-a-lifetime event happens. Over eighty years of experience in martial arts, competitive sports, and coaching comes together in the atmosphere of seeking a deeper awareness of what they already know to be true. What happens next changes everything for me.

This is my journal, of sorts. I have been the benefactor of over four years of Moe and Chris's collaboration. I have played fly-on-the-wall and fly-through-the-air as two giants have, in complete openness and without ego, lectured, questioned, and collaborated.

On the surface, they do not appear to be doing anything differently, but the contrast of the subtle aspects of their skills gave rise to a depth of perception.

I am going to share the little I can perceive. I will do my best to explain with words that which is almost always transmitted by action. My primary hope is that something recorded makes sense to an up-and-coming martial artist such as me. Sometimes it is easier to relate to a peer than an expert. Maybe a few of the experts will use this to remember what it was like to be on the verge of achieving Shodan. My secondary goal is to simply log what is unquestionably the most rapid growth I have made in my martial arts training, lest I ever forget how I made it to where I am going.

I am sure I will be reading this book five years from now and laughing at my lack of understanding. I started this effort in late 2008 and finished at the end of 2010.

Credits first.

Moe, Chris, three "thank you"s.

Thank you for taking the time to entertain the questions that may have slowed down your progress. I can never repay the debt. I hope my role as

Uke with the ability to say, "It did not quite feel the same way when you threw me," in some small way returned part of the favor. You definitely put up with a good many "Do you mean?" questions and seemed to make sense of my grunts, groans, and charades when I simply did not have the words.

Thank you especially for not breaking me in two. It is a testament to your mastery of your respective arts and to the control of your ego that I have come through this with absolutely no injury.

Thank you, it has been fun!

Thank you, Sensei Steve Carlisle. More than any other person, you have taught me how to find the "bunkai," on and off the mat.

A special thank you to Joel, Shawn, and Dave. Glad to have you to talk to on our level.

Thank you to TAA and JAA. Everyone in the organization has in one way or another contributed to my training and love of Tomiki Aikido. See you at the next seminar! (Visit www.Tomiki.org.)

Thank you, George Ledyard. I have attended only one weekend seminar, but I have spent hundreds of hours with your videos. Thank you for revealing so much about this art and for proving that it can be lectured, not just demonstrated.

SOMETHING TO REMEMBER ABOUT THE AUTHOR

I will never forget:

I asked Sensei Carlisle (my first Aikido teacher), "When do I attack Uke?" (Uke = Aikido Training Partner)

Steve replied, "When he stops moving."

I stared at Sensei for a second. I tilted my head inquisitively and objected, "But Uke never stops moving and most times, neither do I!"

Sensei replied, "Motion and stillness are relative. I am here to show you how to make Uke stop."

What I am about to reveal is part of my journey toward understanding that basic concept from which all the striking martial arts emerge. Please keep this in mind as you read. It should answer why I have said something or at least why I feel it was valuable.

HOW TO READ THIS BOOK

This book contains three sections:
- Basic Terms
- The Six Precepts
- The Secret to Aiki

In the Basic Terms, we will discuss some of the language we use in class. These definitions are a first brush with the Precepts. This section will introduce a good many of the basic concepts that create the Precepts. Do not get stuck on lack of detail just yet. You will find explanation in the Basic Terms section that is not presented in the Six Precepts section, but may discover the definitions becoming much clearer as you read through the Precepts.

The Six Precepts are the six primary elements you will find used in almost every technique. A "precept" is an underlying protocol. The Precepts are not themselves techniques, they are a set of rules that improve the technique. We use these six precepts to quickly find the flaws in the execution of a technique, and most importantly, to reverse engineer the movements of others we wish to emulate.

The final section details the secret to Aiki. You could skip to this section first, but it is a real "chicken and egg" scenario. The explanation of the Precepts makes this secret usable, but the precepts are not as illuminating without knowing the secret. You will likely find it difficult to use the secret to Aiki without reading the Precepts. Take your time and absorb it all.

Unless noted, expect that all the techniques mentioned are a reference to the Juu Nana Hon Kata (Tomiki's core seventeen techniques kata). I will use both the number and name of the technique. This would be a good time to warm up your browser if you are not already familiar with the Juu Nana Hon Kata.

Basic Terms

We are going to need a few terms that mean a lot more than just one word, and even a few more that might mean something else to you already and we cannot have that gap between us.

You do not need to agree with me on the definitions, but you do need to know what they mean to me.

In the interest of getting in synch, let us begin creating precision in words.

UKE AND TORI

For the uninitiated, Aikido practice typically involves two persons, each playing one of two roles: Uke and Tori. Uke attacks Tori and Tori (sometimes referred to as Nage) uses Aiki to nullify the attack. When done correctly, this usually results in Uke taking a fall (the art of falling is called Ukemi)

SINGLE- AND DOUBLE-WEIGHTED

Single-weighted, as used in our dojo, is defined as having all, or nearly all, of your weight supported on one leg. Single-weighted is most commonly used in a cat stance. Double-weighted describes having the weight distributed near evenly between the feet. A horse stance is typically a double-weighted stance.

NO-LINE, TRIANGLE, AND THE 20

What is it?

The no-line refers to the line of no resistance in a stance. In a classic horse stance (hips square, double-weighted), the no-line exists parallel to and in between the feet.

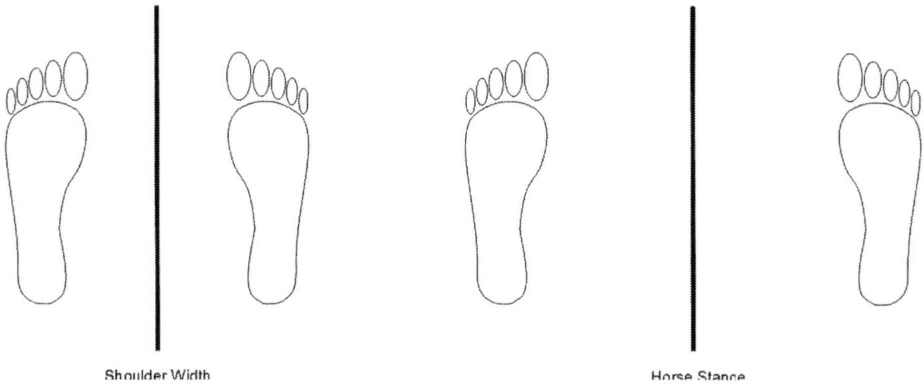

The no-line in respect to the feet in a shoulder's width and horse stance

The Triangle is an overlay we use to help describe the no-line and the 20. The base of the triangle is formed between the feet. The top of the triangle terminates along the no-line at about the distance of the Obi to the floor. (A 6'-tall person would find this point existing roughly three feet out from the body.) This triangle is formed both forward and backward. Combined, they form a diamond.

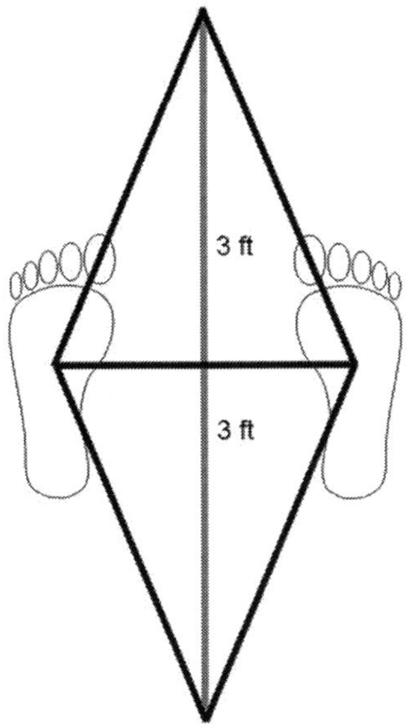

Triangle w/No-Line Shoulder Width Stance

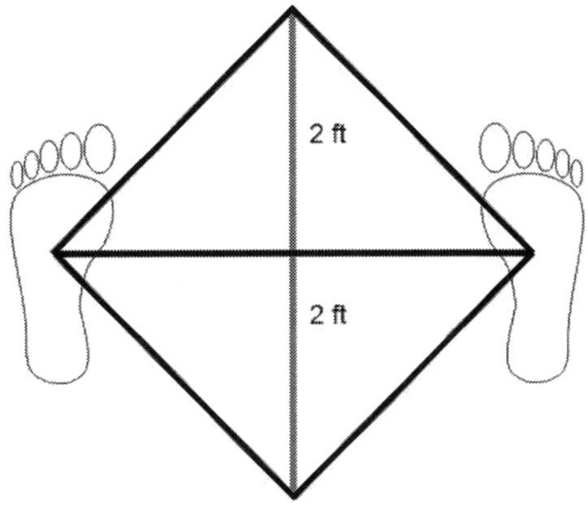

Triangle w/No-Line
Horse Stance

The triangle in respect to the shoulder's width and horse stance

What is special about the no-line and Triangle?

The no-line presents an opportunity to apply force in the direction Uke is least capable of resisting. By drawing out Uke's strength along the no-line at the distance of his triangle point, Uke must step or put all of his attention toward maintaining balance.

Try it! Get into a horse stance and try touching the triangle point without going into a squat position. If you can do it, your arm is probably a bit longer than the norm. In any case, I will bet you could not reach the top of the triangle without significantly lowering your posture and fighting a serious urge to step. Most of us had to step.

There is more.

Here is the tricky part: the triangle point moves as you step.

The no-line is no longer perpendicular to the line drawn between the feet when one foot is in front of the other (double-weighted, not in cat-stance).

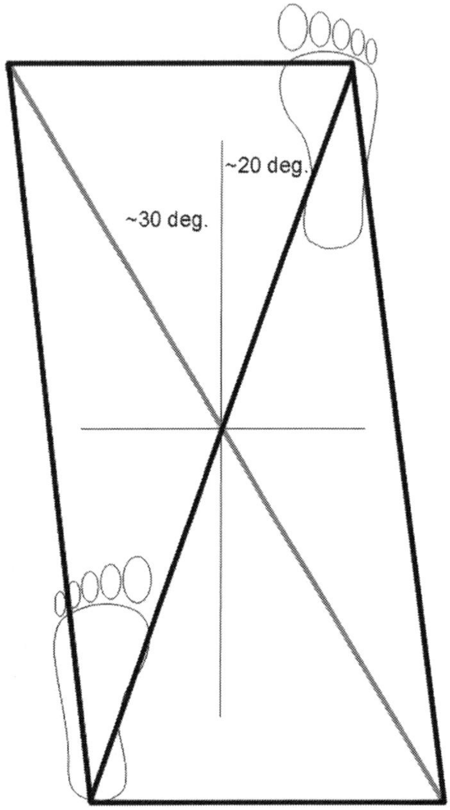

Triangle (with no-line); shoulder-width stance; one foot in front of the other

Note that the no-line is not 45 degrees off of the center line.

You probably noticed the line between the feet shifts to 20 degrees off center. (It is a true perpendicular line in the horse stance.) We call this the "20 line" or simply the "20." It takes a bit more finesse to use compared to the no-line, but offers the other weak angle in the stance. This will become more important further on in this document. Just recognize it is there and start sensing them both. It will not become important until we combine the no-line and 20 to form circles.

One quick word on the distance of the triangle point. What I have detailed is simply a suggestion for learning basic ma-ai in a static motion technique. Adding joint locks and/or momentum can change the distance required to draw out Uke's strength and effect similar neutralization. The important part of the concept is to consistently move Uke along the no-line and 20 path.

CENTRIPETAL ARM

At its heart, centripetal arm is not much more than dropping your arms in a cutting motion.

Hold your arms straight out in any direction. Now let them fall. Where did your hands land? Your hands should have landed somewhere near the top of your thighs, either on your lap, where you keep your six shooters, or somewhere in between. I typically teach this by asking the student to touch their pocket. Specifically, not at the top of the pocket, but at the patch of fabric that sometimes shows through your slacks if your pants are tight.

Someone observing you saw one of two results. If you were standing in place as you dropped your arms, they witnessed your hands traveling in arc. If you rotated as you dropped your hands, your hands followed the path of an inclined plane (just like the threads of a screw).

The centripetal arm is an unbendable arm. It pushes Uke. You should not feel your bicep flex. That would be a pull. The mistake of pulling is most commonly expressed by pulling back the elbow as if practicing a karate punch. Pulling back the elbow can be a tough habit to break.

The secret of centripetal arm is that the hand must drop toward the center of balance (COB). That statement should be revisited after you feel you understand what the COB is.

FORWARD AND REVERSE CAM

I have often found myself pushing as hard as I can into what would seem like the obvious weak point in Uke's structure, only to find I had little to no power. After a decade of hit or miss and bouncing off my opponent, I finally understand why.

The forward and backward cams are the terms that describe the position of the hips.

There are three positions for your hips. The first, the forward cam, looks like you are doing a crunch. Your butt is tucked in and pubic region is pulled up. Make certain you can feel the bottom most part of your buttock flex as you attempt the forward cam. Forward cam has also been described as pulling your belly button up toward your sternum. The backward cam is the exact opposite. Your butt and belly are out (e.g., let your belly button down). The third position is neutral, neither forward nor back.

Pretty simple, huh? It is, once you are made aware.

Ever heard, "focus on your obi," "move from your center," or "it's all in the hips"? It would have saved a bunch of time if the same founts of wisdom included a small explanation of the forward and reverse cam. Let us look at the cam a bit deeper in this next definition: front-wheel drive and the cam.

FRONT-WHEEL DRIVE AND THE CAM

There is a big difference in power between sourcing the momentum of your step with your back leg and when you are "pulling" yourself across the floor with the forward positioned leg. Just what does that mean?

The front-wheel drive step is much more difficult to interrupt. It permits Tori to get below Uke's center of balance and uproot him. In effect, front-wheel drive allows Tori to work with gravity to generate momentum. With gravity on your side, you maximize the effect of your mass in motion and remain grounded.

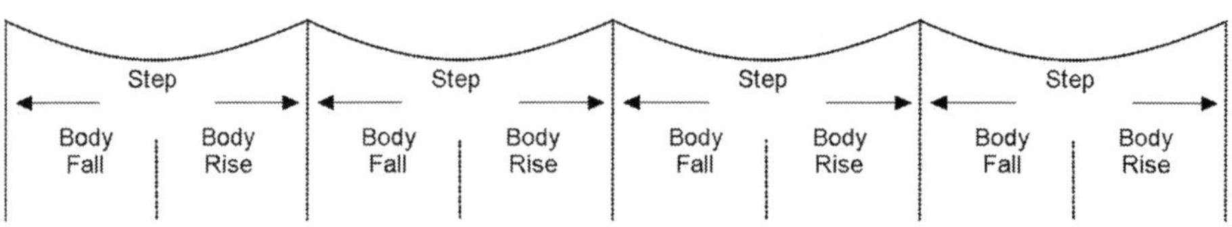

Front-wheel driven step: Center of balance falls first before it swings upward

Rear-wheel drive forces you to "jump" into your next step. At the apex, you are effectively weightless and uprooted. Even a novice has a considerable chance to resist the attack.

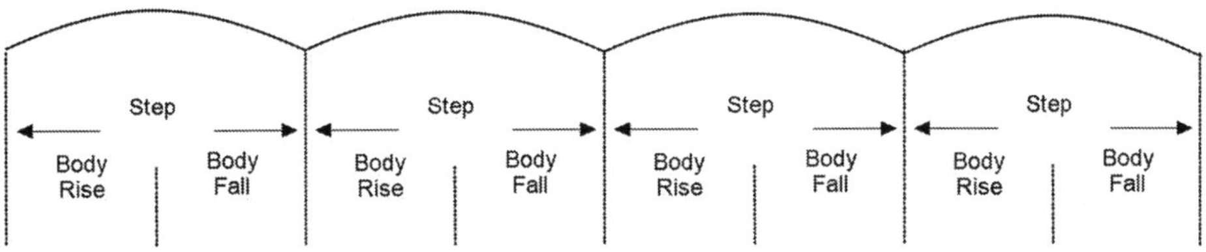

Rear-wheel driven step: Center of balance rises before it jumps forward

Front-wheel drive made much more sense when I started relating this to the many descriptions I had read related to tai chi stepping. In my limited perception, it seemed that, one of my legs was supposed to jut outward simply by weighting the other. Then came the painfully slow transfer of weight from one leg to the next. I was always off balance, and never felt in control. What was missing? Answer: awareness and application of the cam.

Give this a try. Get into a double-weighted stance. Relax. Now sink your weight into your left leg. Feel the weight in your left foot somewhere toward the ball of the foot, bend your left knee a short bit, and forward cam. That little roll of your hips will strengthen your stance and, lo and behold, your right leg should feel the need to jut outward. Voila, you have just learned the appropriate way to get into a cat stance.

Now, grab the floor with the right foot. Your hips will drop toward the floor as your weight transfers toward your right foot. Maintain the cam the whole way. Now you are working with gravity vs. fighting it. At the very end you will be pushing upward with the right foot, and the left side of your body should almost involuntarily catch up with your right side. If so desired, you can let your hips move to neutral or keep the cam and step again.

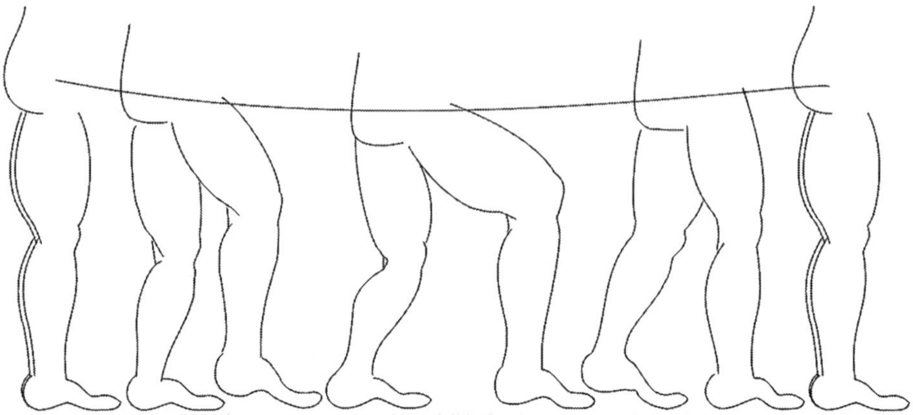

Using front-wheel drive, hips drop and then rise as a step is made

The important part is to maintain the cam the whole measure of the step. You will compromise your effectiveness if you shift to a neutral hip position in mid-step.

Why was that so amazing? Try keeping your hips in neutral, or for even greater contrast, try using the reverse cam (stick your butt out) and make that step. You should have a significantly clear understanding of just how dramatically the position of your hips affects your stability.

Additional help: Try replacing the conscious thought of shifting weight from one leg to the other with focusing upon doing a constant cam in the direction you want to go. You should find that your legs will move on their own. In the example above, your right leg will catch your weight and the left leg will eventually catch up with the rest of you. You will also gain the benefit of constantly applying your weight on your opponent. You will be "moving from your center." Let us explore the concept of the center.

THE SAGITTAL PLANE; THE FIRST BELT HOOP

Before you read this short definition, suspend your disbelief for a moment and pretend that center of balance is the same thing as center of mass. Are you fully in suspension? Okay, read on.

Where do you think of when asked, "Where is your center?" Did a spot a few inches below and just behind your belly button come to mind?

Energetically and in a horse stance, you would be correct. I cannot say much more about the energy aspects of your center, but as far as your center of balance, I know it moves. In order to move, for a period of time you are going to have more weight on one foot than the other (this also applies to when you get in a cat stance, or when you kick, throw a ball, etc.), the center of balance is not in the middle any longer. So where does it go?

Balance a straight piece of pipe on your finger. The weight is equal throughout the structure. Your finger is in the middle of the pipe. Now try balancing a baseball bat. See the difference? Your finger will be somewhere on the tapering, nearest the thick part of the bat. This same thing happens as you put the weight on one side of your body. Your center of balance shifts toward the "heavy" side. Just how far does it shift? Not too far, about the width of your palm. If you are wearing jeans, you will find it located near the first belt hoop.

The sagittal plane describes a plane that divides your body into left and right. In a double-weighted condition (horse stance), your center of balance is just under your belly button and both sides of your body are equal. When you move to the cat stance, your center of balance and that line dividing your body shifts to that "first belt hoop." In class, we like to (admittedly improperly) infer that the sagittal plane drifts to the first belt hoop. When in a cat stance, the sagittal plane spans from the arch of the weighted foot, inside the knee, up to your first belt hoop, just inside your nipple, and up to your ear.

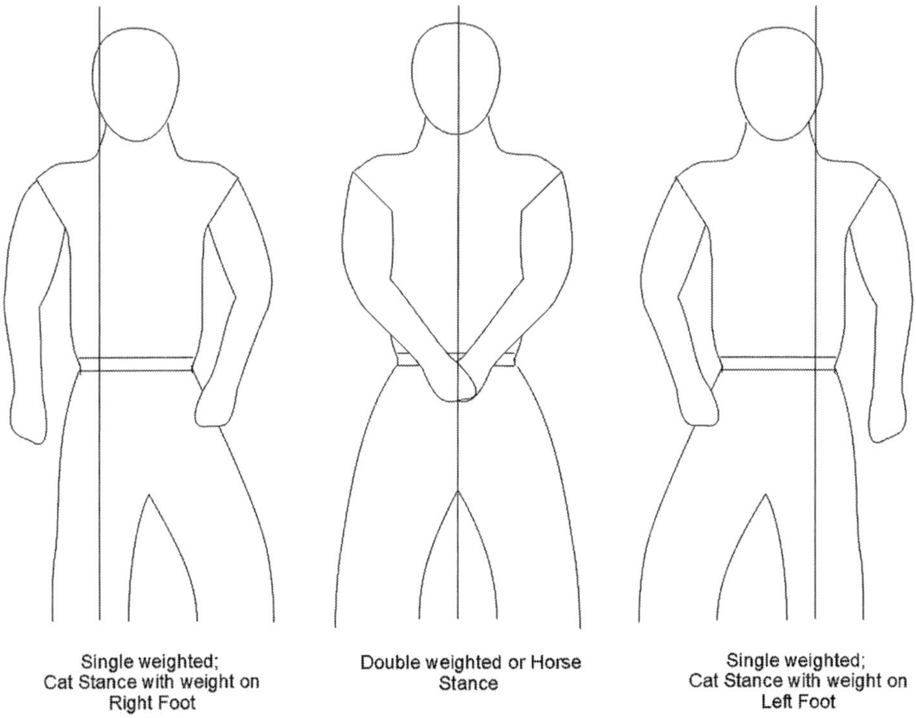

Sagittal plane position within Uke's body (Uke facing us)

If the sagittal plane moves, it also makes sense to investigate the coronal plane (the one that divides you into front and back). I am no expert, but more times than not, I find that keeping the weight on the balls of the feet works best in most situations. With the weight on the balls of the feet, I sense the weight moving toward the front of the body. Combine that with the lateral movement of the sagittal plane, and you get the first belt hoop. Your center of balance is almost on the surface on the front of your body.

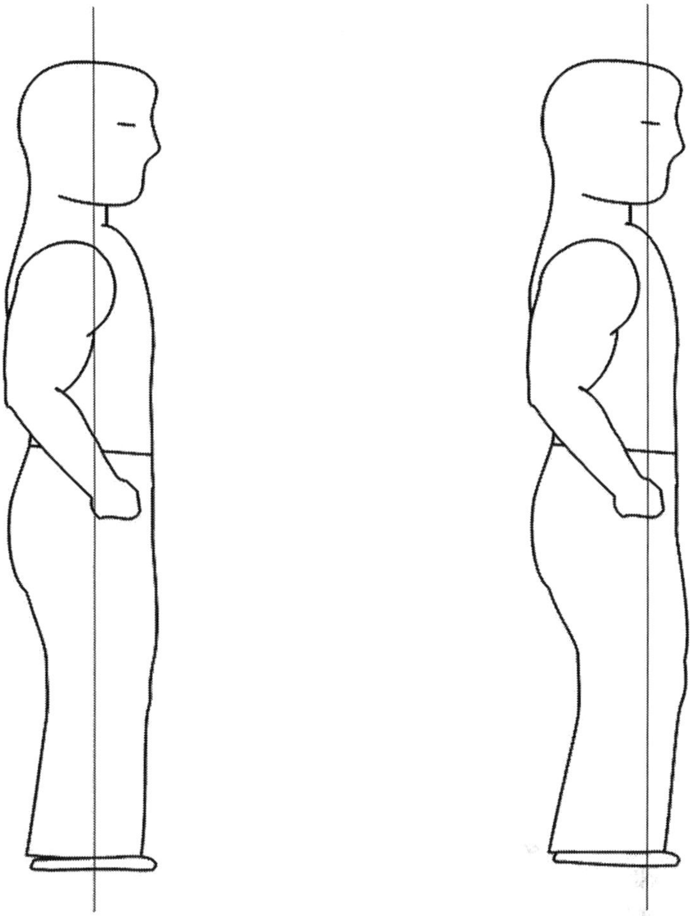

Coronal plane shifts as weight moves from the center toward the balls of the feet

I have heard Aikido described as drawing Uke into your center of balance and control. I feel very liberated to know where that center is.

It also pays to understand that it is difficult to generate strength in your hands when they cross the sagittal plane. Experiment for yourself. Get in a right-foot-weighted cat stance. How much power is in your right hand when it crosses past the newly settled sagittal plane? Your left hand should feel much sturdier all the way across your true mid-line.

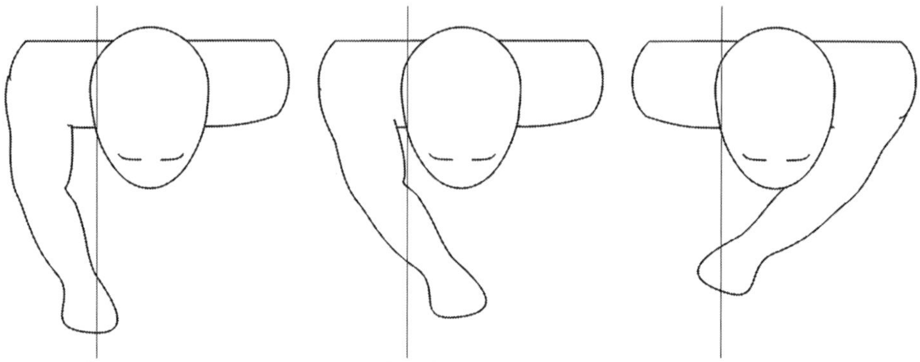

Where the hands are strongest in a right-foot-weighted stance

CENTER OF BALANCE INTO LEVERS AND HINGES

Awareness of how your center of balance moves within your body is a key element of understanding a hip-wheel turn and how the hip-wheel turn applies pressure.

Start with the weight on the left leg (post left). The center of balance moves across the body as you turn and shift weight to the right leg.

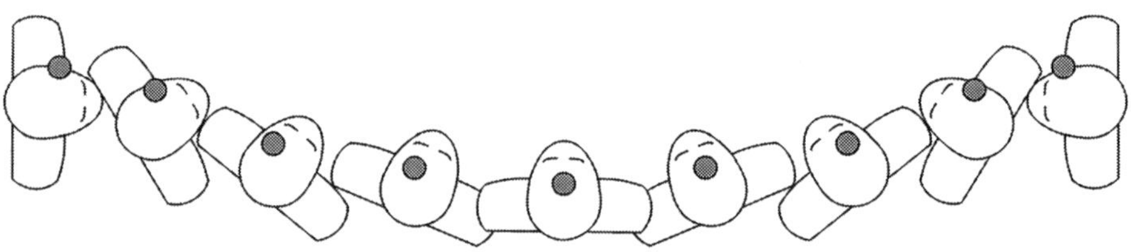

The path of your center of balance (gray dot) during a hip-wheel turn

Think of the hip-wheel turn as an opportunity to place one side of your body behind Uke's mass and move him (with mechanical advantage of a lever).

The first belt hoop (the position of your center of balance in a single-weighted stance) divides your body into a short and long side.

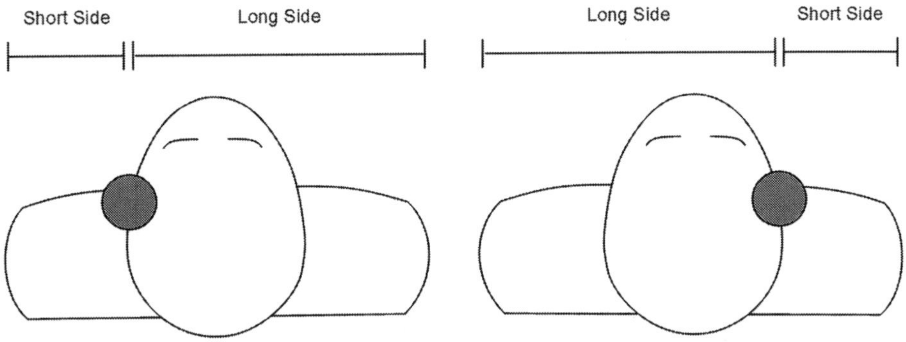

Left-weighted "post left," left side long, right side short
Right-weighted "post right," left side long, right side short

Your first belt hoop (aka sagittal plane, center of balance) acts like a fulcrum between the "short" and "long" side of your body. Torque is created by one side of the body chasing the other around the axis of your first belt hoop. Your body is behaving like a first-class lever (e.g., a crowbar).

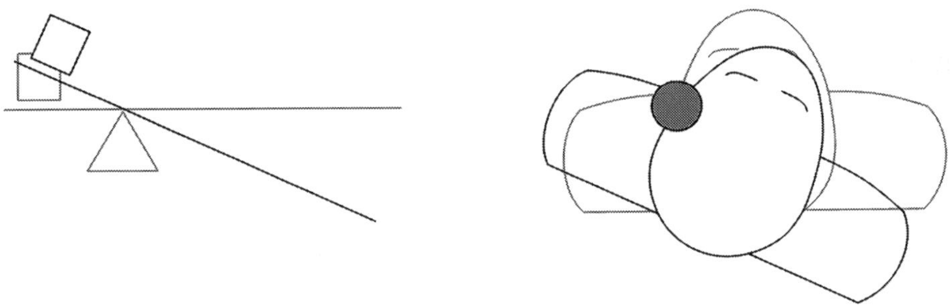

Your body as a lever

What happens when the fulcrum is on the end of the lever? You get a hinge!

Tori creates a hinge when he puts his focus on the outside of the hip instead of his first belt hoop and spins. It looks like a "bump and run" maneuver similar to when a football running back hits a would-be tackler and spins. We have all done it, and Uke stands there smiling. Do not be a hinge!

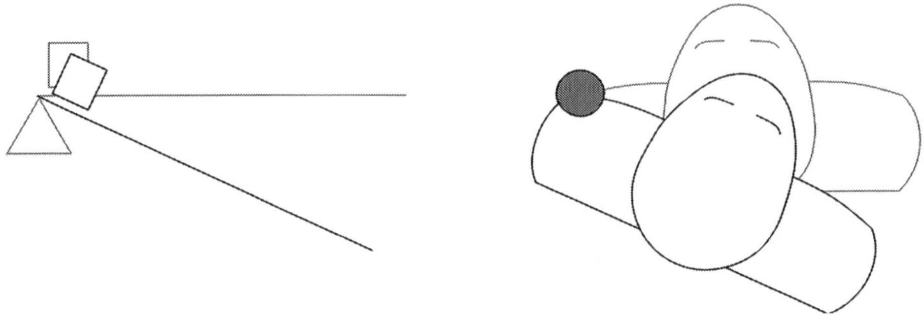

Your body as a hinge

A hinge is a class 2 lever and, for the purposes of most Aiki practice, not nearly as effective at moving our intended objects. It is the difference between using a wheel-barrow (class 2 lever, COB on point of the shoulder) and a crowbar (class 1 lever, COB on your first belt hoop).

SPINDLES AND GIMBALS

When creating rotational energy, your body behaves much like the spool of a fishing reel. In a manner of speaking, you wrap Uke around yourself.

Additionally, you accelerate Uke's body by making him orbit around your center. You get to move a short distance (in this case, "move" means rotate"), and Uke moves a lot further to keep up.

The spindle is an upright cylindrical concept. If I have learned anything from Moe, it is that Aikido is a vertical art. We began to use the term "gimbal" to describe angling the axis of the spindle so that it influences a drop or rise as Uke orbits. Include the concept of centripetal arms, and you begin to realize how rotational energy is vastly different than linear.

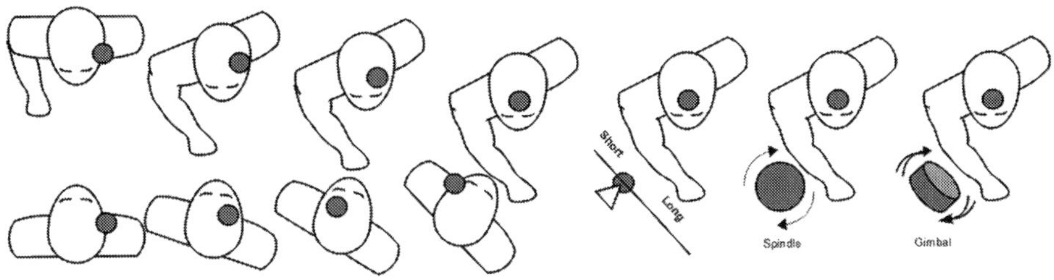

Spindles, gimbals, and the center of balance

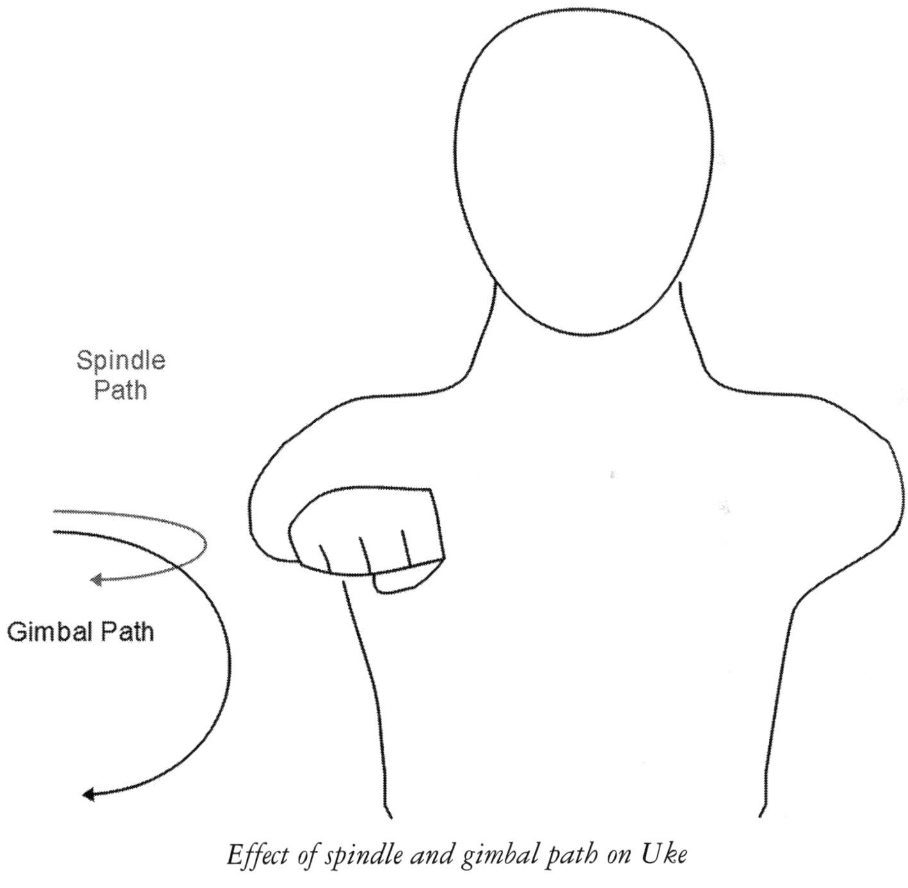

Effect of spindle and gimbal path on Uke

SWORD CUT AND DEAD BLOW HAMMER

First another disclaimer, I want to reiterate that I am not an expert. Dave is our resident sword expert, and he has revealed to us many different types of sword cuts. We have worked with more than a few styles and have concentrated the most on the one I am about to describe. We feel it has the most application toward Aiki (and is the one that Chris uses almost exclusively). For now, let us call it the "sword cut," even though we all know that there are many other perspectives on how to move a sword.

The sword cut and the dead-blow hammer describe how to meet force and how to generate additional momentum.

The sword cut begins with the sword elevated above the head. In lieu of simply dropping the arms, the hips are lowered by bending the knees. Dropping the hips draws the arms downward. Shoulders relax as the arms fall (centripetally), the butt of the sword reaches the same height as the bottom of the sternum. At that point, the tip of the sword is allowed to begin arcing outward. At the same instant you allow the tip of the sword to arc, you begin to rise up by straightening the legs. This action creates a lever with the pivot in your right hand, left hand and body on one side, and the length of the sword on the other. The "body rise" enhances the momentum of the sword arc. (We call this body rise "ratcheting up.")

It might help to imagine that the left hand is on the short side of the sword and the body rise is driving the momentum behind the short side of the lever. (See the "levers and hinges" section.) I sometimes describe it as lifting up on one side of a teeter-totter.

I am becoming aware of multiple endings to the sword cut, but this is the one I am most cognizant of at this time. The sword arcs until the desired height is reached. The body rise stops and a second, slighter body drop (cam) directs your entire mass behind the sword for a Tsuki attack.

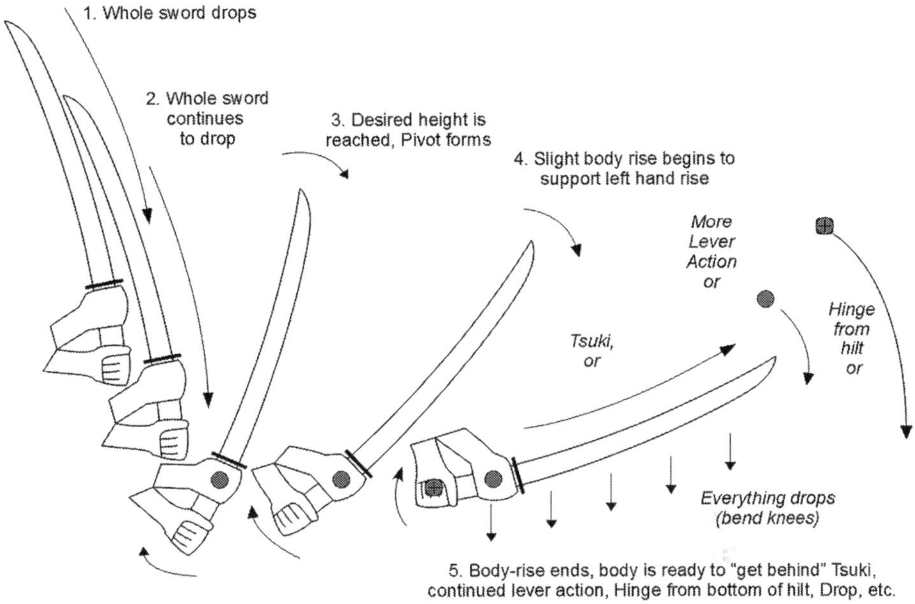

My understanding of the sword cut

The dead-blow hammer has a hollow head filled with heavy slug that freely floats to either side of the head. The handle attaches in the middle. It looks like a sledge hammer.

The hammer is raised, and the weight is in neutral. As the hammer is dropped, the weighted slug slides to the back of the hammer. At the point that the hammer hits the nail, the head stops, but the slug keeps moving toward the front until it adds an additional hit to the nail.

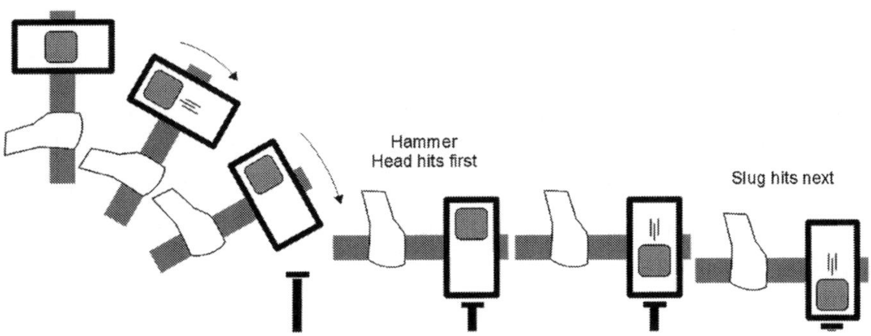

The dead-blow hammer

The common trait between the sword cut and the dead-blow hammer is that secondary motion that "gets behind" the initial force and drives it just a bit further than the initial contact.

HEAVY HANDS

The sword cut and the dead-blow hammer are only part of a greater understanding. I will let you in on the secret behind it all. The short version is they create heavy hands.

Using heavy hands is how to amplify your weight. The trick is to suggest where the weight will be applied, let Uke react, and then make it unwieldy for Uke to support it.

This is part of the answer to, "How do I make Uke stop?" and a great start toward learning advanced striking and throwing.

Imagine a dumbbell with only one weight attached. Grab the imaginary dumbbell by the end missing a weight. It should look in your mind a lot like you are holding a hammer, but it is not described as a hammer for a very important reason: we are going to hit with our hand and not the weight.

Raise your hand with the imaginary weight straight up. Begin to let your hand fall centripetally. Hit the intended object with the butt of the bar. On contact, allow the imaginary dumbbell weight to arc outward and "pull" you over the point of contact.

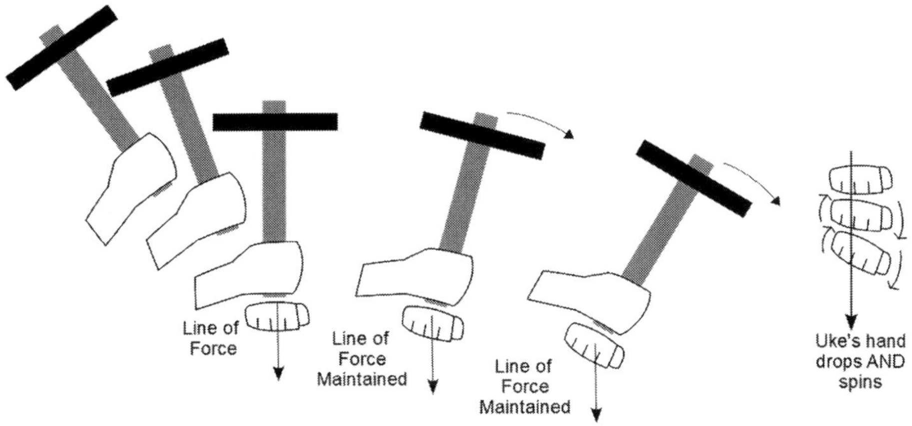

Heavy hand applied to Uke's outstretched arm

Focus on the pivot and the action beyond the point of contact. The initial contact tells Uke where to set up structure. Uke creates structure and guards against the initial conflict. The real attack follows with a pulse in an awkward direction in relation to that structure.

Imagine trying to catch a 50-pound sack of beans. Where do you attempt to catch the weight? In the middle, of course! What happens when the beans slide to one side? The weight becomes awkward for the structure.

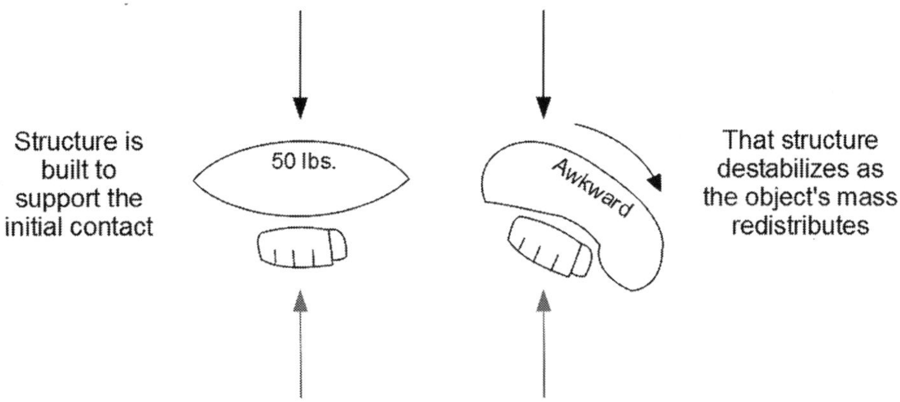

Effect of shifting weight on an arm

If one can fall over a point of contact, why not fall under? So enters the monkey bars.

Monkey bars sets up the initial contact the same way, but instead of falling over the point of contact, fall under. Watch a monkey swing from branch to branch. A strong branch will not budge but watch the weaker branches bend or even break if the structure is not appropriate. Would you consider Uke's outstretched arm a strong branch? I do not.

You can roll Uke in any direction using these methodologies, if you know where the weaknesses are in Uke's structure. (Rectangles, snakes, and the no-line/20 are good examples of where the weaknesses are.)

RECTANGLES AND SNAKES

Rectangles

It is fairly obvious that the torso can be perceived as a rectangle. The hips and shoulders form four corners. The upper and lower arm are also rectangular.

On the forearm, the crease of the wrist and the crease of the elbow create the short ends of the rectangle. With your hand palm up (bones uncrossed), the forearm is a lot like piece of two-by-four.

The upper arm rectangle is another two-by-four. Technically, there is only one bone in this part of your arm (the humerus bone). The rectangle of the upper arm is formed by the shoulder (front and back deltoids muscles) and the elbow (tips of the bicep and triceps muscles).

It can be important to realize that the upper and lower rectangles are out of phase. The forearm sits with the larger, four-inch side of the two-by-four parallel to the floor. The upper arm is sitting with the shorter, two-inch side on the floor. Applying heavy hands to the arm is most effective when the pressure is placed on the "corners" of these rectangles.

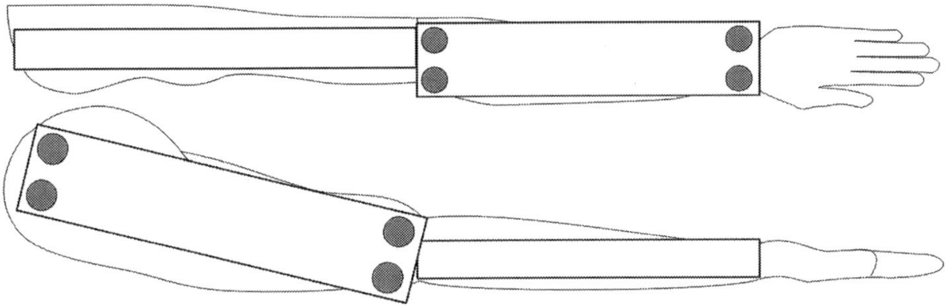

Four corners of the upper and lower right arm

Snakes

Better than pressing heavy hands on one of the corners is to take that corner and move it along the line of the snakes. The snakes intertwine along your arms in much the same way as they do in the medical symbol of the snakes and the stick.

Hold your arm out, palm up. Draw a line from the corner of your wrist closest to your thumb over to the elbow corner closest to your body. Continue tracing to the upper arm rectangle. The snake will jump down to the outside of the arm at the bottom of the elbow. Keep tracing that line to the front corner of the shoulder. (Just in front of your collarbone.)

The three other snakes should be easy to trace. Start number two on the opposite side of the wrist from where you started number one (on the bottom of your hand, at the "V" of the web between index finger and thumb).

The next diagram is a bit confusing, but I think you can get it.

Torque applied to Uke's body along the snakes will most efficiently impact his strength and ability to maintain structure.

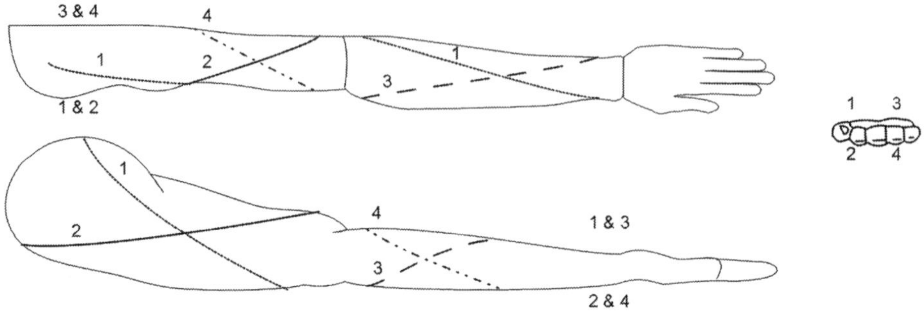

The snakes run along the inside of the forearm to the outside of the upper arm

PARALLELISM

Parallelism is moving parallel to the no-line or 20 line. Provided Uke has structure, you do not necessarily have to be on the line to affect his stability. It is important to move Uke along at least one of these paths from the instant of contact. Uke will give up on the attack and attempt to maintain balance the instant that he is lead along these lines. Uke will create structure as he attempts to maintain stability. That structure will reduce Uke's ability to attack and offers us opportunity to progress into more complex attacks on Uke's stability.

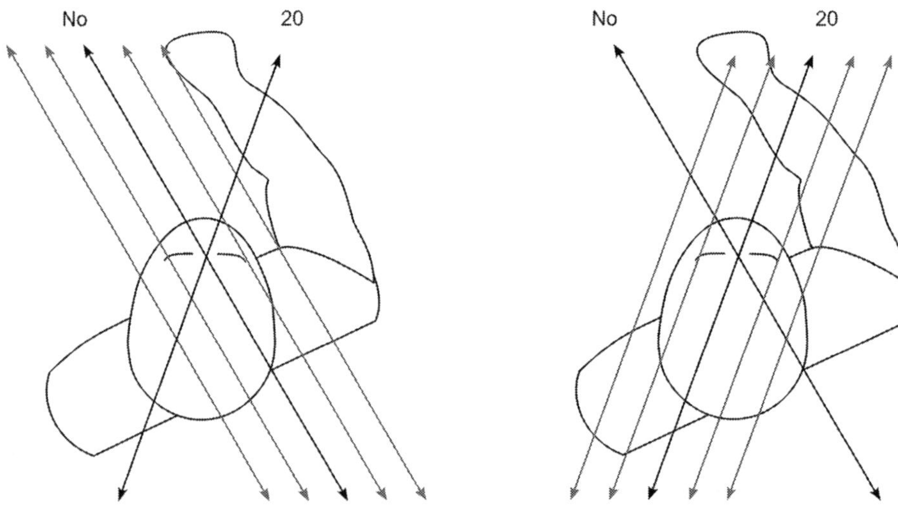

Lines parallel to the 20 and the no-line

OUTER CURVE, THE OTHER CURVES, AND THE FOOTBALLS

This is going to take a bit of explanation, settle in for it, but know that we are to working toward an understanding of the following diagram of the four footballs.

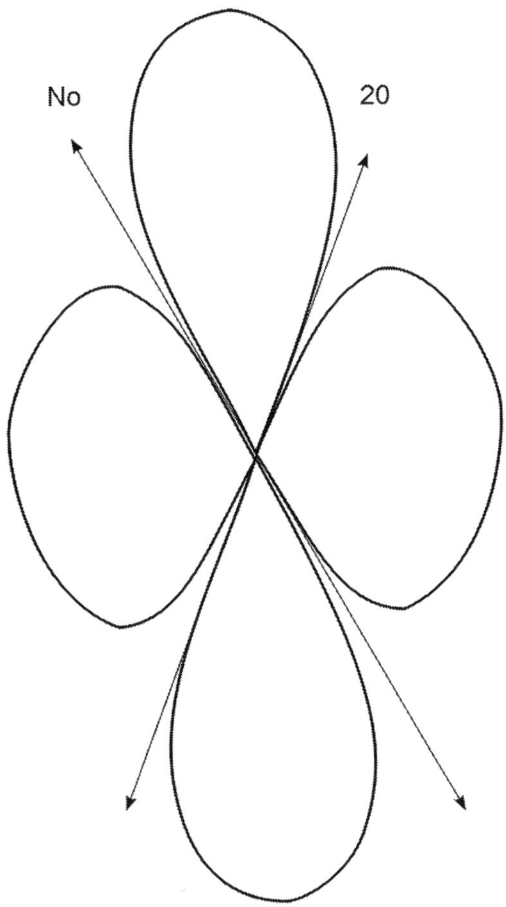

The four basic curves create the footballs (aka the lotus petals)

Uke has his best chance of defending himself when we try to throw him with a linear, one-dimensional force. Moving Uke one-dimensionally (even along the no- and 20 lines) will typically result in Uke stepping and reposition his structure.

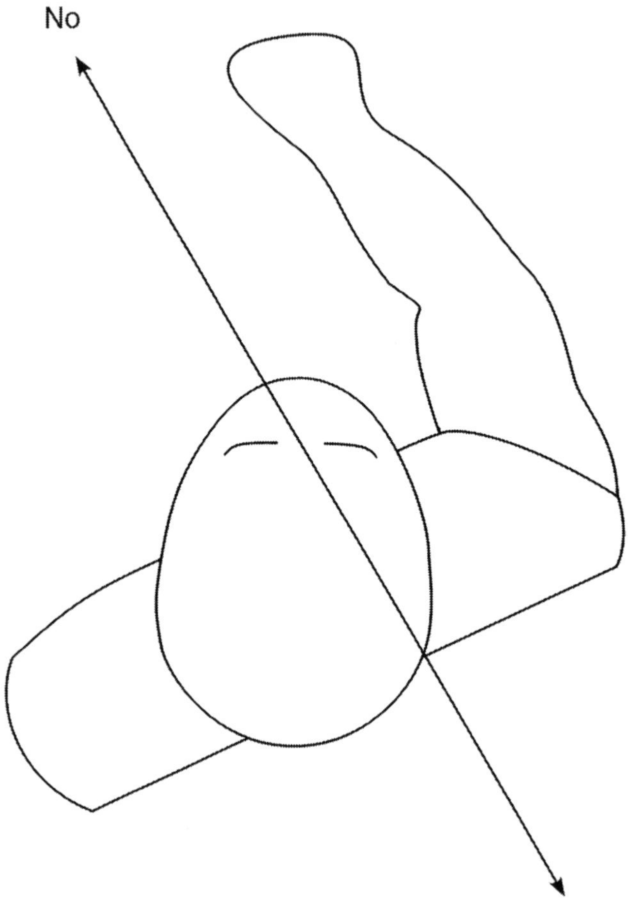

Singular, linear force; no rising or dropping

Unfortunately, for most of us, this one-dimensional, linear force is the common reflex when we act as Tori.

So if we want to improve our chances of throwing Uke, we want to mix it up a bit by offering Uke more than one motion at a time.

How do we move in two directions at once? We move circularly, or, for the purposes of Aiki, we move along a curve.

Let us take a look at how a curve is created and then detail where these curves exist in reference to Uke. We will save a look at how to use them for the precepts sections.

What makes a curve?

The curves themselves do not really exist. What we are experiencing is actually the result of simultaneously using the no-line and the 20. In other words, the curves are created by varying the force of two linear vectors.

Let us talk vectors (in layman's terms—apologies up front to the physics majors).

From a simplistic point of view, a resultant force is created when two or more forces act upon a singular object.

If the two forces are moving along the same direction, they add to each other and create a greater resultant force.

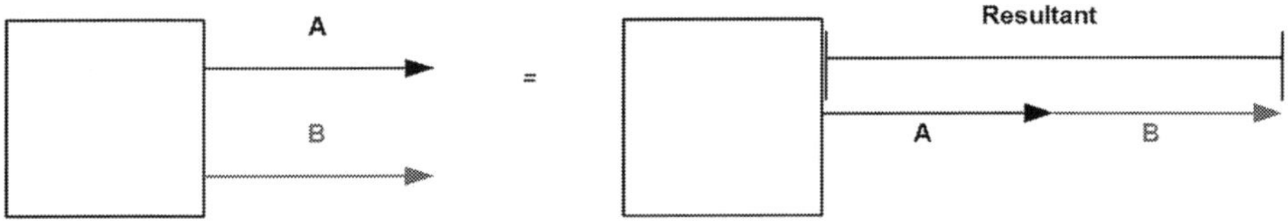

Force A and Force B moving in the same direction create a stronger resultant force.

When these forces move in different directions the resultant force does not directly follow either of the forces that created it.

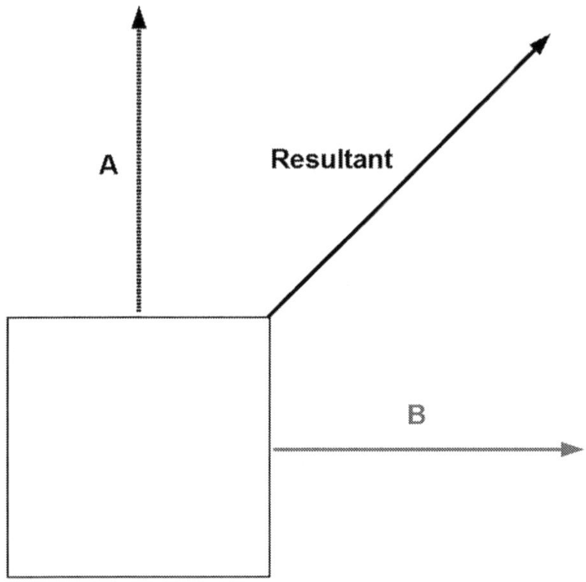

Force A and Force B moving in different directions create a combined force in a different direction

In Aiki, the curves are a resultant force. In other words, each curve is an effect of two causes.

How do we use two almost perpendicular linear forces to create a curve? (How do we use the 20 and the no-line to create a curve?) By constantly changing the amount of force used in each direction.

Let us use the edge of a clock as an example.

If the Force A and Force B change in their intensity, and eventually reverse in direction, the clock (circle) can be drawn as such:

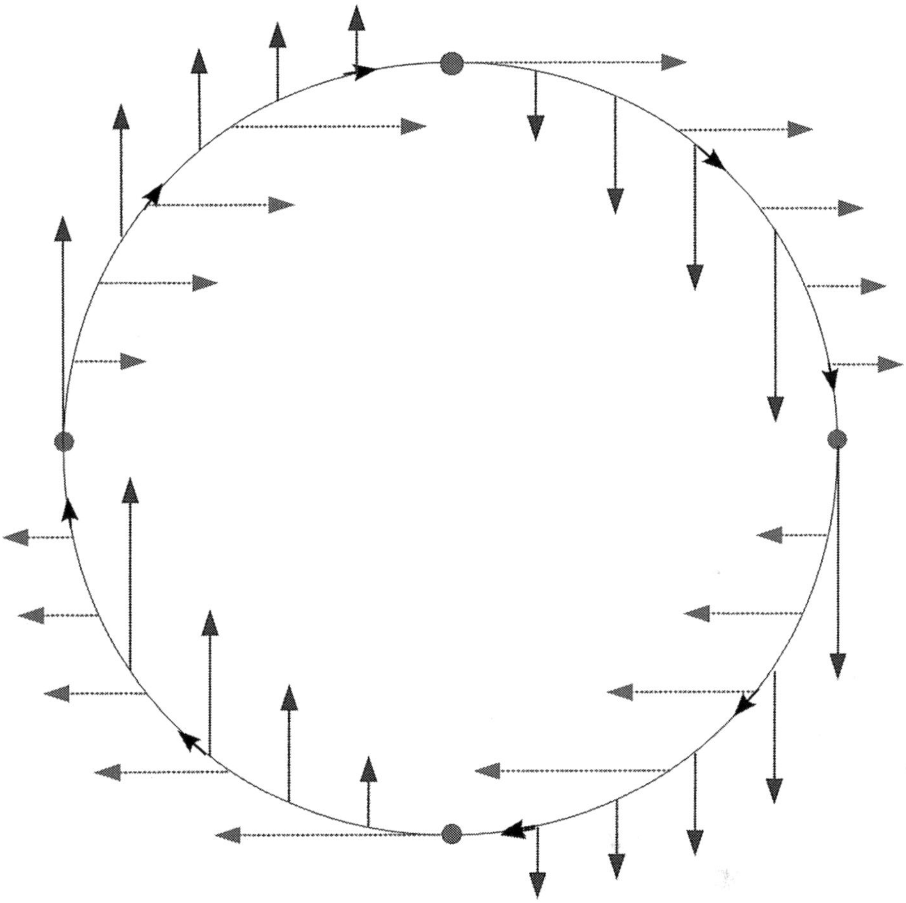

The circle is the resultant force of two constantly changing forces: clockwise

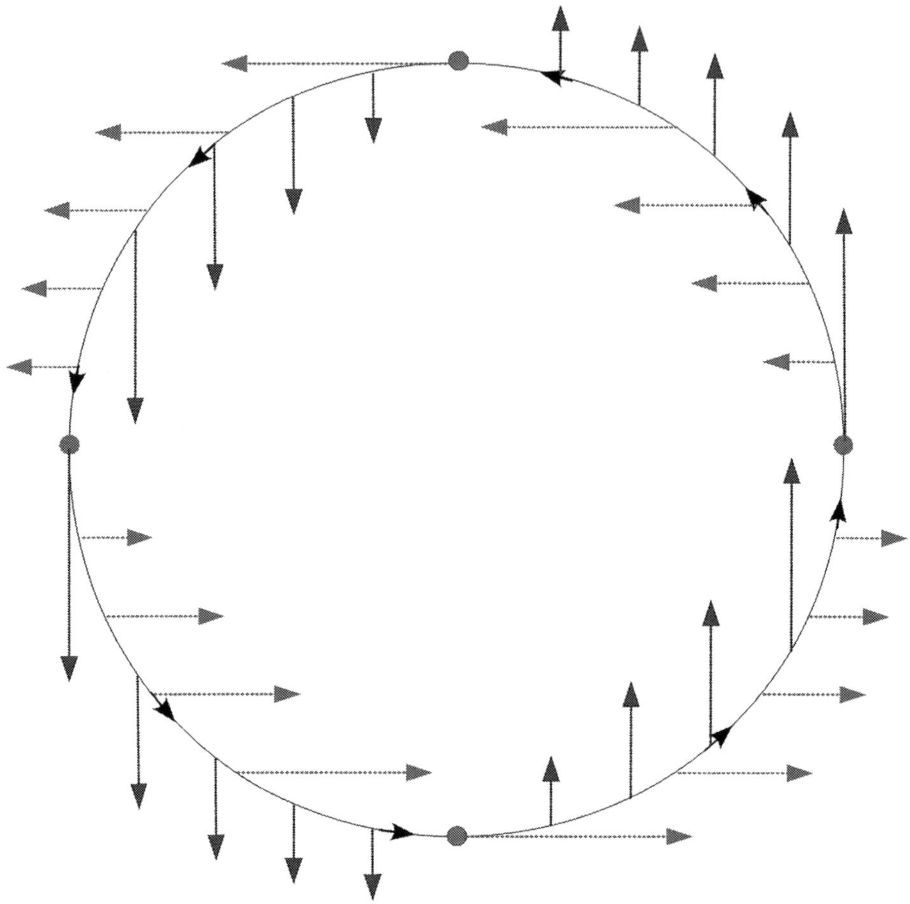

The circle is the resultant force of two constantly changing forces: counterclockwise

Notice that horizontal force changes direction at the same time the vertical force peaks and vice versa.

The Curves are a simultaneous attack on the two weakest dimensions of Uke's structure: the no-line and the 20. A curve is the effect; the 20 and no-line are the cause.

Let us look at the two forward curves and how they produce a football.

Outer curve

In this curve, we start along the 20 before engaging the no-line and complete a circle by varying the force along the 20 and no-line directions. This curve is most useful when performing Oshitaoshi #6. I call it the "outer curve."

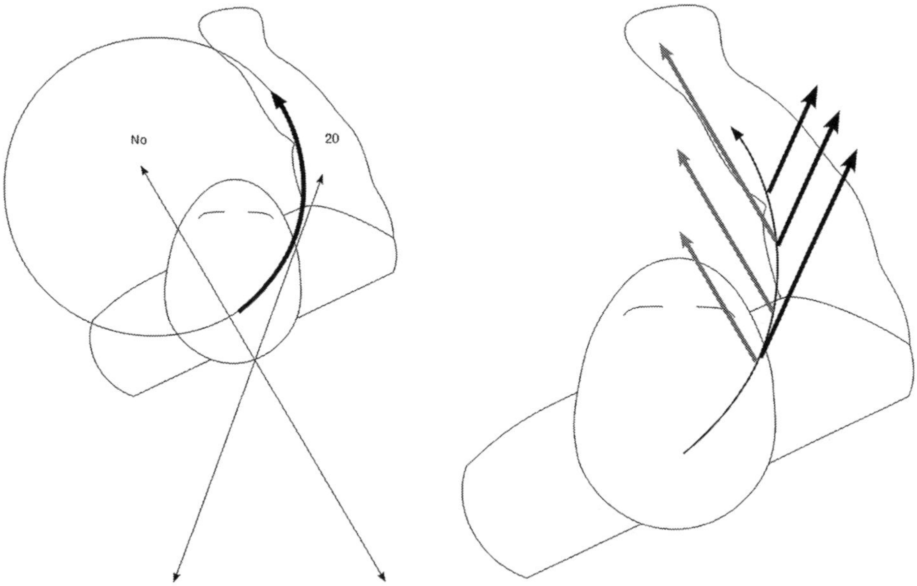

Uke and the outer curve

Inner curve

If we start forward with the no-line and move to the 20 we get an equally effective curve called the inner curve.

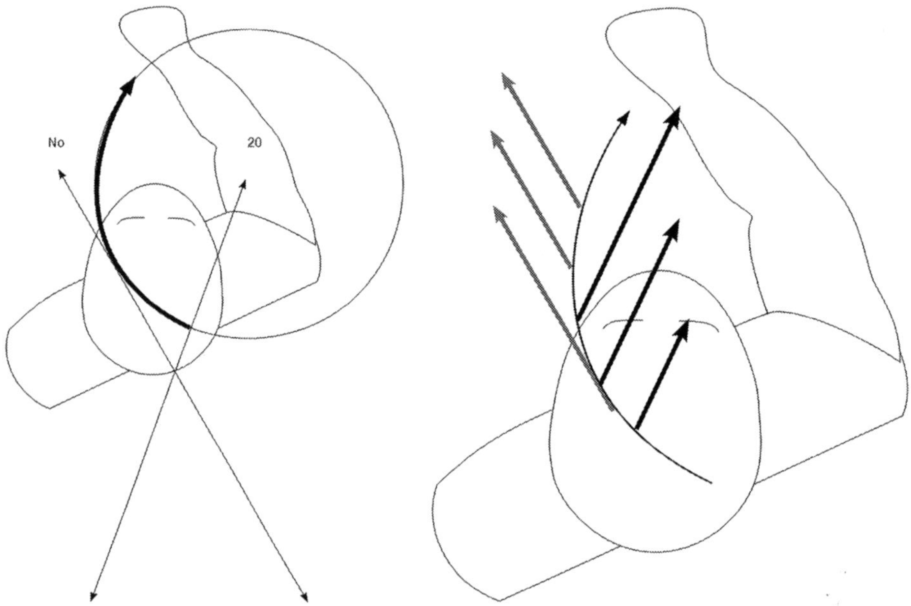

Uke and the inner curve

I sense the inner curve when starting Shihonage #14 and Maeotoshi #15 in traditional kata format.

Football

If you put these two curves together you become aware of what we originally called the lotus petal, but that sounded too flowery, so we started calling it the football.

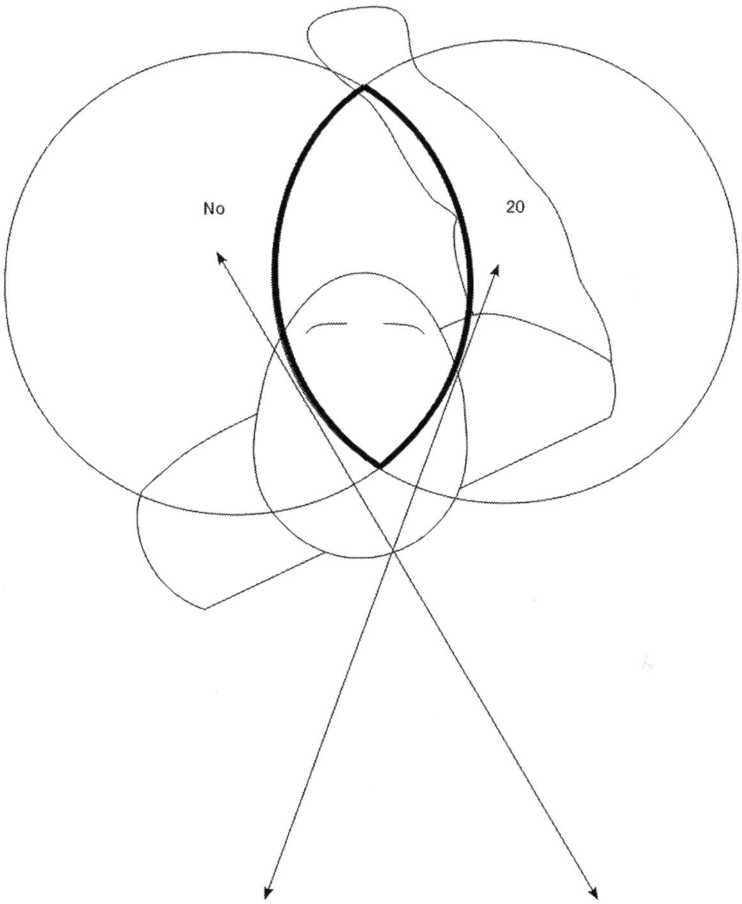

The football: union of the outer and inner curve

If the two front-side curves are resultants of the no-line and 20 in front of you, we should assume that two curves form from the no-line and 20 as they extend toward the rear. I will skip the long explanation and simply draw the complement to the outer curve without much investigative text. Suffice to say: those with a bit of imagination might draw some artistic conclusions as well. Here is what we come up with:

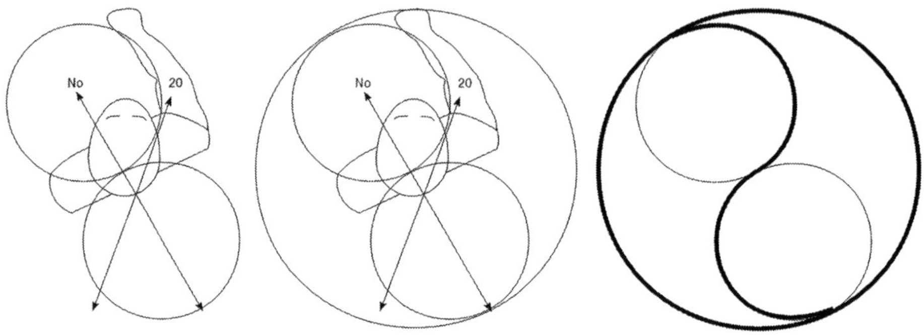

Playing artistically with the outer curve

Do not get excited. The yin/yang symbol really does not exist here in such a proportional shape.

The circles themselves are inaccurate. The circles are nearest to perfect circles when Uke is in a horse stance (where the no- and 20 lines are perpendicular), but are grossly distorted when Uke has one foot in front of the other.

The diagram that has the most martial application is actually this one:

The footballs, also known as the lotus petals

You might see why, at first, we called this the lotus petals.

The footballs depicted are approximations. The shape of the footballs depends on where Uke's weight is in relation to his feet. There are no footballs when Uke is on one foot, because there are no curves when Uke is on one foot. (Feet act as a triangle. More on that later.) Use the diagram as a point of reference only, not as an absolute.

BASIC AIKI-AGE, AIKI-SAGE (TIP-TO AND TIP-OVER)

This is a first brush with these two important concepts.

Pronounced "eye-key ahh-gay" and "eye-key sahh-gay," Aiki-Age and Aiki-Sage constitute the practical application of heavy hands. They generate vertical pressure on Uke's center of balance, and as such, are a critical part of weakening Uke's stance.

The understanding is typically easy. It is building the coordination that offers the most challenge. Aiki-Age and Aiki-Sage are subtle. The drills are sometimes difficult to perform, even with understanding and an instructor. Do your best and take comfort in the knowledge that, later in this book, we dedicate an entire chapter to this precept.

Aiki has the effect of making Uke feel awkwardly burdened, unstable, or trying to catch himself.

How do Aiki-Age and Aiki-Sage help Uke produce this effect?

Aiki-Age

Imagine a fifty-gallon steel barrel partially full of water (maybe half full). The lip of the barrel should be at about chest height. The barrel is rigid and heavy (twenty-five gallons of water weighs about 200 pounds). It is also not too easy to get your arms around—not something you are easily going pick up and move.

The easiest way to move a barrel is to tip it and roll it on its edge. Seems pretty obvious, but have you stopped to take an in-depth look at how we tip a barrel?

Imagine standing about half an arm's length away from the barrel. Tip the barrel toward yourself and look inside. What did your body have to do to make the barrel tip?

Did your arms go limp? No.

Did your shoulders rise up? No.

Did it help to grip tightly and squeeze? No.

Did your hands try to bend the top of barrel like wringing a towel? No.

(Then why do we try all those things when trying to tip Uke?)

All you had to do was gently cup your hands, rest some weight on the lip of the barrel, relax, drop your shoulders, then elbows, and bent your knees slightly. (Chris calls this "sequenced relaxation.")

The barrel was a bit heavy to move at first, but did you feel the barrel "go light" again? Did you spill the contents of the barrel or did you hold it suspended once it "felt light"? How much pressure was the barrel putting on your hands to keep it "suspended on its edge"? Could you have spilled it if you wanted to? Could you have put it back on its base again? Could you have spun it like a wheel and moved where you desired?

This analogy offers insight to a condition we desire to create within Uke called "balanced instability," but just as important, it describes how Aiki-Age creates that condition. "Age" is "tipping the barrel toward yourself" or "looking in the barrel." Others in the organization like to call it "tip-to," short for "*tip-to*ward yourself."

I know you think you understand, and I will bet that you do, but let us add to the awareness.

The part of the barrel lip that you were in contact with traveled along an arc. Did the arc ever go higher than the top of the barrel? (Hint: no.)

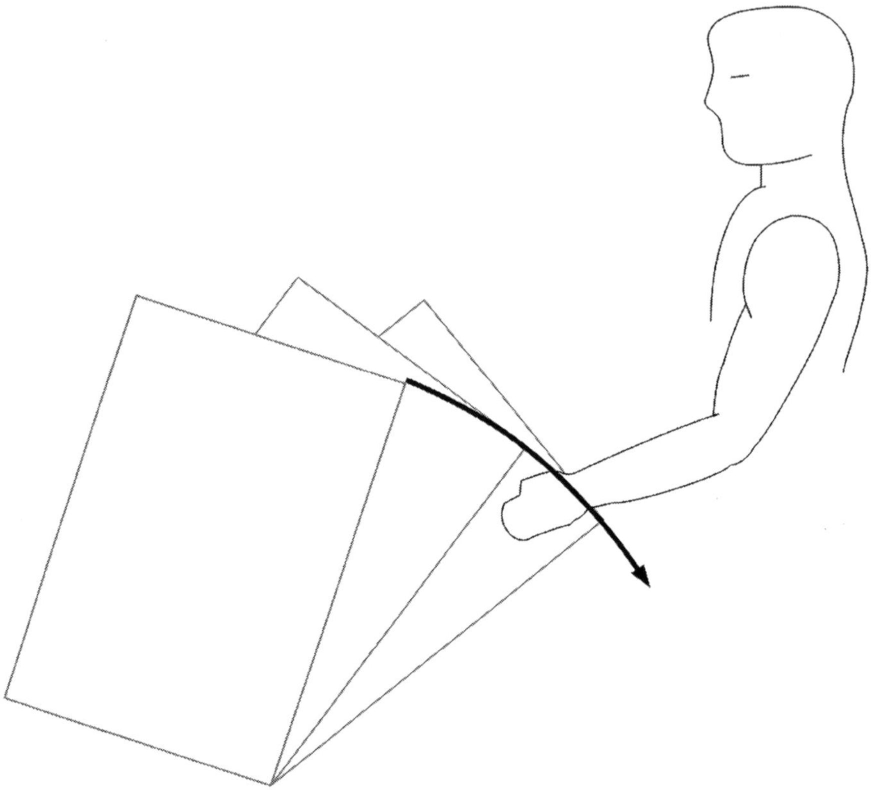

The barrel as it tips toward us; the arc is never higher than the top of the barrel

Additionally, pay close attention to the fact that your hands will have to travel the same arc that the barrel's lip does. It is important to remember this as you attempt the Aiki-Age drill on Uke.

What would happen to the barrel if we allow our hands to drift off of the arc and move upward as we tip the barrel? Answer: our hands lose contact with the barrel and the barrel will either return to the original position, or, if the barrel was far enough along the arc, the barrel will spill over.

It should go without saying that it would not have helped us to attempt to push inward along the edge of the barrel in an attempt to crush the barrel as it was being tipped toward us. We should be focusing on making the barrel topple, not destroying its shape and structure.

These two analogies have a direct correlation to our Aiki-Age drill.

Uke behaves much like this steel drum, but with some very interesting differences. Let us apply "Age" to Uke and see if you can point them out.

Have a friend stand in horse stance with arms out in a circle, grasping one hand in the other. (Just like putting someone in a bear hug.) Have them get comfortable, root into the floor, and keep this pose somewhat rigid throughout the drill (like having unbendable arms).

For our first try, have Uke maintain this structure: Shoulders are somewhat rigid, and do not let the hands drop. Uke should do his best to keep his feet in place. There should be no stepping until we force them to step.

Stand directly in front, facing each other. Rest your hands on Uke's arms with one hand on each side of Uke's hands. Now "tip the barrel" so you can look inside.

Most persons do not get it right the first time. Instead of tipping Uke, they try to "pull" Uke toward themselves. (Their arms move like they were elbowing someone behind them. That is not it.) Still others do their best to push down on Uke's arms and compress Uke like a spring. Still others act like they are trying to rip down a basketball hoop. None of these methods are what we are after.

When performed correctly, Uke will come off his heels and onto his toes. At some point it you will feel Uke "lean" on you.

This applies even if we allow Uke to get somewhat loose (not limp!) in the shoulders. The arc created by dropping your elbows should keep Uke's arms outward.

Uke should feel like he is holding up a five-foot stack of plates and all the plates shifted away from him (and toward you). In other words, Uke should feel awkward, unstable.

A properly applied Aiki-Age makes Uke look a bit like this:

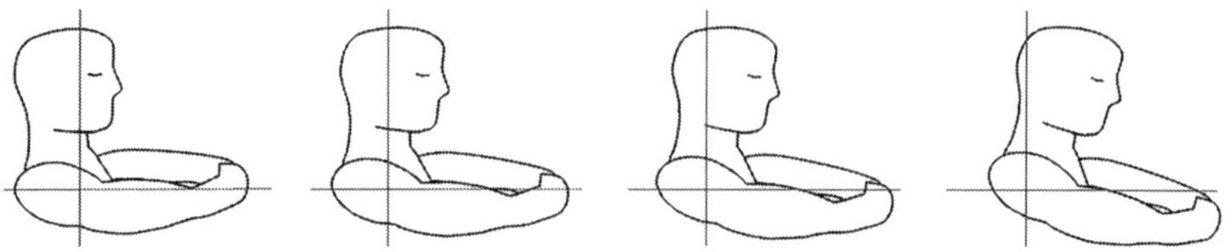

Uke's position as Aiki-Age drill is applied

Assuming you are starting to get it, did you notice any differences between tipping a barrel and tipping Uke?

The first should be that Uke is easier to tip than a barrel. The barrel's base is a lot wider and much more stable. Uke's arms are floating where there is no support (no feet). In contrast, the barrel's frame is under the point where you contact it.

If you performed the drill facing Uke while he was in a horse stance, you were standing on his no-line. Take note of that. It is the easiest line to tip Uke on.

Do not believe me? Set up the drill once again, but this time, before you tip, have Uke get in a right foot forward stance and root with equal weight on each foot.

It is a bit harder to tip Uke while facing Uke head-on and he is in a foot forward stance.

Now, have Uke freeze like a statue for a second while you reposition counterclockwise about thirty degrees off center and try again.

That is the magic of the no-line. See if you can find the 20 and tip again. I expect that this exploration will tie together Aiki-Age and the 20 and no-lines for you.

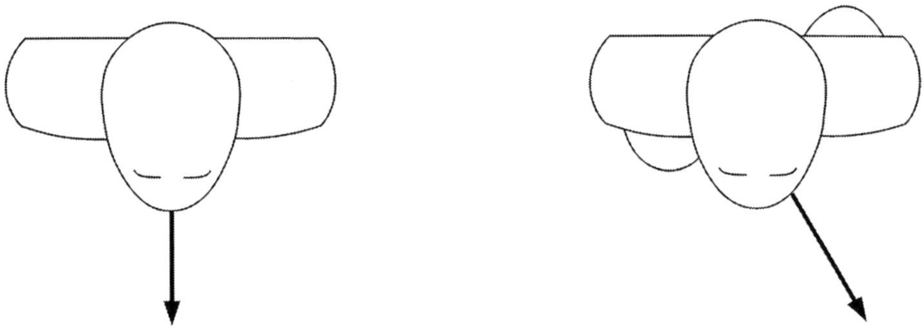

Easiest direction to tip Uke when in horse stance, easiest in right foot forward stance

Aiki-Sage

Aiki-Sage is the complementary action to Aiki-Age. If you can tip the barrel toward you, you should be able to tip it away from you.

Aiki-Sage is sometimes called tip-over or tip-away.

Let us imagine pushing that same, heavy fifty-gallon drum away from ourselves.

In which direction do we need to push to efficiently topple the barrel?

That is right! We need to push in an arc! (Assuming you would rather the barrel support itself most of the time. I mean, I guess we could have tried to grab the lip closest to us and pick up the barrel. That would take a great deal of strength. Let us agree that picking up the barrel is a bad idea)

The arc we follow in Aiki-Sage is a bit different than the one we followed in Aiki-Age. In Aiki-Sage, the arc rises before it falls.

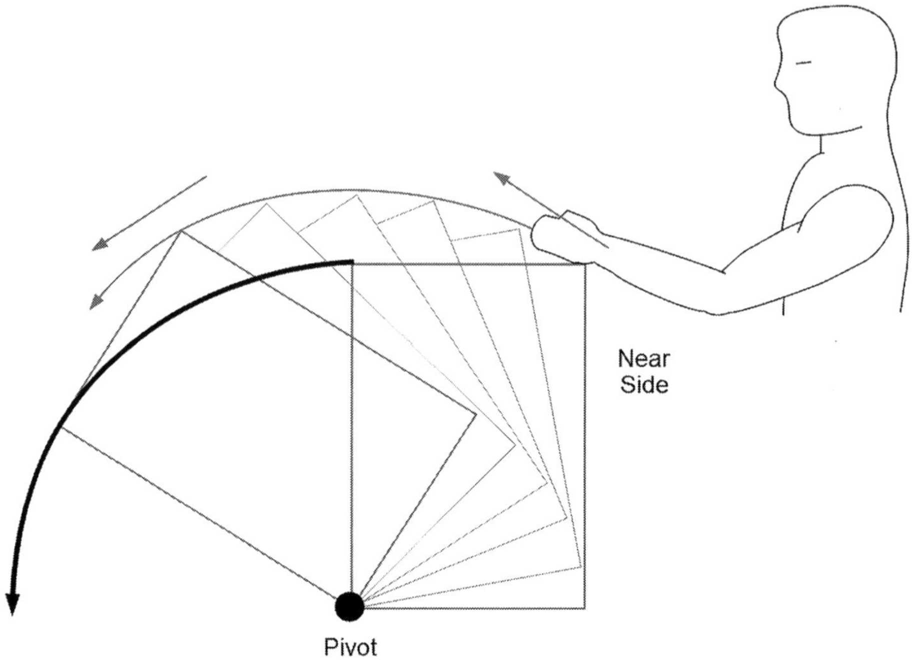

Aiki-Sage arc rises before it falls

Technically, from the perspective of the barrel's lip opposite of where we attach, the arc only ever traveled downward. This is a function of where the pivot is in relation to where we attach.

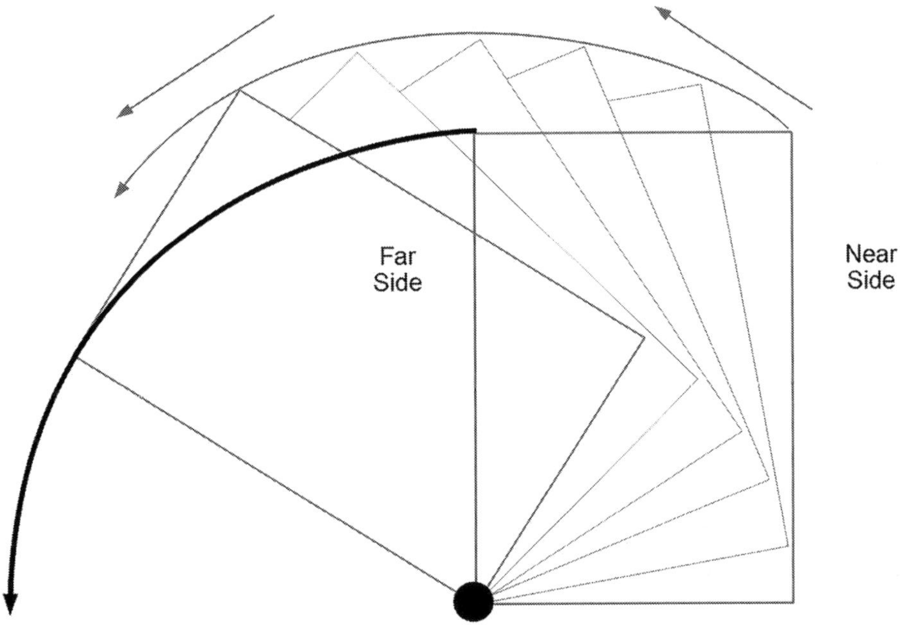

Toppling the barrel with Aiki-Sage; near side rises and falls, far side only falls

The tipping over action of Aiki-Sage is better described as a wave. The wave will both pick up and push down on an object.

Aiki-Sage behaves just like a wave

Set up exactly as you did for the Aiki-Age drill, but this time, try to move Uke in Aiki-Sage.

A properly applied Aiki-Sage makes Uke look a bit like this:

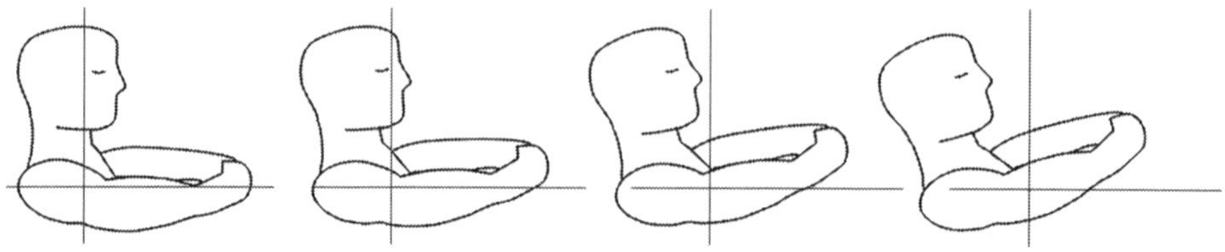

Aiki-Sage applied correctly

Aiki-Sage truly is the essence of Shomenate #1. You can throw Shomenate with an Aiki-Age, but it is not a very common method

Fear not if you are having trouble with these drills. There is much more to add that assists with these drills. We are still only defining the basics.

CONNECTION AND BRIDGE

I have been told many times that Aikido techniques do not work without connection.

Being open minded, I have accepted that statement, but have always asked, "What exactly is this connection?"

In response, I have received many blank stares and even a few attempts to put the feeling into words. Most times it resulted in a demonstration (without words) that sent me flying across the room, but still wondering what the connection is.

After much research, here is the definition: Connection is the ability to guide or direct Uke's inertia.

Pretty simple, huh? You may have heard that definition before, but wait! Did you ask the follow-up question: "How do I create a connection?" Did you ever get a response? More than likely, you received more demonstration, or "You can kind of feel it when…" These are frustrating as it describes how to know when you have it, but does not describe how to get it.

Let us get specific. The definition of how to create connection is: affixing two bodies together such that one is supporting the other.

That should make things a bit clearer, but even that is a high-level goal or 50,000 foot view.

Let us get even more precise and break that definition into two steps: 1) create a bridge, then 2) Aiki-Age/Sage.

The bridge—affixing two bodies together

(Disclaimer: Technically, you do not actually have to physically touch Uke to knock him down. I have experienced this as Uke more than a few times, but am not capable of that (yet!). I am not going to even try to explain it. For the rest of us, it relies on actual contact.)

Think for a moment about a bridge. Three entities exist: the bridge and the two roads that it connects.

Would the bridge have function if it were flimsy and easily snapped in half? No, it must have some form of structure or rigidity. Would the bridge have function if it unhinged itself from either side? No, it would have to stay attached. The same applies in Aikido.

In Aiki, the bridge is the conduit by which one person affects force on the other (and vice versa!). We have a few options in how we create the bridge.

In Aikido, three prevalent types of contact create a bridge: 1) arm-to-arm (arm = from fingertips to your shoulder), 2) arm-to-torso (including head), or 3) torso-to-torso.

The primary difference is in how many joints are involved. The fewer joints involved, the more likely that you will be able to create and maintain the bridge structure.

This is important, because it is critical to maintain a bridge throughout the application of a technique.

Keeping the structure

As described earlier, a bridge has to have some amount of structure or rigidity. Ever try to push a rope down the road? It does not work. We need some structure if we hope to push Uke down the road.

Creating structure in a torso-to-torso contact is typically easy because our bodies are rigid. The structure is almost implied. It is fairly easy to maintain the structure, as there are very few joints that can flex and collapse the bridge.

How do we create and maintain structure in the more complex arm-to-arm contact? Unbendable arm works on Tori's side of the equation, but what about Uke's arm? What keeps Uke from collapsing his arm? The answer is: joint locks, Uke attempting to block Tori's strike, and, my favorite, Uke trying to keep his balance.

The fact that torso-to-torso contact has the least amount of joints involved does not imply that a technique based on this contact is any easier than a different type of contact (e.g., arm-to-arm). What it does imply is that it is easier to maintain the bridge in a torso-to-torso technique (e.g. Gedanate #4 of the Tomiki 17 kata). We still need skill at using the bridge to make it effective.

Do not forget to stay attached

Even if the bridge has structure, it still is not complete until it is attached. This attachment is made in one of two ways.

The first is easy: grab! Either Tori or Uke can grab. Lose or break the grip and you lose the attachment. The grab is most important when we begin to move away from Uke and stretch the limbs taut (extension connection).

The second method is maintaining pressure on both sides of the bridge. This is like holding a ruler between the palms your hands. The ruler will not drop provided you constantly compress the ruler, but falls the moment one hand moves away from the other (compression connection).

Such that one is supporting the other—Age/Sage

Now that we have attached our bridge to Uke, how do we finish the job and get to support one another? We use Aiki-Age or Aiki-Sage.

Age/Sage is used to create one of two support situations that result in our control over Uke.

The first situation is resting your weight on Uke where it is unwieldy for him to support you (yang connection). This is a lot like riding a skateboard. We put our weight on the object, and it moves with us as we push ourselves along.

The second is convincing Uke to support himself on the strength of your structure (yin connection). This is like dragging a suitcase with wheels on it. The suitcase has wheels on the ground, but would fall if not for your grasp. The suitcase goes everywhere you go.

I like those analogies because you have seen them work and you have seen them fail. Ever fall off a skateboard or have your suitcase wheels get stuck? All of the sudden the skateboard or suitcase owns you!

Most techniques rely solely on one type of support. I find that toggling between yin or yang connection in the middle of a technique is tricky. (Not impossible, but very tricky, you have to be in the right spot.) Trying to toggle between these typically ends up in breaking the connection altogether, but that realization comes much later.

Let us bring this back around to something we described in detail earlier in this document.

Which simple machine typically comes to mind when you think of lifting or supporting an object with a rigid structure? A lever!

Perfect, but which particular type of lever? An inclined plane! (A ramp.)

I can hear you scream, "What? An inclined plane and a lever are different simple machines!"

Technically, you are correct, but I know one thing, with just a stick and a fulcrum you can create either machine at will. With a little fancy movement, you can make a first-class lever act like an inclined plane. In fact, that is what we are about to do.

Let us play around a bit and discover that Aiki-Age and Aiki-Sage are not much more than using an inclined plane to direct Uke.

How is Age/Sage like an inclined plane?

How about we make triple use of our time here? Let us:

1. Introduce the basics of another of the precepts called lever arms.
2. Dive deeper into the Aiki-Age drill.
3. Complete the thought of how Age/Sage is like an inclined plane.

Step one of creating connection says that we have to first create a bridge with an attachment between Uke and ourselves.

This is kata, so Uke's unbendable arms again form the lip of the barrel and his basic structure is already there.

Next we complete the bridge by attaching to Uke. Making contact with Uke and dropping some weight on Uke's arms forms the attachment part of the connection. It might help to imagine yourself draping your hand over your suitcase handle.

Now, you might have guessed it already, but your arm is going to become a lever. The lever's fulcrum is formed at the point of contact between Uke and Tori's arm (Tori's wrist). You can think of Tori's hand as the short side of the lever and the rest of the body (not just the arm, all the way to the feet) as the long side.

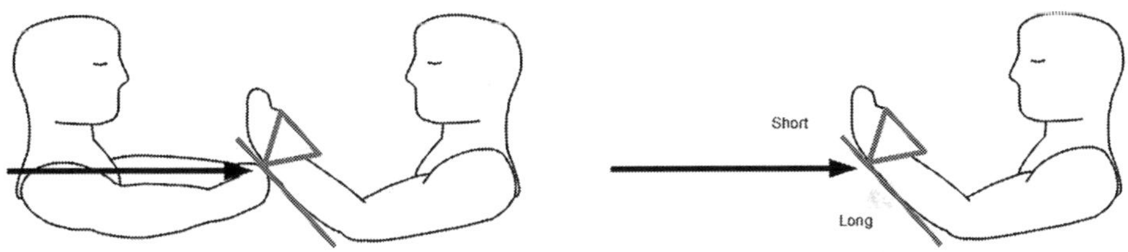

Lever arm; point of contact becomes the fulcrum; lever arm has a short and long side

I hope you challenged me just now by asking, "But how is the lever useful if the force is applied at the fulcrum and not on the ends?"

This is where we break for a bit to understand the difference between a lever and an inclined plane. Then we tie the whole drill together again.

The lever

Consider a teeter-totter. When two equally heavy persons sit on the ends, the ends will rise and fall with the slightest upward push from the person with their feet on the ground. The ends of the teeter-totter are basically weightless, or in other words, balanced. The fulcrum is fully supporting the plank and the people on the ends. The people gain the benefit of having fun with little effort. This should bring to mind the earlier analogy of balancing a pipe on your finger.

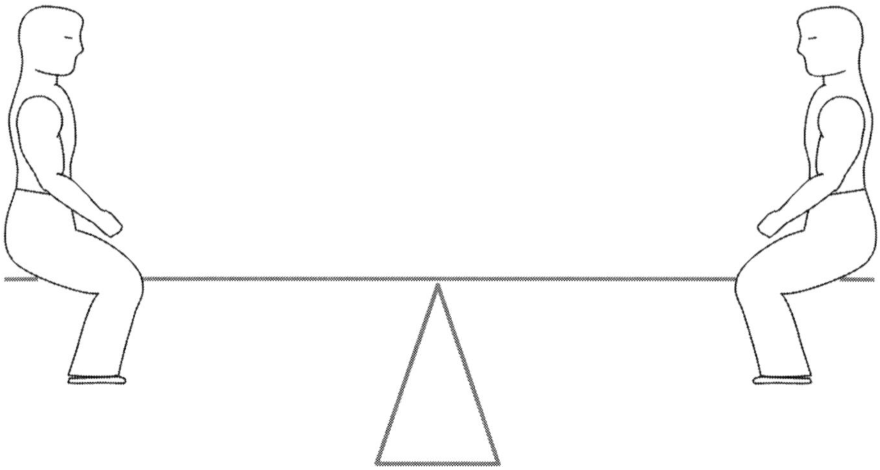

Two equally weighted persons on opposite sides, equally distant from the fulcrum create "balance"

If we introduce a much heavier person to one side of this teeter-totter, the balance is destroyed and the teeter-totter will create a perpetual lean.

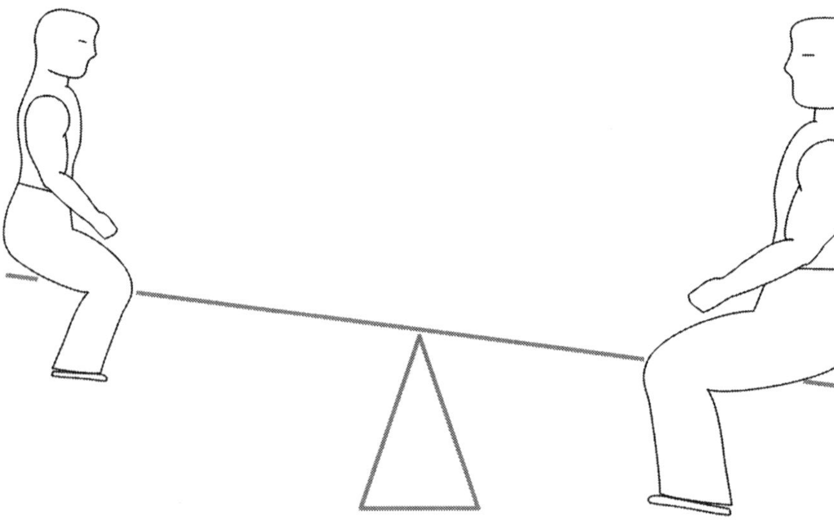

A heavier weight on one side of the teeter-totter creates an imbalance

In order to bring this 'back to balance, we leverage (pun intended) mechanical advantage by lengthening the side of the teeter-totter with the lighter person to make up for the lack of weight. (Basically, we re-position to balance the torque.)

Balance can be restored by repositioning the fulcrum along the length of the lever arm

This is the magic of levers and mechanical advantage. A lighter weight can be balanced or equally forceful as a greater weight on the opposite side of the fulcrum. We can again create rising and falling motions with the slightest outside force (e.g., when one of the riders pushes against the ground).

Take the time to impress this lever analogy upon yourself. We will be coming back to this particular analogy in a future discussion regarding your sagittal plane, the cat stance, and what it takes to really use your center. (Preview: Sagittal plane is the fulcrum, do not support Uke on the ends!)

The inclined plane

This is where I drive the physics majors really crazy, but who cares? It is my book. For the purposes of defining architecture for Aiki, this explanation is going to work fine. (Although I do admit that the physics majors are correct and I am wrong; in my heart I still do not subscribe to normal force. In my mind, all the inclined plane can do is try to do is keep its form, and thus, keep you from hitting the ground. As long as you are not sliding down the slope, the only question is can your base stay under your center of balance (COB) and keep it supported. I must be missing something in the conversion of pressure into the base of the object, but standing on a slope still feels like it is pushing upward in opposition to gravity. This is why I studied electronics. I digress; let us get on with the heretical physics.)

Now, what is the inclined plane doing that the lever is not? In a word, ricochet!

The inclined plane is good for redirecting the oncoming force in a particular direction.

In the case of the picture below, we will use the word upward to describe the direction to which the inclined plane deflects the incoming force.

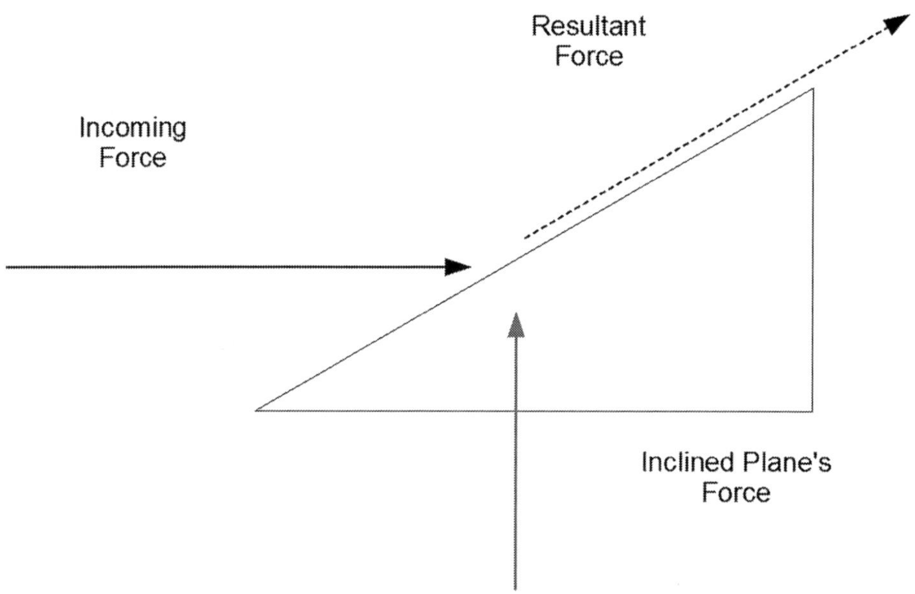

Inclined plane pushes upward

In this particular diagram, as the incoming force comes in contact with the inclined plane, the inclined plane holds its form and directs the force along the surface of the inclined plane.

The key element to understanding the inclined plane is that it accepts a contact from the outside force and moves it along a particular trajectory. Where the lever uses varying weights on either side of the fulcrum to move something, the inclined plane stays resolute and supports, better said, guides the force into a new direction.

The best analogy I can think of is climbing stairs. As you step forward, the next step of the stairs is supporting your weight as you extend your leg and straighten yourself out. You can travel up or down the stairs, but never fall through them.

What do you call a completely vertical inclined plane? A wall! Do not laugh too hard. It is very common for an Aikido practitioner to present Uke with a wall instead of a staircase (collision vs. Irimi).

If we are in synch on the differences between the lever and the inclined plane, let us play mad scientist and make a hybrid.

Using the lever as an inclined plane

Back to where we started. Let us return to the Age/Sage drill.

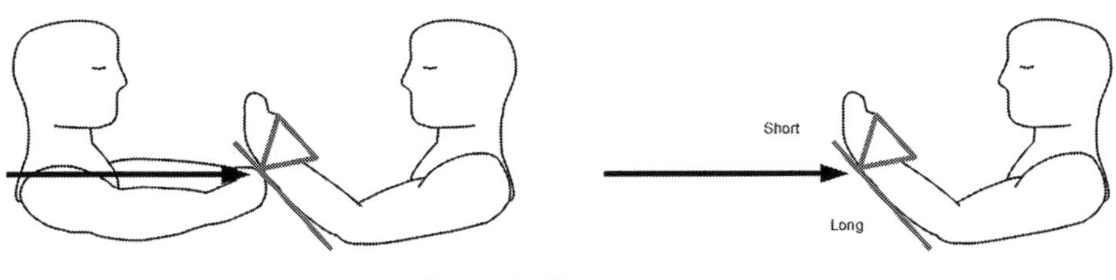

Age/Sage drill starting point

Notice that Uke's force makes contact with our arm (the lever) at the point of the fulcrum. This is desirable, because the point of the fulcrum is place where the lever acts like an inclined plane. The fulcrum remains resolute and, in this case, applies a downward, angular force on Uke as Uke tries to move forward.

Aiki relies on the fact that even a modestly sized person can easily root him or herself into the ground and, with arms extended, present a sizable and rather unmovable force. Of course, we must remember to present a staircase rather than a wall.

It is a natural tendency to treat Age/Sage like a punch or push. Most Aikidoka will try to drive force into the oncoming object. When they do so, they in effect, are presenting a head-on collision with Uke.

This is fine if Uke is not defending, is significantly smaller than we are, or we are hitting Uke in a vulnerable area of the body. Most times, we get run over or Uke simply uses the resistance to regain stability and reposition.

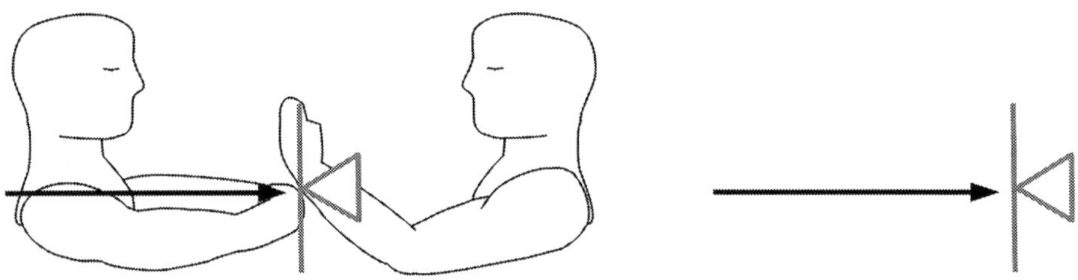

Tori presenting a wall and creating a collision

Another common complication: Tori uses the wrong angle at the wrong time.

We want Uke's inertia to continue toward us as we guide that force to an unwieldy position.

We want the initial contact to start Uke moving along the face of the lever, but we have to be careful.

If we maintain the same angle for too long, Uke will move his force along the face of the lever until he reaches the point where Uke is moving the teeter-totter. The fulcrum acts as a hinge, and the further Uke moves along that path, the more torque he gains. Eventually Uke will uproot or move through this type of block (and we get hit).

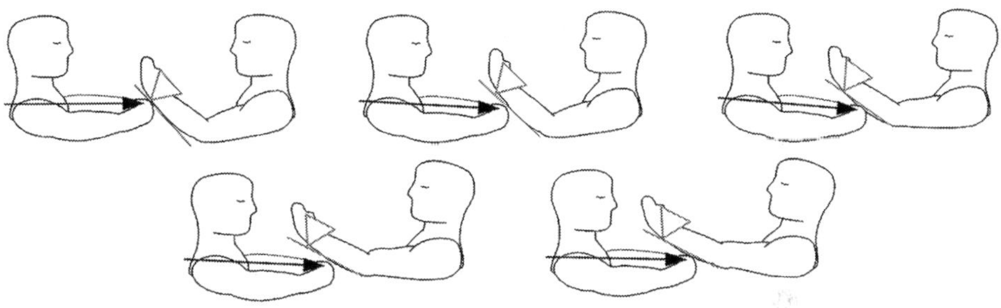

Uke slips too far along the teeter-totter and starts to uproot Tori's structure

The moment the fulcrum redirects Uke's force; we need to continually re-position that fulcrum in such a way as to ride Uke's force into the ground (or other unwieldy position). We start as the underside of a staircase and finish as a wall.

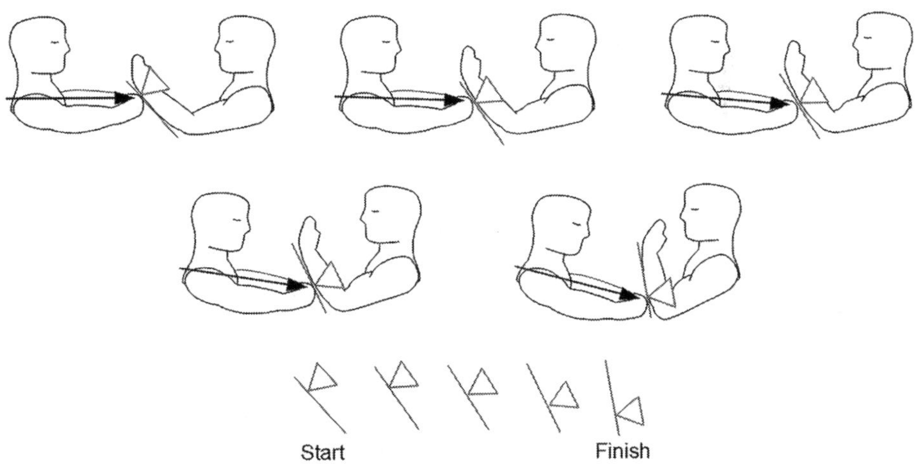

First version of Aiki-Age using lever arms; first lever Age

Optimally, Uke should be falling forward and trying to catch himself with his hand(s). Of course, since the surface we initially offer to Uke is like the underside of a staircase, Uke cannot find enough resistance to completely regain stability by pushing against our arm. Uke will find that his momentum is still carrying forward.

If we adjust appropriately, Uke will find enough force to believe he can right himself, but ultimately, he cannot. Uke continually finds himself unstable.

Aiki-Age using the four lever arms

Let us take a quick look at lever arms.

We can use lever arms to create both Aiki-Age and Aiki-Sage.

The drill we just described is the first of four lever arms.

This first one starts like the underside of a staircase and ends as a wall. Let us call that one first lever Age.

The second lever Age starts the same way, but lieu of finishing like a wall, we allow Uke to slip underneath. Uke falls first as Tori collapses onto Uke. Tori adds his weight and guides Uke downward.

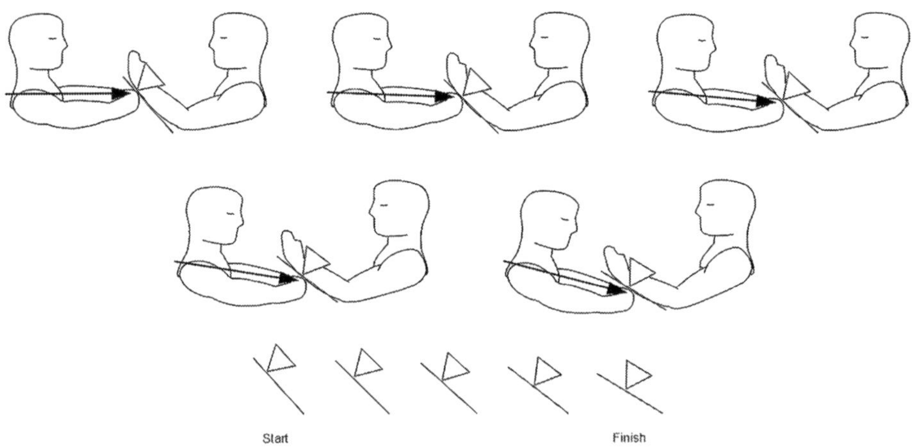

Second version of Aiki-Age using lever arms; second lever Age

Put yourself in the mindset of building a house with a deck of playing cards. The house of cards is a complex array of two cards leaning against each other.

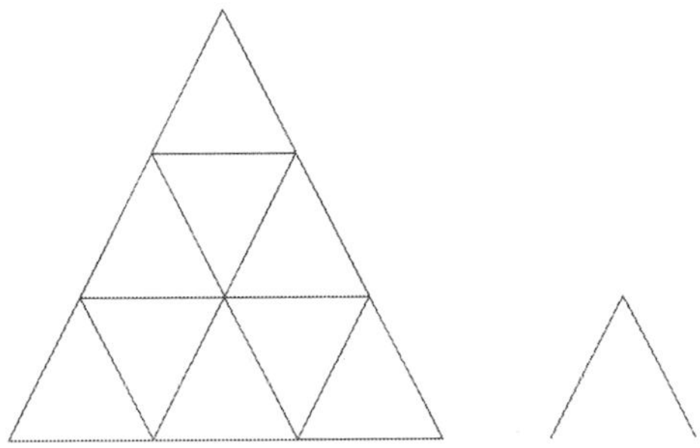

House of cards; two cards leaning on each other

Two cards leaning on each other is not the most stable structure. (Hence the fun and challenge of building a house of cards.) It completely relies on friction to maintain the structure. The friction on the bottom of the cards keeps the base of the triangle from expanding, and the friction at the top where the two cards meet keeps one card from toppling the other.

What is one possible result when base is stable, but the friction at the top of the cards is not perfect? Second lever Age!

Suppose the card on the left is Uke and the one on right is Tori. As the card on the left begins to slide downward along the face of the card on the right, it temporarily supports the card on the right. The left-side card falls first and the right-side card lands on top.

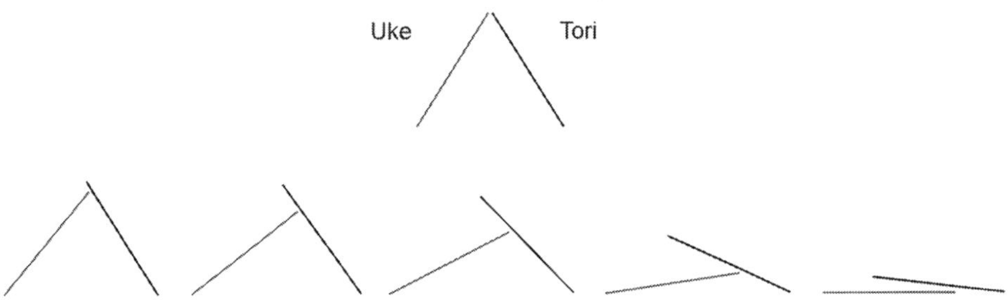

Second lever Age as a pair of cards

The cards will fall in a much more perfect arc than a human will, but the principle is the same.

Second lever Age is a bit easier to understand and perform than the first lever Age.

If we take step back and apply the card analogy on first Age, it resembles the left-side card falling downward first. As the left-side card falls, it will push the right-side card to a full vertical position (i.e., the left-side card stands the right-side card up).

First lever Age as a pair of cards

Who knew cards had any application in Aiki?

Since the first two Ages start with Tori over Uke, it only stands to reason to ask, "How do we achieve the same goal when Tori starts under Uke?"

The third lever Aiki-Age starts with Tori under Uke. This is the reason we nicknamed it under-Age. Essentially, it is a lot like rolling Uke down a hill, or as I like to describe it, letting Uke lean on a table that is missing a leg.

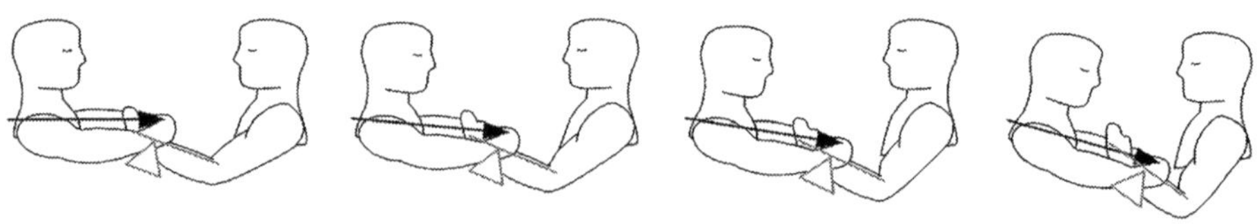

Third lever Age

Notice that the point of contact starts as the fulcrum. In this way, Uke gains confidence that he can support himself. The trick is to move that fulcrum so that Uke falls off the table (and toward your elbow).

Third lever Age is similar to first lever Age, in that your arm is guiding Uke to the ground by eventually moving your forearm toward a vertical position.

There is no way to truly measure this, but this under-Age is probably the most common version of Age. Most of the Aikido kata start with a Mochi or grab that puts Uke in the upper or on-top position. (Typically, Uke grabs a wrist.) The trick is to create the sensation of rolling Uke's grasp from your wrist down to the inside of your elbow. (That trick may make more sense when we explore using the rings much later in this book.)

There is a fourth lever arm Age.

If you can allow Uke to fall off the fulcrum toward you, the same methodology can be used make Uke fall away from you. Toward or away, the result is almost identical.

We beat the last three lever-arm-based Aiki-Ages to death. I hope it will suffice to say that the fourth lever Age is sister to the third lever Age with the exception that fourth lever Age allows Uke to fall off the other side of the teeter-totter.

Align your index finger with the radius bone and point at the spot you want Uke to fall into. Let Uke slide toward your finger.

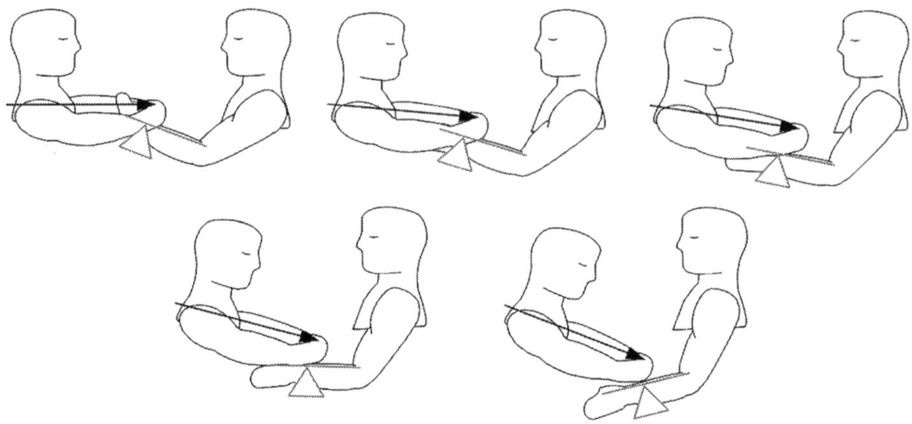

Fourth lever Age

Leverage the lever arms to effect an Aiki-Age or Aiki-Sage. This will complete step two of how to create connection and will leave you with a bridge that permits either Uke or us to lean on the other.

Now that you have connection, you are free to begin most Aiki techniques.

In summary of the connection and bridge

You can create a bridge and not have connection, but there is no connection without a bridge.

A bridge can be created through a joint-lock, grab, strike, block, or even Uke's reflexes (I think this is how Sensei throws Uke without even touching him).

In short, the bridge is the conduit we use to apply force to Uke.

Connection is formed when we use the bridge to lean on Uke or when he leans on us. Aiki-Age and Aiki-Sage are how we create the lean and complete the connection.

Connection cannot exist without the bridge. The bridge comes first. You can gain and then lose the lean, but still maintain the same bridge.

Although, the most common reason for losing connection is the destruction of the bridge.

Creating connection is entering. Once you have entered (gained influence of Uke's center of balance), you should have a sufficiently superior position to be faced with the moral dilemma of what to do next.

The beginning phases of the striking arts rely solely on the bridge (the bridge can be the strike itself). The later phases of striking use connection to improve accuracy, deliver increased force, maximize damage, and most importantly, to keep from getting hit. This is the lesson Sensei Carlisle was trying to teach me when he told me to strike when Uke stops moving.

DESTABILIZING UKE

Destabilizing Uke means we are moving Uke's center of balance to the edge of where he is supported by his stance.

Like plastic army men, each of us has a base that defines the area in which we are stable.

The base takes on three primary shapes: a diamond, a rectangle, and the triangle in our feet. Our stance defines which shape is in effect.

The theory is quite simple. We remain standing (not falling) for as long as we keep our center of balance over (supported by) our base.

The base shapes

Unless supported by an active gyro, nothing I can think of in this world stands on any less than three points. (A top is a gyro. It can stand on one point as long as it spins. A bicycle has two gyros as it moves.)

So you say you can stand on one foot? Talented you, but have you ever stopped to take a good look at feet you stand on?

Try walking on the sidewalk for a while in white socks. Take notice of where your socks get dirty. Do you see the triangles?

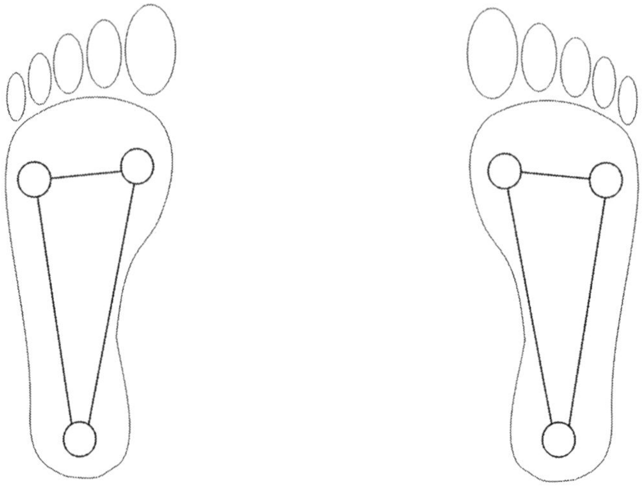

The triangles in our feet

It is important to understand that our feet are, in effect, tripods.

Why is this important? The shape of our base is a combination of the support provided by these tripods.

It should be obvious that standing on one foot means we are supporting all of our weight over one of these triangles.

What if we share our weight across both feet?

In a side-by-side stance (horse stance), the two triangles combine to create a rectangle (trapezoid).

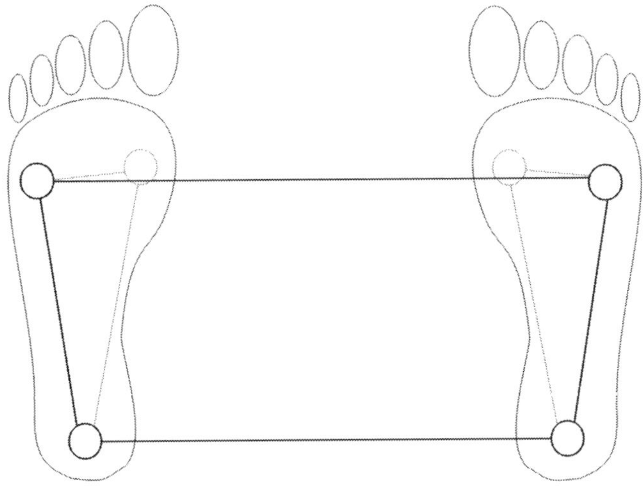

The rectangle base

With one foot forward, they form a diamond. Not the typical diamond. It looks more like a solitaire diamond from the side. A not so perfect diamond, but a diamond none-the-less.

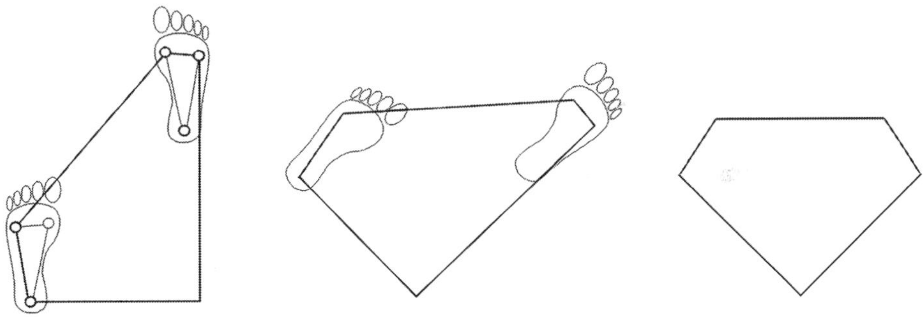

The diamond base

Moving our center to the edge

The next few statements are likely going to sound crazy, but trust me, they will make more sense after you read the precepts. Take this on faith and use your imagination until then.

Your center of balance (COB) is a ball that moves around inside the space of your pelvis. Your pelvis is like a flat sheet of ice, parallel to the floor, and the center of balance glides on the surface. (It is important to note that the center of balance does not roll; it glides without spinning.)

We control the motion of the COB. The control of the COB is better known as shifting our weight.

We lose stability as our COB moves closer to the edge of the base shape supporting it, to the point that we have to step once the COB moves or is projected outside that base.

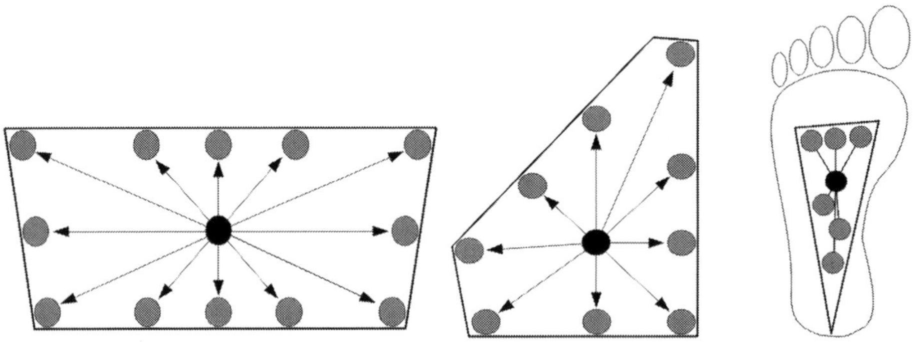

Reducing the base; moving the COB to the edges of the base shape

IN CONCLUSION OF BASIC TERMS

We have covered only a few of the terms we use in class. The language of our class is constantly evolving. New terms arise, and we keep improving our understanding of the old.

Some of this likely seemed like random thoughts, but expect that we did not waste any time. The concepts are about to come together in a much bigger way.

Now, on to the precepts.

The Six Precepts

ANOTHER APPROACH TO LEARNING

I was (and still am) completely frustrated with being told, "Just do this," as if this were the only way to teach Aikido. I am not very good at learning by feeling (kinesthetic learning). There are too many variables involved to see what is missing. I need a logical approach. Need gave rise to invention.

The precepts are a tool to add cognitive awareness to how you move. The goal is to assist in learning the kinesthetic part(s) of Aikido more wholly and quickly. The precepts assist in reverse engineering motion. When someone says, "do this," you will have a way to analyze exactly what "this" means.

These precepts relate specifically to learning Aiki. The precepts are a foundation that should be in place while attempting to learn the other more advanced aspects of Aikido such as timing, breathing, relaxing, pressure points, etc.

What you are about to read was compiled over four years. It took some time to find the Six Precepts. They came slowly and out of order. Sometimes I understood them physically, but took months to find words to describe them. Other times, I knew what I wanted to do long before I could train my body to do it.

The explanations are a constant work in progress. The awareness and understanding of the Precepts continues to deepen. The analogy that makes sense to one person means nothing to another, so we create new explanations. The explanations included are the most widely relatable explanations I know.

Three quick notices before we begin. First, I wish I had more time to refine the explanations. Second, I wish you would not have to try to learn this from a book. Discussion, Q&A, and tailoring the explanations to your background are a far better way to engage this material. Lastly, sincere condolences as you apply the Precepts. Trust me on this. Your brain will adapt very quickly, but your body will need some time to catch up.

In fact, some of the motions you have already mastered kinesthetically will crumble and disappear as you engage your mind with your motion. Do not worry! The temporary "loss" seems to be a path to greater ability. I cannot duplicate Moe (yet!), but I can tell you with certainty that I am progressing steadily. The moves that have boomeranged back are consistent and extremely repeatable.

You can expect to experience this setback each time you add attention to a different Precept, but keep with it. It is somewhat like juggling. Keeping one or two Precepts in the air is not that difficult. It is the third and fourth one that starts the challenge.

In all things, train to expand your awareness; appropriateness will follow.

What is a Precept?

The Precepts are the key mechanical elements of controlling another person's balance and stability.

These Six Precepts are important elements of adding Aiki to your techniques.

The Six are ordered into three pairs. The first pair describes where Uke is weak. The second pair describes where you are strong. The last pair are the connection builders.

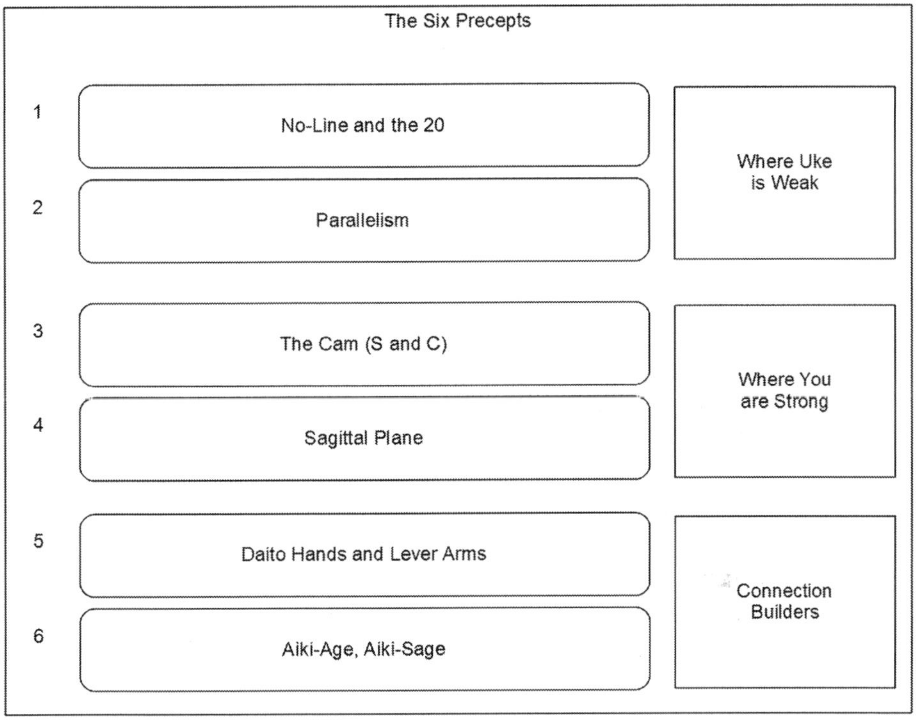

The Six Precepts

Expect to find a quick review of the Precept and a quick drill to help feel the concept. We then tie together each pair of Precepts into more advanced concepts.

Unless noted, expect that all the techniques mentioned in the application of the Precepts will be a reference to the Juu Nana Hon Kata (Tomiki's core seventeen techniques kata). I will use both the number and name of the technique. Keep your browser at the ready if you are not already familiar with the Juu Nana Hon Kata.

WHERE UKE IS WEAK

Precept 1: no-line and the 20

Every stance has its strong and weak lines. It is a function of being a biped equally weighted (or nearly equally weighted) on two feet.

The no-line and the 20 are the lines where we are least capable of generating force. As such, these are the directions in which we are most likely to lose stability.

Both Tori and Uke are subject to this (in)ability.

The no-line and the 20 are named due to their position in a forward-foot stance.

With one foot in front of the other, the no-line extends forward and backward as it passes between the feet. The no-line crosses the center-line at about thirty degrees off center. The 20 passes through the feet and crosses the center-line at nearly twenty degrees. The 20 also extends in two directions. The 20 is sometimes described as bringing Uke over his little toe. The 20 also extends over the heel of Uke's rear foot.

In a horse stance, the no-line again goes between the feet, and the 20 moves through the feet.

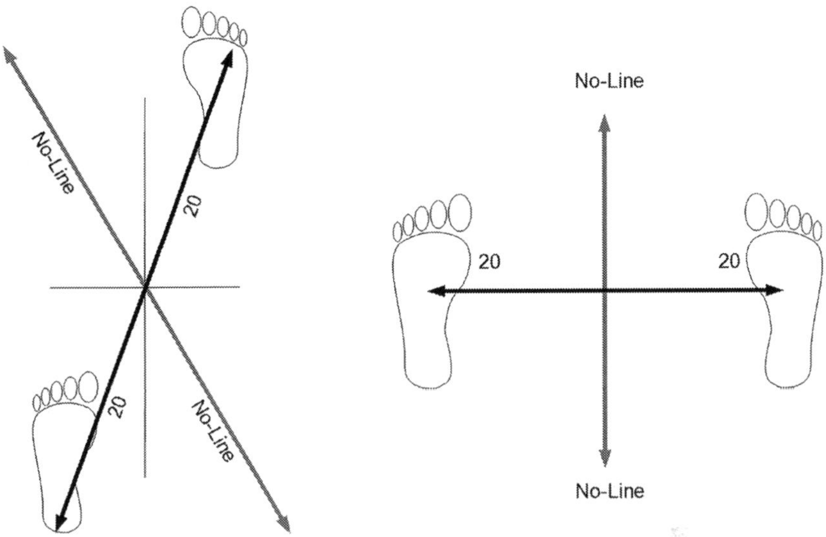

No-line and 20 in a right-foot forward and horse stance

There are many ways to get a keen sense of where the no-line is. The simplest solo method is to try touching the floor along the path of the no-line. Any stance will work as long as you keep your feet in place and maintain near to equal weight on your feet. You should feel yourself making significant adjustments in stance and overall weight shift to avoid stepping or falling.

The best method for experiencing the no-line is to use a partner.

Have Uke stand in a right-foot forward-stance. Uke's goal is to remain equally weighted and not move his feet.

Put your hand on Uke's chest and begin pushing Uke along the center-line. Uke should be easily able to present resistance at this point. Now, while maintaining this pressure, begin to orbit Uke counter-clockwise. As you step in this circular path around Uke, you will find a point where Uke is unable to offer much, if any, resistance. This is the no-line.

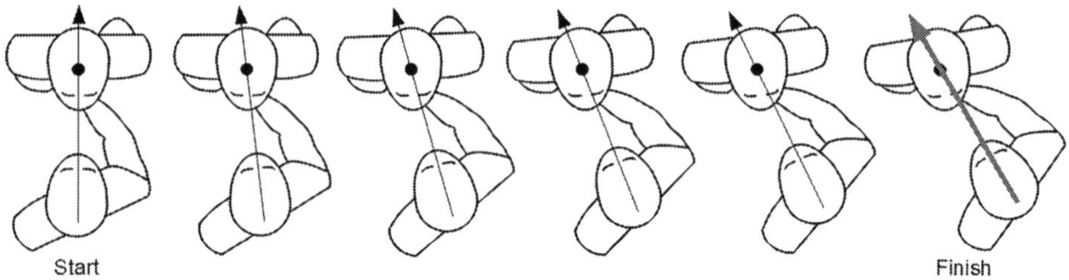

No-line drill: Tori orbits Uke to sense the no-line

Try it again, but this time, instead of pushing on Uke's chest, grab his shirt in the middle of his chest and pull Uke as you orbit.

Shomenate relies heavily on the no-line (#1 of the Tomiki 17). In many ways, the aforementioned drill is Shomenate. Instead of many steps used in the drill, Tori should use a single turn-step (tenkan-ashi) to move into the final position. This single-step version is the most appropriate way to turn the drill into a functional move. Practice the initial drill. Once you have a feel for the no-line, begin performing the drill with one step. Evolve to Uke stepping in, then with Uke punching, kicking, etc.

I find it helpful to use a line on the floor to teach the no-line. As Uke, position yourself so that the line on the floor (seam in the mat) is the no-line. Once in position, hold both arms straight outward to allow Tori to line himself up with your center-line. The outward arms will additionally serve as a way to judge the Ma-Ai. Once Uke is in place, drop your arms and practice accordingly. (Tori orbits using one or multiple steps, or Uke steps back and starts into a one-step sparring exercise, e.g., throws a punch, kick, etc., as Tori moves into position.)

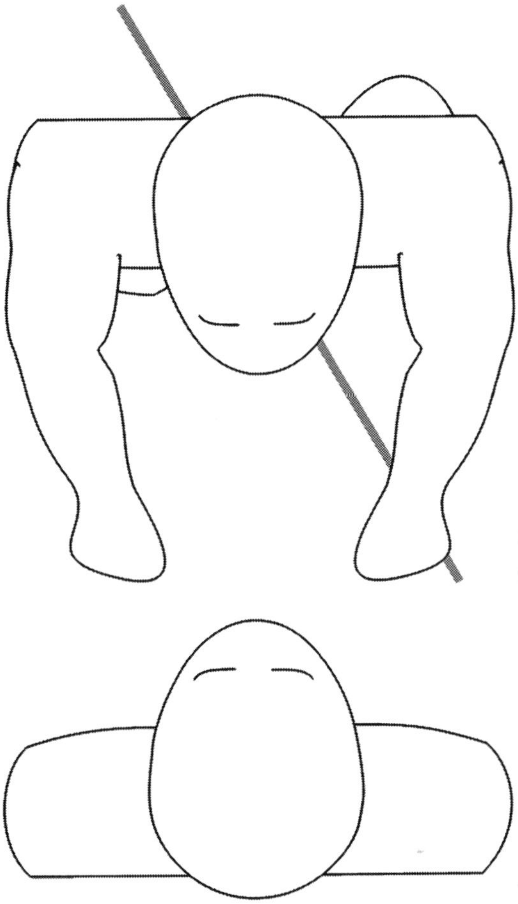

Uke uses a mat seam to give Tori visual cue of the no-line; Tori lines up between the arms

For now, the measure of success when using the no-line should be that you make Uke step. Although the no-line is the basis of many techniques, it itself is not enough to throw Uke. It takes more than one precept to make a throw.

The 20 is not much harder to recognize. The same drills we used for the no-line apply. We simply orbit Uke clockwise. Pull Uke to lead him over the toe and push him to move him over his back heel.

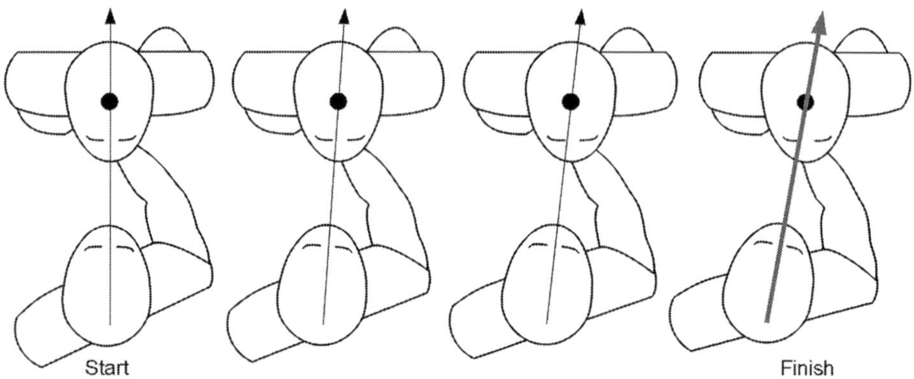

The 20 drill: Tori orbits Uke clockwise

This drill is the main ingredient of Aigamaeate #2. Uke steps and punches right. Tori will turn-step to the left and push Uke along the 20.

You can turn that drill into Gyakugamaeate #3 by striking with the left arm. Use the 20 to make the throw.

Of course, re-position yourself a bit and you can use the same seam in the mat to help teach the 20.

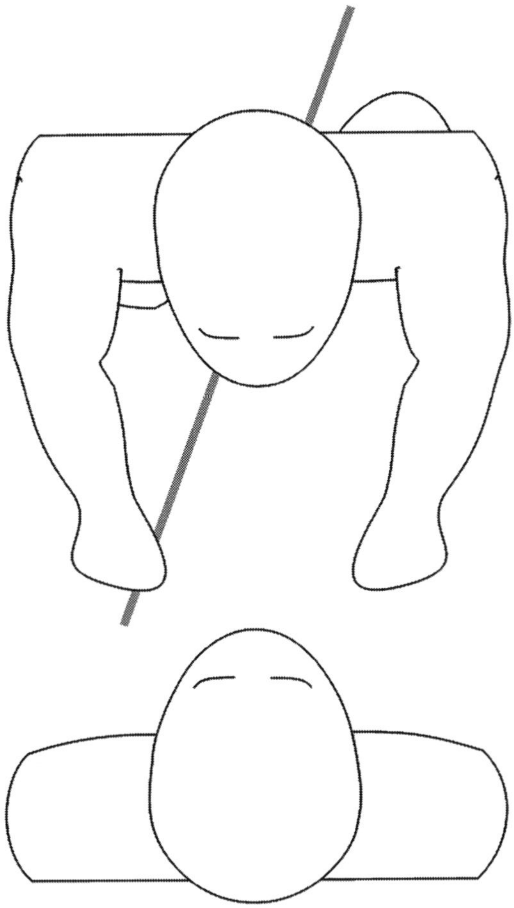

Using a seam in a mat to line up for the 20

Awareness of this weakness in our stance is important in all aspects of sports. Yoga practice is enhanced when you understand where you can and cannot focus your weight. In any double-weighted pose, leaning in the direction of the no-line or 20 will result in having to step. (Try warrior pose, but instead of putting your arms directly forward and backward, place your arms parallel to the no-line. If you have not already noticed the change in your stability, get ready to step as you have someone put the slightest amount of pressure down on one or your hands.)

One last thought before we move on. Keep in mind that the no-line moves as Uke walks.

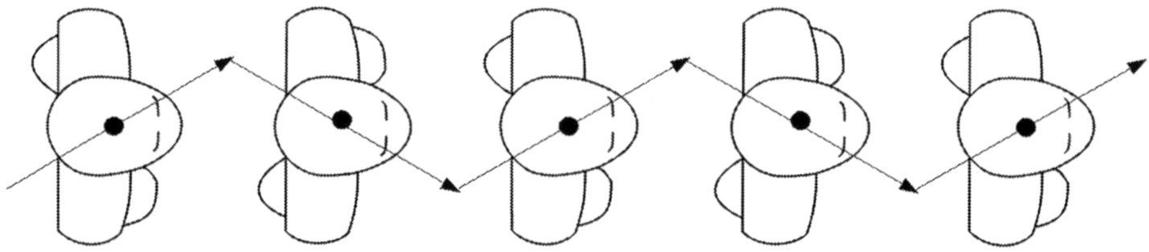

No-line moves with Uke as he walks

You can learn to anticipate where the no-line and 20 will be as Uke steps.

Precept 2: Parallelism

Perhaps the easiest Precept to understand but surprisingly troublesome to get correct is Parallelism.

Parallelism is the answer to, "What do I do when I am not directly on the no-line or 20?"

Parallelism is taking Uke along a line parallel to the weak lines in his stance.

Stealing from our basic terms section, Parallelism for the no-line and 20 looks like this:

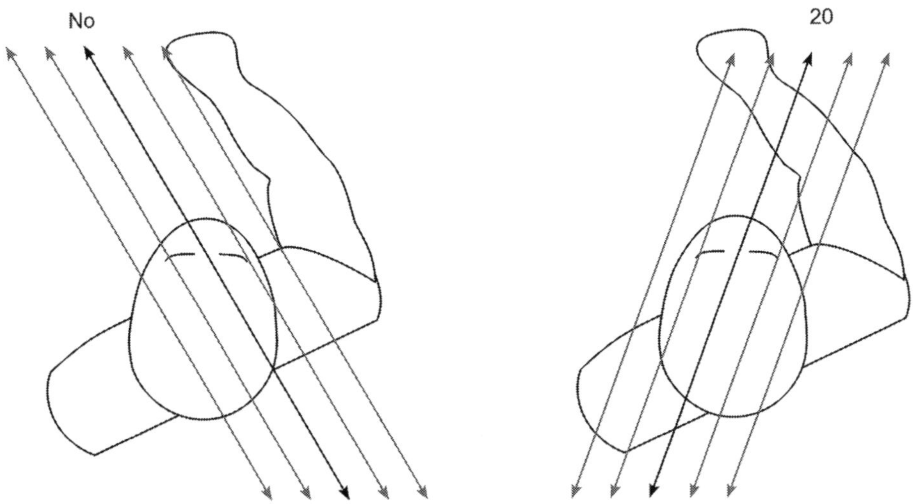

Parallelism is applying force to Uke parallel to the weak lines in his stance

Parallelism requires a good bit of spatial and body awareness. This includes awareness of Uke's body as well as your own.

I think this is a good time to include a drill.

The basic Parallelism drill is similar to Sumiotoshi #16.

In this drill, we will start from a static position. Line up facing each other in a right-foot-forward stance, right arm extended, and touching wrist to wrist. Uke stays double-weighted and does his best not to move his feet.

Grasp Uke's wrist with both hands, step leftward, and lead Uke down the 20 just far enough to take the slack out of his arm. At this point we are directly on the 20 and Uke should be only slightly off balance.

Did you remember to bring both of your feet together? Good! Now step left along the parallel no-line and do your best to throw Uke.

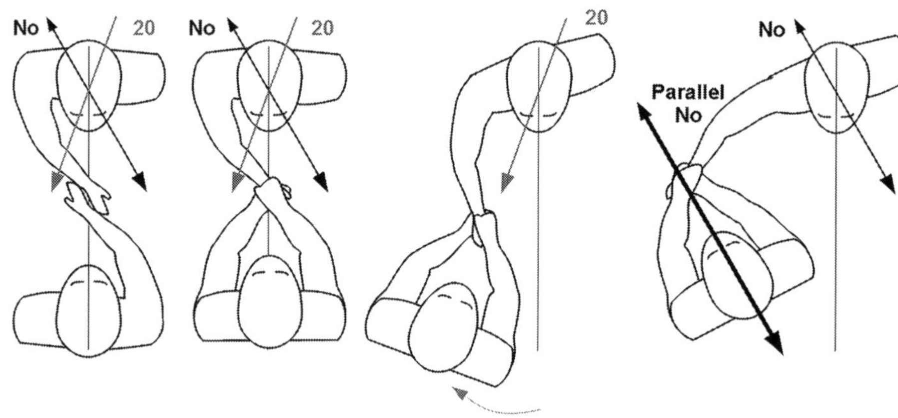

Parallelism drill

The most common mistake made at this point is moving toward the no-line in lieu of parallel to it.

Another common mistake is the temptation to follow the rotation of Uke's arm.

The most common cause for both of these is a lack awareness of where the no-line is.

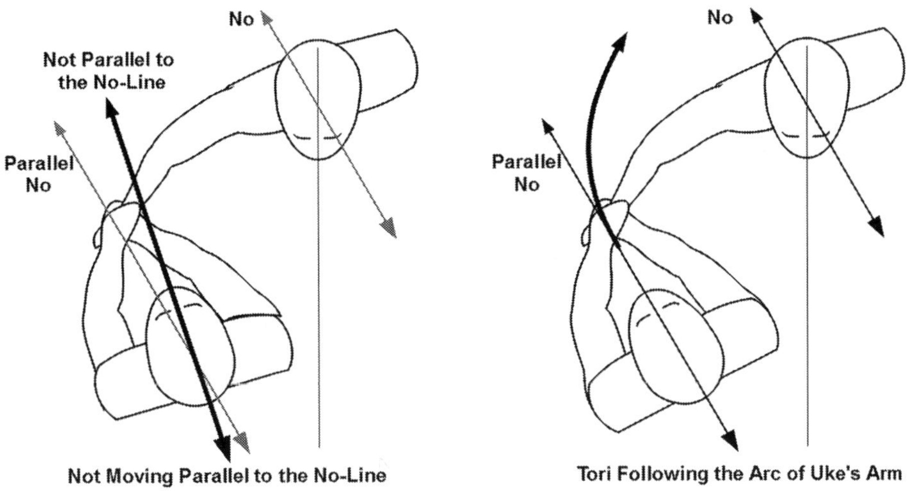

Common issues in Parallelism drill

I have taught this more than a few times and I can say with confidence that it may require a visual cue to finally get a feel for where the no-line is.

If you do find a correction is required, this is the best time to have Uke align his no-line with a seam in the mat. As Tori, it may help to put yourself in a bowling mindset. Throw a straight ball (no spin) toward an imaginary headpin that is equally far from the no-line as you are.

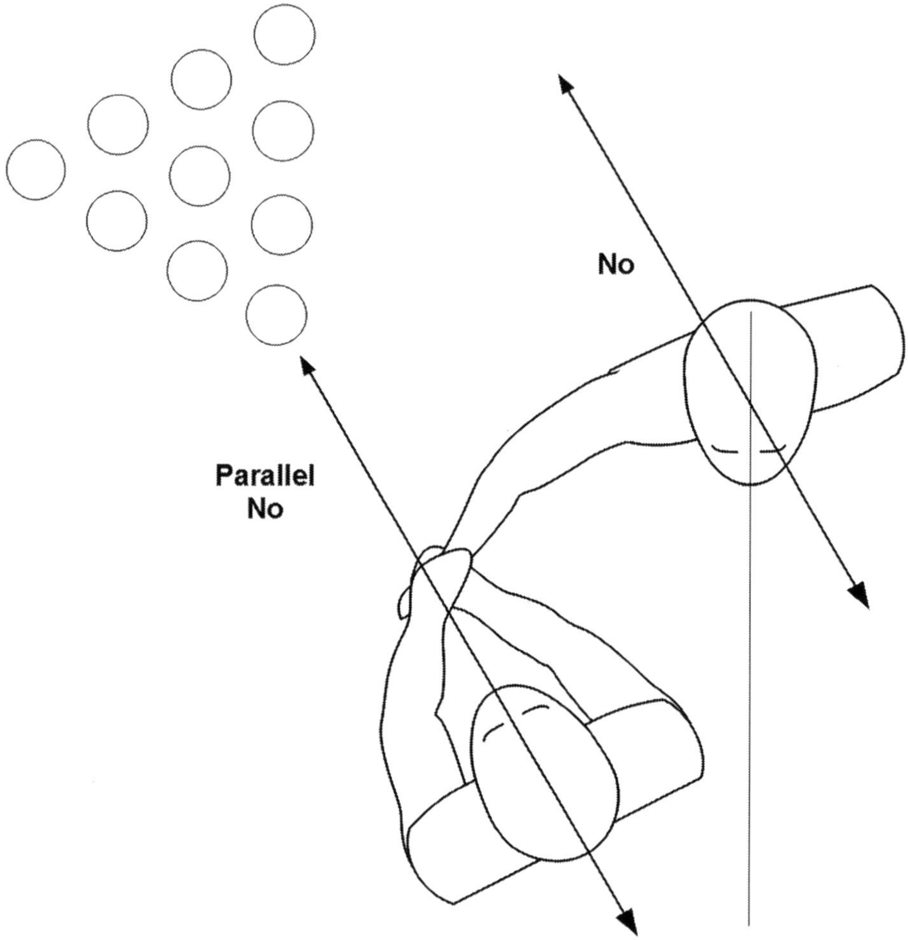

Using a bowling analogy to keep parallel to the no-line

Start looking for Parallelism in your Sensei's motion. You will likely find the same thing I did: Sensei has such awareness of this line that he/she can move almost anywhere and still maintain the integrity of moving Uke's center parallel to the weak lines in the stance. (Sensei may not be cognitively aware of what he/she is doing!)

Parallelism shows itself in many places. You are likely using Parallelism any time you are relying on contact with Uke's appendages versus his torso/head.

Tier 1 Advanced

You did not think the first two Precepts stopped there did you?

It could end there, if that were all you wanted. You can get a lot of mileage from these quick, linear examples of where Uke is weak.

We are about to explore how Precepts 1 and 2 become circular.

Rotational no and 20: The curves!

Quick review of a few key concepts in the basic terms section:

1. The curves are how we use the no-line and 20 at the same time.
2. Frontward and backward for both the no-line and 20 equals four directions.
3. Four directions, four curves.
4. The curves are not perfect circles (unless you are in a horse stance).
5. The lotus or football patterns arise as you consider how the curves overlap each other.

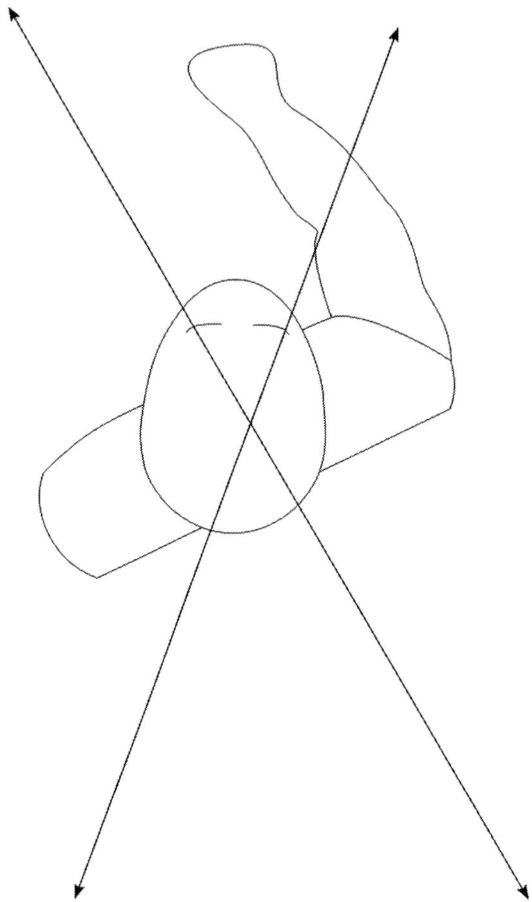

Four (linear) directions

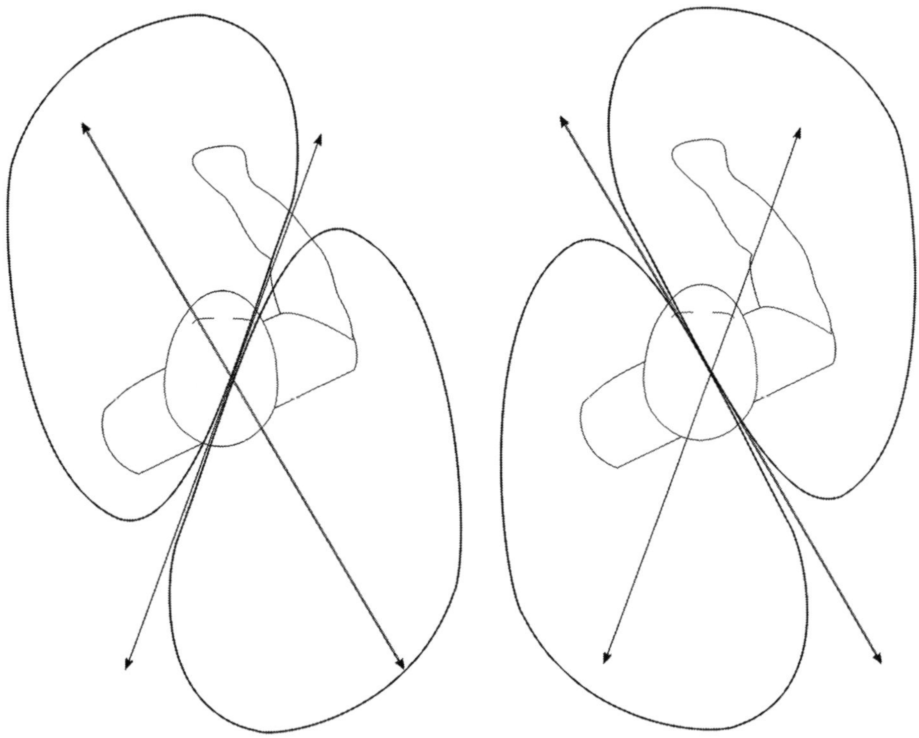

The four curves

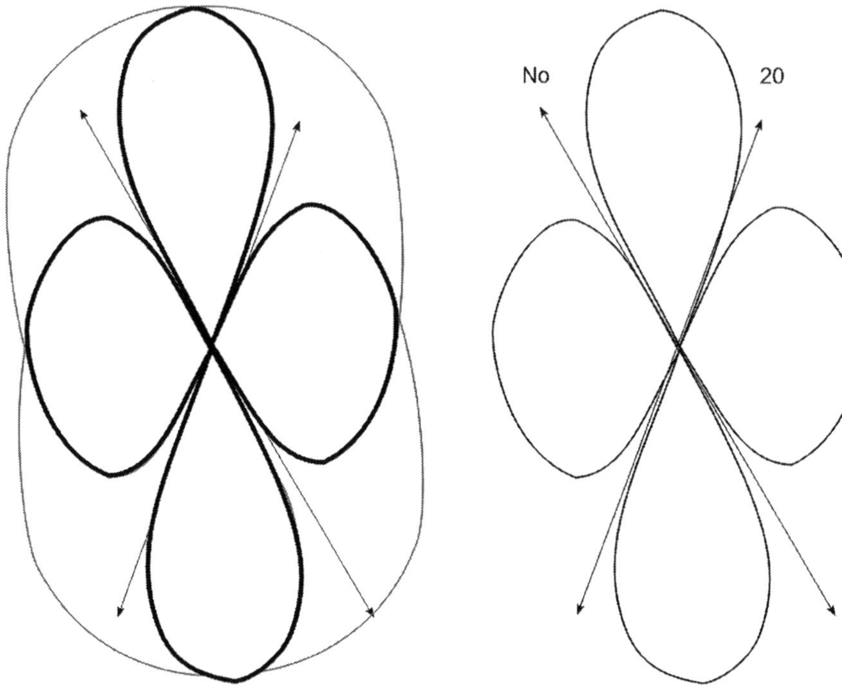

The footballs (lotus) formed by the overlap of the curves

All caught up? Good! Now to answer the question on the front of your mind: "Why do I care about the curves?"

Why use the curve?

Most Aikidoka train to do a great job of stopping the first fist from hitting them squarely, but they stop short at considering that Uke has two hands. Stopping Uke's first strike leaves his second hand free to swing around and deliver the follow-up blow.

Coming in contact with Uke should result in control of Uke's entire body. This is where the curves come in.

The typical sequence of events is as follows. Tori will maintain distance from Uke, such that Uke has to take a step in order to strike Tori (basic Ma-Ai). Uke attacks and Tori engages.

The common engagement is Tori slipping the initial attack and positioning for a throw.

Below is a representation of Tori slipping to the outside of Uke's right arm as Uke attacks with a right-arm, right-foot forward punch.

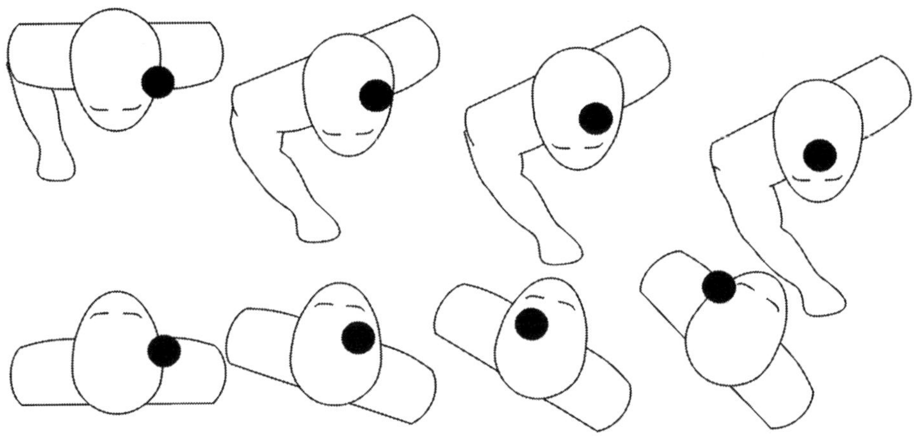

Uke attacks right-hand, right-foot step, Tori positions

We have not covered this yet, but for the purposes of explanation, the dot over each participant is the center of balance (COB).

Tori has successfully slipped the attack. In order for Uke to launch his left hand, Uke has to rotate his body clockwise around his center of balance.

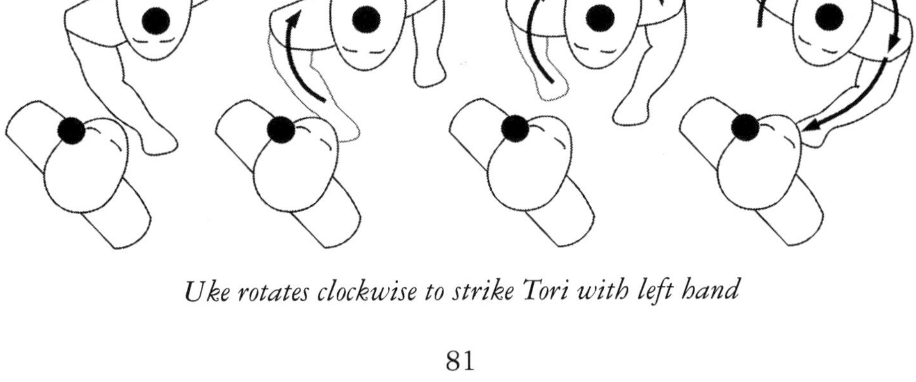

Uke rotates clockwise to strike Tori with left hand

How do we keep Uke from launching the second attack? In other words, how do we control Uke's center and not just Uke's arm?

The short answer: Slide Uke along the edge of one of the football curves (lotus petals).

"What do I mean by 'Slide'?" you ask.

Sliding has two parts: 1) spinning Uke's center while 2) drawing his center toward the weak lines of his stance.

Spinning Uke is like pulling the rope that starts your lawn mower. You are not tugging on the center of the wheel directly. You spin the wheel by tugging on the outer circumference. Much like spinning the hub of a bicycle wheel by running your hands over the rubber tire.

The first part of spinning uses Uke's arm (or some other part of his body) as the outer edge that ultimately spins his center.

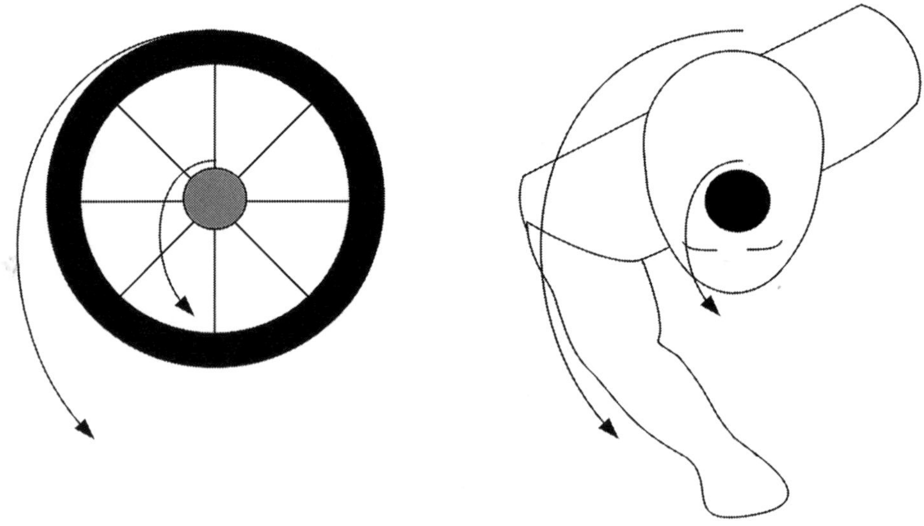

Spinning a tire as similar to spinning Uke around his center

The second part of sliding, drawing Uke's center toward the weak lines in the stance, should be fairly obvious by now. In lieu of simply moving toward the no-line or 20, we attack both by following a curve.

Let us use the outside edge of the forward football as an example of a weak line in Uke's stance. (In other words, let us take a look at using the outer curve.)

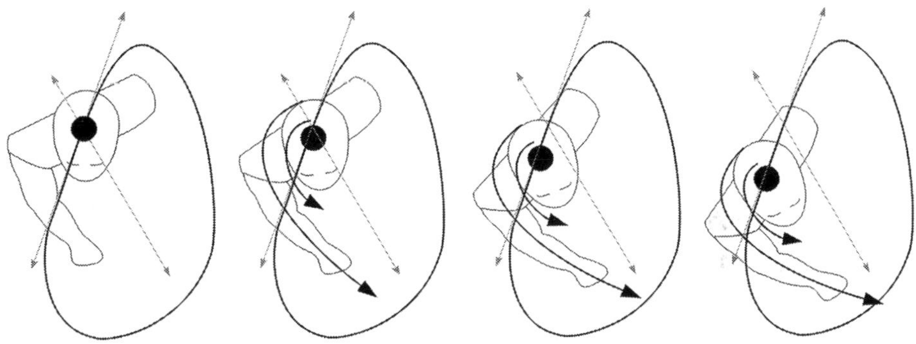

Sliding Uke: spinning his center as you draw him along the outer curve

This spin is a critical part of sliding. The spin creates a centripetal force that keeps Uke's opposite hand from reaching across to strike you.

Some additional thoughts on sliding.

- Sliding Uke along the curve maintains Uke's forward momentum to the point at which he cannot easily retreat backward in the same path he arrived.
- Sliding Uke along the curve is a rotational approach. As such, great distances are covered within a confined space. This is all the more reason why rotational control of Uke requires a good bit of practice to get it correct. It is easy to go too far.
- Uke is not spinning (revolving) at a high rate of speed. He does not need to. We simply need to keep him flowing counterclockwise (in this example). In fact, Uke never actually gets to finish a single revolution.

- Sometimes all you need is a spin. You do not necessarily have to draw Uke's center along a curve. You can use the spin to torsion Uke's hip and then throw Uke by applying force on the no-line or 20.

Not keeping Uke's center spinning counter-clockwise (in this example) is the primary issue encountered when learning this technique. Consider what happens when we collide with Uke's attack in lieu of accepting and guiding the force into a slide.

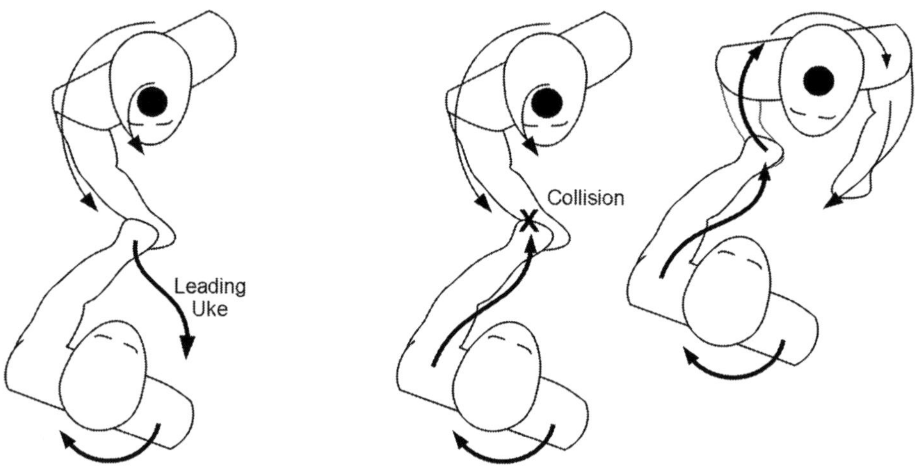

Accepting and leading Uke's attack contrasted with colliding with Uke

So now that we understand each other when we say slide or spin, let us take a look to understand what makes all this sliding work.

Controlling the hips

Although the control of the Uke's torso is very powerful, it is control of Uke's center that we are really interested in.

A bit of background story here, bear with me.

A while ago, I felt that many of the techniques we were playing with involved control of the first thoracic vertebrae (the one just below your neck).

I was working on "T1" theory for a short while, but knew that something was wrong. I had never heard anyone mention that your power came from between the shoulders, but I was grasping for something. I was stuck in the shoulder area. The shoulders are close to eye level, I was still two Precepts shy of six, and had not discovered the secret to Aiki.

During the same time I was investigating T1 theory, we were analyzing the supination and pronation of Uke's foot in various techniques (i.e., how Uke puts his foot down as he steps). Something useful was here, but I was not able to apply that information.

So after a few months of working simultaneously at the top and bottom, I stopped to take a look in between.

The result was that it finally dawned on me why sliding is so effective: it is all in the hips!

To be even more specific, it was an understanding of what happened to Uke's hips that was the key.

I started asking questions. If control of Uke's center is the goal, and the center was somewhere in his hips, how do I lock the joint where the center resides? How and when were Moe and Chris doing it?

A bit of careful observation was all it took.

The short answer: they were spinning Uke on his weighted foot.

I noticed that, as Sensei spun my center, my knee would get tense and then, more importantly, the thigh/hip bone (femur) would rotate to its extremity. In other words, the thighbone would lock against the front or back of the pelvis.

It began to be apparent that they were applying a gaeshi or hineri rotation on the leg in the same manner that they use rotation on my wrist (e.g., the rotation of the wrist leads to locking the elbow and eventually to locking the shoulder).

The masters were obviously using joint locks on the upper body to avoid being hit and to direct Uke's movement. It became clear that, when using rotational entries (sliding Uke), they use the upper body to direct the weight onto the appropriate leg and use the floor to apply locks to the lower joints.

Show you? Okay, but you will have to allow me a small bit of freedom of artistic expression. We are going to work with range of motion as opposed to actual bone structure.

From the top-down perspective, the femur and pelvis can be imagined to look a lot like this:

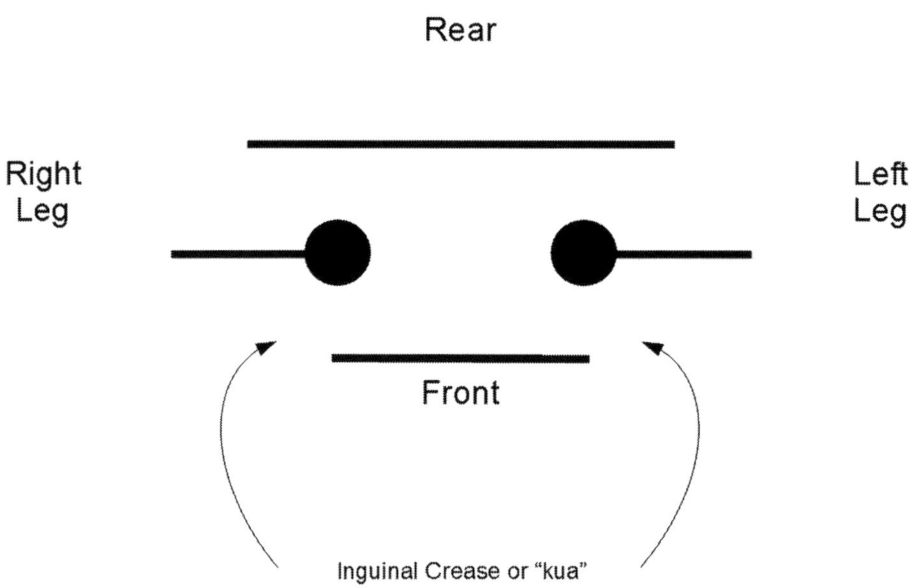

Top-down view of the hips and the tops of the femurs

The femur can rotate in its socket in three dimensions. The direction we are most interested in for this discussion is depicted below.

The rounded head of the femur sits in the hip socket and the other end (your hip) is free to arc forward or backward. Most persons describe this motion as opening or closing the hip (or Kua/Inguinal Crease). The effect on your foot can be described as toes out as you open your hips, and toes in on the closing.

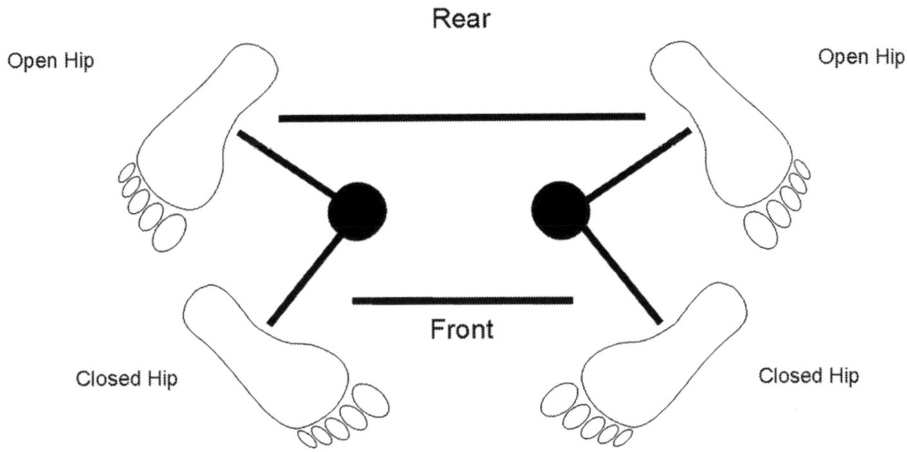

Opening and closing the hips

We are taking some liberties here. Notice the proximity of the top of the femur to the edges of the pelvis. I am fairly certain that the femur cannot actually contact the pelvis at those extremities. The two lines that represent the pelvis are just indications of where the hip has reached its limit of motion in this dimension.

Now, have you ever been told, "Point your toes in the direction you want to go"? Did you ask why?

Besides the obvious protection of your knee joint, the reason is that your leg, from hip to toes, basically acts like a wheel.

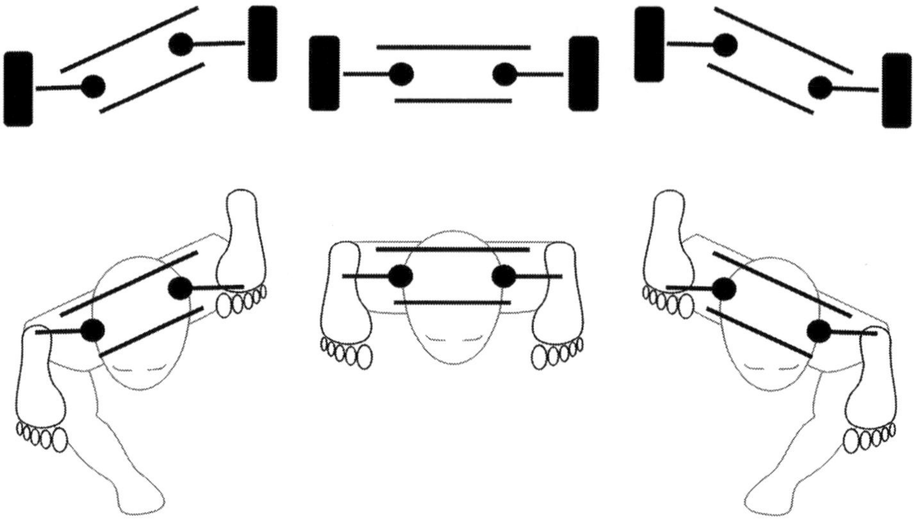

Your feet and hips depicted as a wheel

Neat little axle we have for a set of hips, huh?

What happens when a bicyclist suddenly turns the wheel sideways? He tumbles! This is the result of his mass moving laterally in lieu of in line with the wheel.

It is very similar with your hips. I said similar, not exact. You see, the bike is a solid frame. Your hips allow the femur a bit more play. The additional dimension of the ball joint allows you to cross your legs.

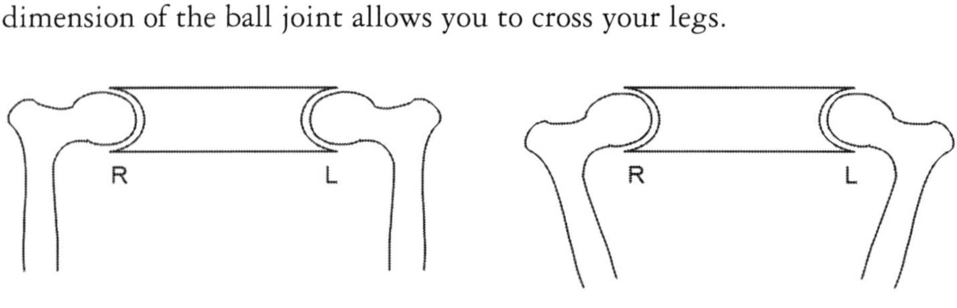

The position of the femurs in relation to the hip in a normal and scissor-leg stance

The scissoring of the legs is how you karaoke (forward and rear) cross-step.

How do we control Uke's ability to scissor or cross-step? How do we make Uke rigid enough to fall?

Simple! This scissoring of the legs is extremely awkward, to the point of almost impossible, when the hips are not in a neutral position. In other words, the karaoke step does not work when Uke's hips are at the full open or closed position.

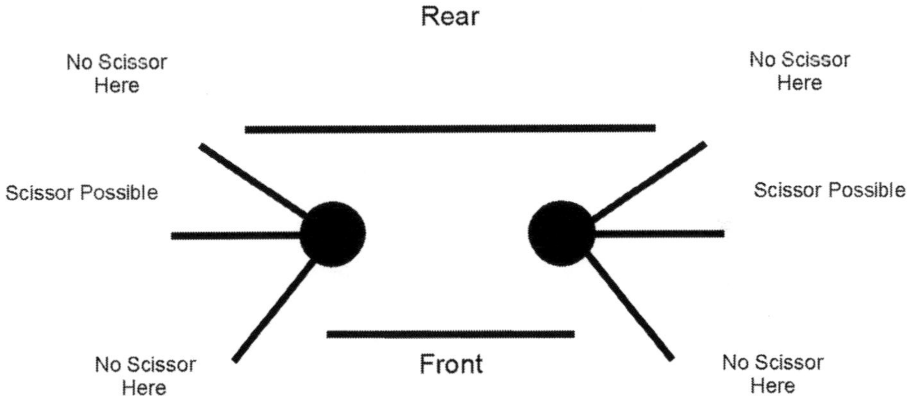

Your hips must be in or near neutral to allow scissor (karaoke) step

Thanks for coming back. If this is the first time you are reading this, I am almost certain that you just spent a few minutes locking out your hips to test what you just read.

Now that you understand in your mind and in your body, what do you notice about this picture?

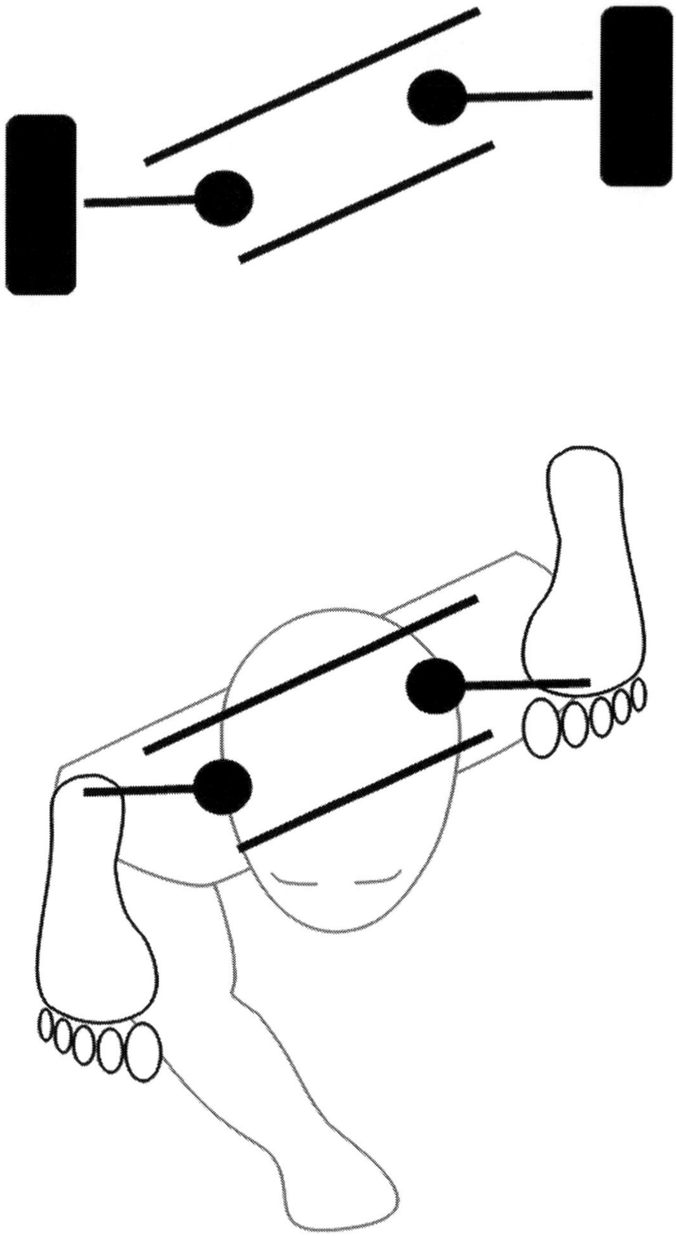

Uke is in right-side-forward stance; right hip nearly open, left hip nearly closed

Read the caption again. Take notice of how close the hips are to being open and closed. We do not have to spin Uke much further to make the right hip fully open and not too much further to get the left hip closed.

If we want to help Uke open or close his hips, we need to weight one of his legs and spin him. Weighting his leg plants his foot into the ground. In effect, you have used the floor to grab his foot.

Put Uke's weight into his right foot and spin him counterclockwise around the axis of his center.

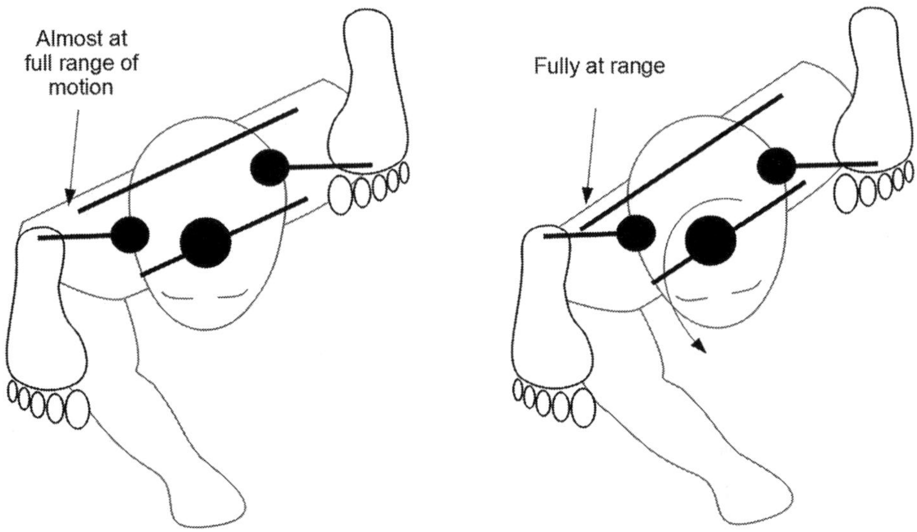

Spinning Uke around his center as you pin his foot to floor opens his right hip

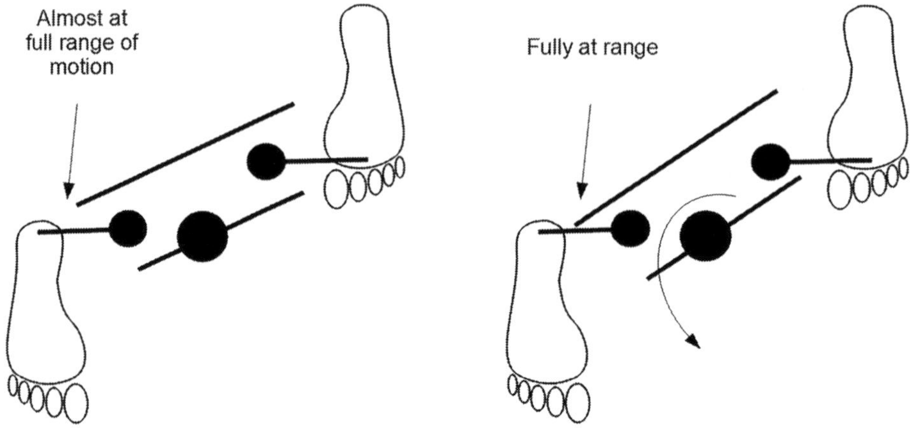

Same picture as above but with upper body removed

Can you see the spin causing Uke's right hip to fully open? Uke cannot karaoke step. In fact, you will find that Uke is very likely to throw his shoulders back in a reflexive attempt to gain stability.

Many instructors will describe the situation as opening a hole in Uke's stance. When Uke's right-hip goes fully open, his tailbone starts to tuck under and there is a soft spot in his stance just behind his right hip. Move Uke's body toward that soft spot and watch him crumble. It should not take much force to make him crumble.

I am going to skip giving an example of closing Uke's (left) hip. It is not as common in the basic seventeen kata. I sense the left hip moving to full close as I get thrown in Tenkai Oshitaoshi (#6, but instead of pushing across Uke, we turn outward and bring Uke along for the ride) or with very certain people, in Maeotoshi #15. (Chris Parkerson is the primary culprit. Chris likes the small circle, small movement throws.) In both situations, the left leg is fully closed, and they lead my head forward as they direct my fall. I am sure you can find it if you play a bit.

The scissoring and opening/closing of Uke's hips are the two most important directions we need to be aware of controlling if we want to throw consistently. Start analyzing yourself (and others) in terms of where did you/they put Uke's hips.

Tangent topic: You may understand better why certain styles of fighting are so adamant about squaring the hips and shoulders. You might see some relevance to the tai chi's external harmonies.

WHERE YOU ARE STRONG

Precept 3: The cam (S and C)

Understanding Uke's hips is a great segue to understanding your own hips.

I am beginning to understand that power comes from your center. The trick has always been in knowing where the center is and how to move it.

A great deal of force can be generated from your legs, but it cannot reach your upper extremities unless it is channeled upward. The hips are a common place to lose the connection to the floor (and nothing can hit you harder than the floor).

The cam is how to position your pelvis in such a way that you can drop forward and backward. The cam positions us to linearly project the force of the weight drop (e.g., into a step or punch). Drop stepping is efficient, relaxed, and easily the most powerful way I know of to move. The cam is integral to how we step and even in how we "move without moving."

The S and C are next in the progression. The S and the C continue the delivery to your shoulders. The position of your shoulders is important. You can be perfect in your footwork, aligned in the hips, and still have the shoulders and spine betray your technique before you even get to use your arms.

Let us take a look at the cam, how the cam applies to an Aiki (drop) step, and then tackle the S and C.

The cam

There are three important positions in the pelvis: backward, neutral, and forward.

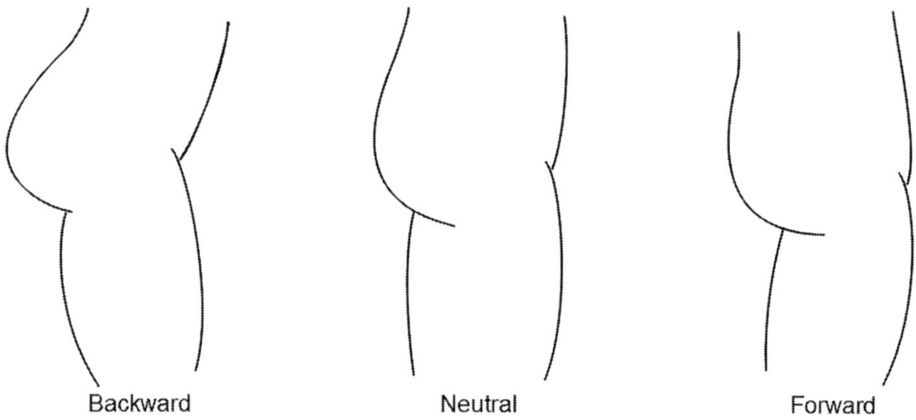

Three positions of the pelvis

The cam is rolling the pelvis to either the forward or backward position. (Forward cam, backward cam.) That is it, literally, but there is more happening behind the scenes.

Fully rocking our pelvis backward or forward is merely the effect. The purpose and cause for these positions is the deliberate drop of the hips over the femur. Let us take a closer look at our skeleton and notice that we are not simply tilting our pelvis.

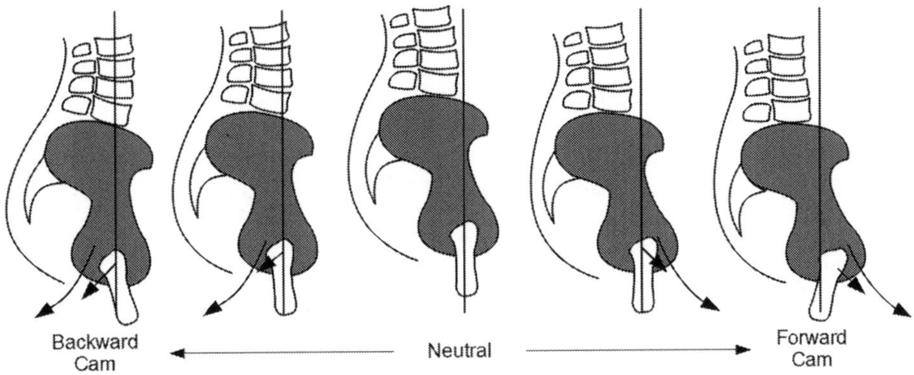

Moving from neutral hip to forward and backward cam positions

The above diagram expresses the action more subtly than I had hoped, but I expect you notice that the femur rotates in the hip socket and allows the pelvis/torso to fall on either side of the femur. The knees will bend and allow even more room for the femur to get behind the pelvis (in solid gray) and continue projecting the pelvis/torso in the desired direction (forward/backward) as the torso falls.

In the forward step, our intent is to drop or our torso between our leg and the object in front of us. The leg and the object in front will bear the weight. In most cases, the object in front of is not capable of supporting that weight (it is not easy to hold a person up, especially if we are falling onto Uke's no-line!).

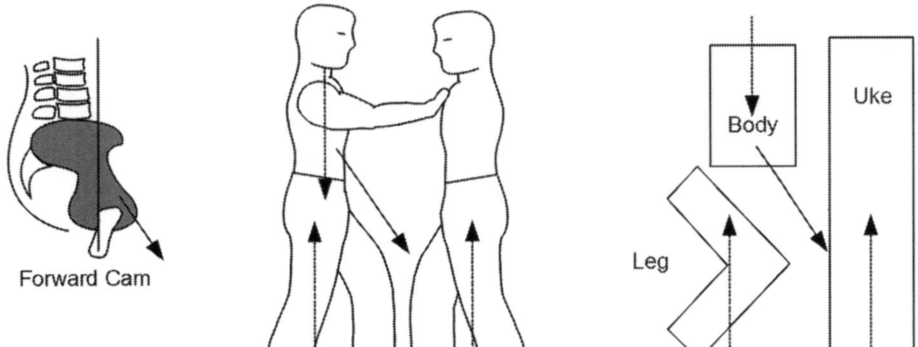

Relaxing and wedging the torso between the leg and Uke

Hips in the neutral, or worse yet, reverse cam have diminished effect on Uke when we attempt to move forward.

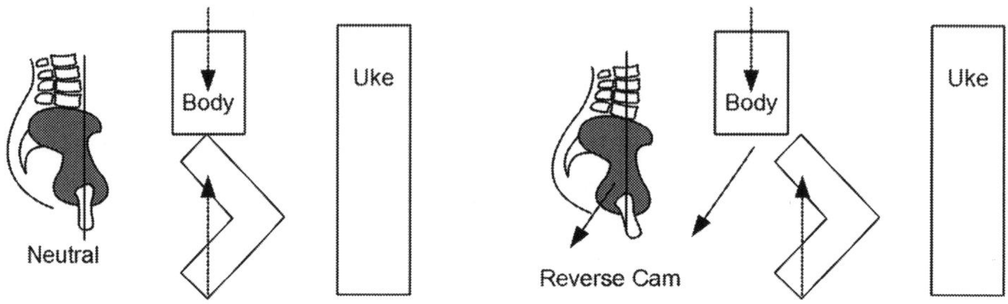

Neutral and reverse cam have diminished effect on Uke as we move forward

The key point to recognize is that we are using our weight and not our strength. The leg must support the motion, but the active ingredient here is wedging our torso between our leg and Uke.

To fully understand the application of the cam, we have to study how we step.

The Aiki (drop) step

There are two parts to Aiki (or drop) stepping: the drop and front-wheel drive.

Let us study a forward-right step (stepping forward with the right foot).

Aiki step: The drop

We begin by weighting the left hip, tilting the pelvis forward (forward cam), then dropping the torso over the left femur. Simple, elegant, and imbued with a hidden magic.

The pelvis is a solid object. A forward cam that pushes the bottom of the pelvis forward affects both the left and right sides of the pelvis as well.

The hidden magic is that as you cam and fall over the weighted left hip joint, your unweighted right leg will begin thrusting forward and toward position to catch yourself at the bottom of the swing. (This is a great way to get into a cat stance.)

As the pelvis falls over the left femur, the entire mass of the torso is deflected forward, and the weight begins to shift from the left hip socket to the right. (And yes, I consciously wrote hip socket. More information on that topic in the next precept.)

At the bottom of the swing, you will be equally weighted. That completes the drop.

How do we continue the swing upward? Front-wheel drive!

Aiki step: front-wheel drive

It is at this point the left leg takes a break and the right leg takes over. The right leg should begin to pull you onto its full support. The left leg should remain relaxed and will be dragged or hangs as we complete the weight shift. The legs close as the left leg catches up to the rest of your body.

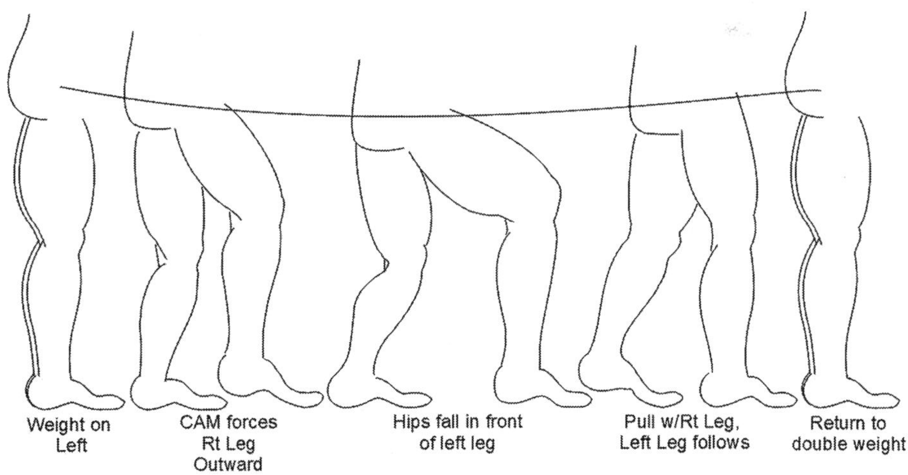

Forward cam drop step

The front-wheel drive feels like you are dragging your rear leg. Mainly because you are! It is a hip thrust and pull of the forward leg that completes the step. I sometimes describe the Aiki step as the Igor step. If you exaggerate a bit, you can mimic the stereotypical walk of mad-scientist's servant with a bad leg.

The picture above depicts returning to neutral hips, but that does not have to be the case. A slight cam can be kept indefinitely, or at least through a multiple of consecutive steps. (It is typical to hold a slight cam for at least two steps in the Tomiki basic seventeen kata.)

Take a quick look at the next diagram and become aware of the wave-like path created by Aiki stepping.

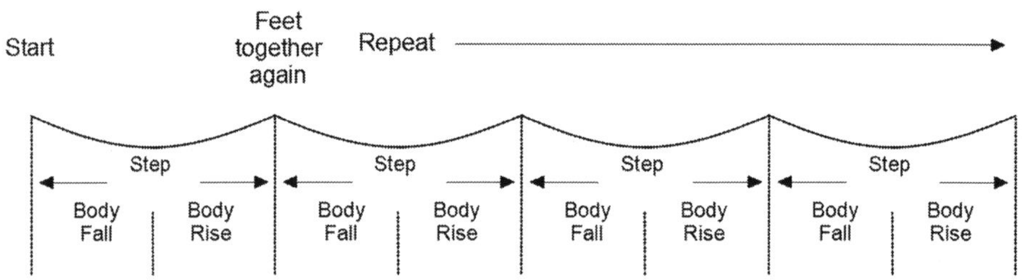

Aiki drop step path; the body falls before it rise; weight swings from one position to the other

Where is the difficulty?

What is the opposite of front-wheel drive? Rear-wheel drive. Real-wheel drive can be a real problem.

Rear-wheel drive can be described as a hop, pushing off starting blocks, or a skating motion.

In short, rear-wheel drive is weak in comparison, and it is not as easy to avoid as you might think. Rear-wheel drive is a hard habit to break because it is the common method people use to walk.

Rear-wheel drive can be applied at two points in a step.

When rear-wheel drive is applied at the start of the step. We throw ourselves through the air and become weightless at the middle of our step. Weightless in the middle of a step is not desirable in Aikido.

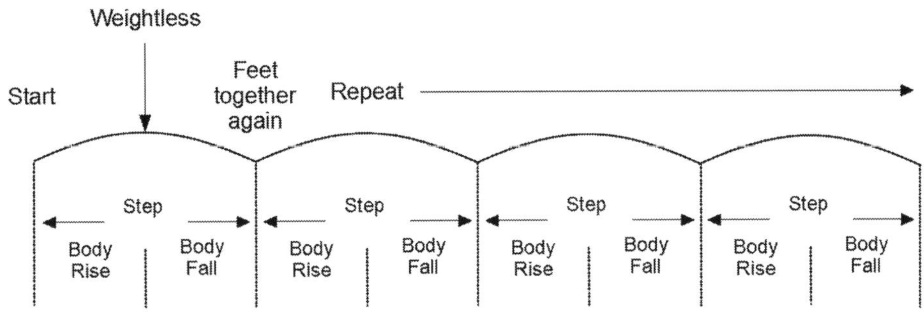

Rear-wheel drive applied at the start of a step;
Tori hops between steps and is weightless at the top

Look around a bit and you will find that many people push off of their back foot and hop everywhere they go.

If you can resist the temptation to use rear-wheel drive at the start and become aware of falling first, the initial drop of the Aiki step is easy to duplicate.

The next hurdle is to avoid getting to the bottom and then using the left (rear) leg to propel the body onto the right (forward) leg.

Propelling yourself using the rear leg is again a jumping action. The rear leg is vaulting you to the top, and we lose the momentum of our weight swinging upward.

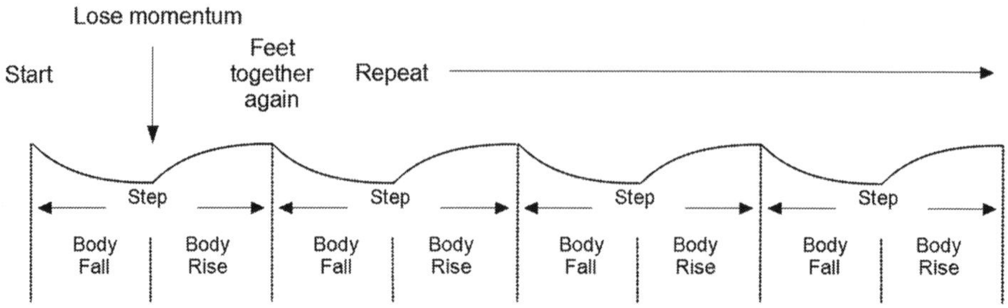

Rear-wheel drive applied at the bottom of the step; we lose the momentum of our weight swing

Trying to jump out of the bottom of the Aiki step makes it easy for Uke to simply smack you down.

Keep in mind that in the Aiki step, the left leg supports the drop; the right leg supports the rise.

Aiki stepping relies on swinging your weight. Because you are swinging your weight, you remain heavy throughout the step. You peak at the finish of the step (when your feet come back together), versus rear-wheel drive where we peak in the middle, weightless, with our legs apart.

Aiki step in reverse

Everything we just put into the forward step applies in reverse.

We will not go into detail about the reverse cam yet. Expect more study on the reverse mode as we describe the S and C. I will leave you with a reminder of this picture and the thought that, in the reverse cam, we are putting the weight (torso) on the opposite (rear) side of the femur.

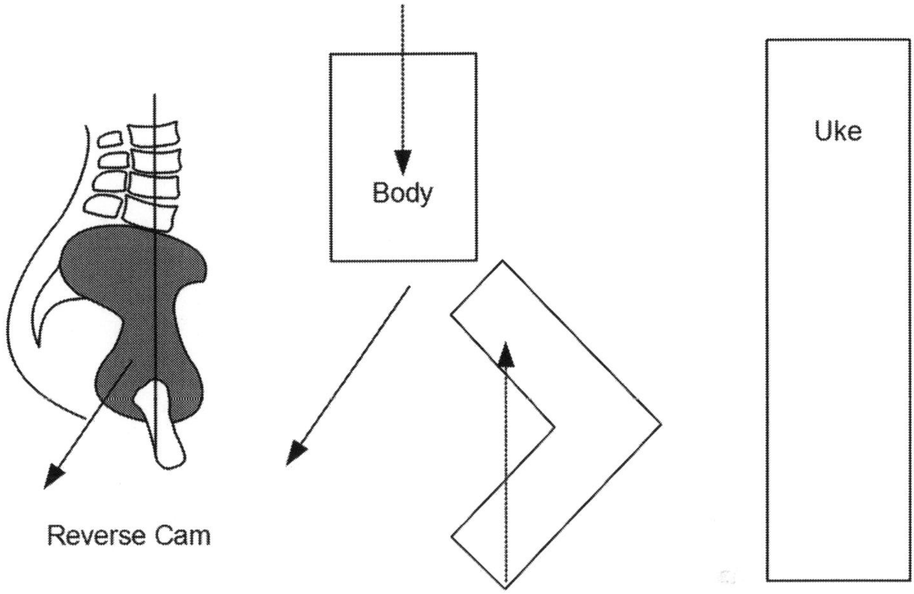

Direction of the power generated in reverse cam

Closing comment: In my opinion, drop stepping is how you should be stepping when practicing tai chi. The cam allows you to control the speed of your movement in constant contact with the floor, and positions the hip so that you can most easily transition weight from one foot to the other. Fast or slow, it does not matter. Play with the cam next time you practice. See if you agree.

Aiki step drill

Front-wheel drive is subtle and requires some attention.

We are going to take the time to build awareness of both front- and rear-wheel drive.

The good news is that this drill has a near one hundred per cent success rate at making front-wheel drive painfully obvious. The even better news, it is a very simple drill.

The Aiki step drill focuses on the latter half of a step; the part that requires rising up with front-wheel drive. This latter half of a step is the one that typically generates the most frustration.

Do not worry if you have issue with the initial drop; you will get plenty of practice with the entire step in the push drill that we learn after the S and C discussion.

Let us explore how not to step by using rear-wheel drive first.

Stand, legs apart, knees almost straight, even weighted. Shoulder width or less between the feet is fine. Toes forward. Get comfortable.

Notice that both of the hip joints (Kua/first belt hoop) support the weight, and that, in the sense of the Aiki step, we are at the bottom of the swing. Ready?

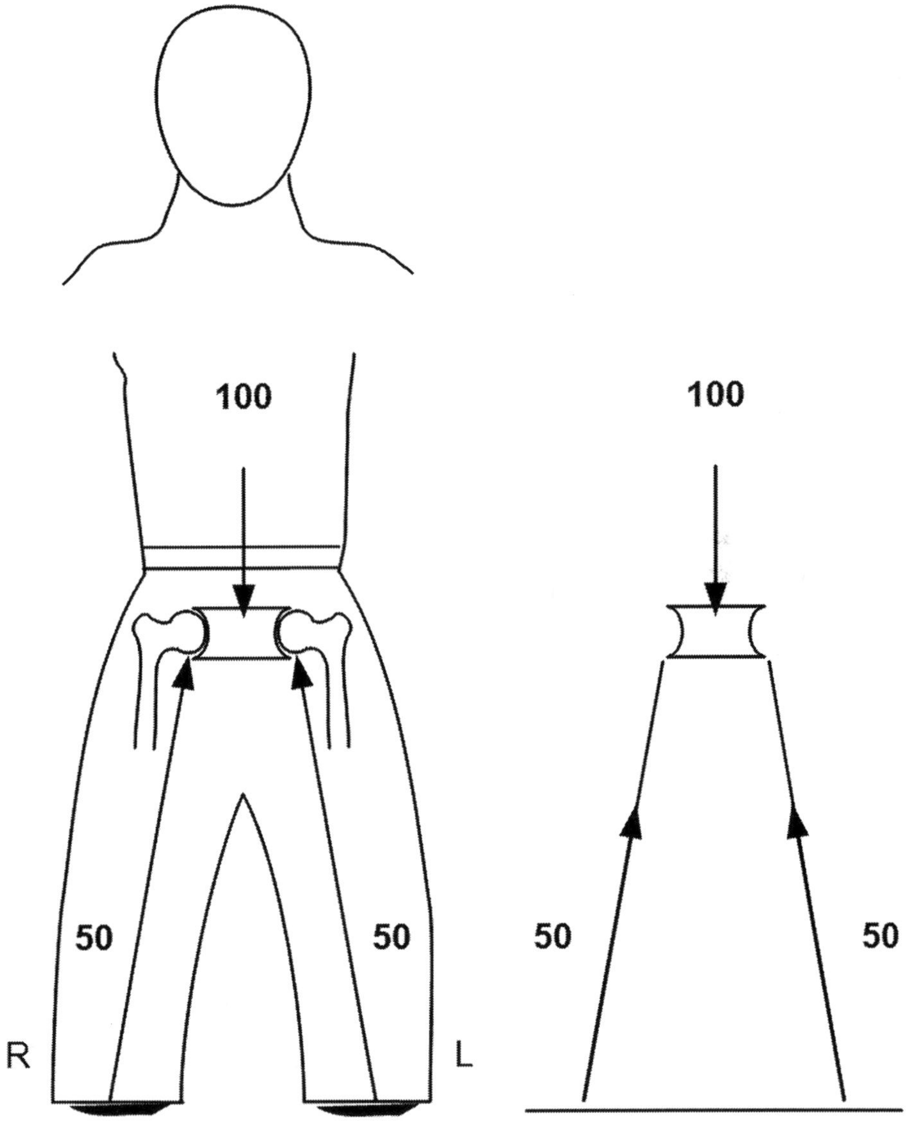

Legs apart, legs almost straight, equal weighted stance

Simply flex your left calf to extend your toe and lift the left heel off the floor. Your weight should shift from the middle to your right side, balance yourself on the right side.

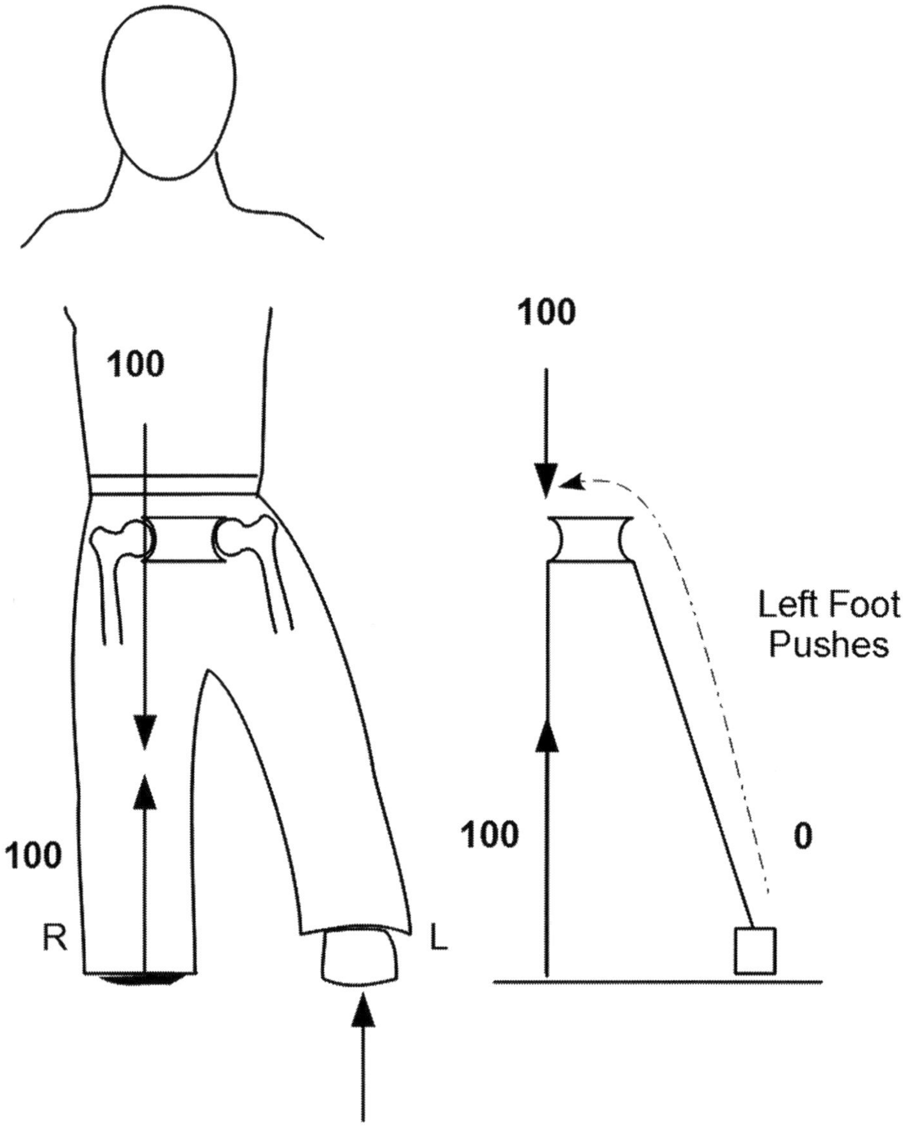

Extend left foot (lift left heel) to move to right-side single-weighted stance

That was rear-wheel drive. Really. Not much to it. For many of us, this is how we step every day; jumping, ever so slightly, from hip to hip with every step.

Did you feel the left foot (rear foot in relation to which direction we were moving) push upward and nudge our weight over to the right side? The rear foot drove us to the right (rear-wheel drive).

We are going to return to this very same ending position when using front-wheel drive, but we get here a different way.

Now let us try this with front-wheel drive. Reset yourself to the double-weighted position.

This time, keep your left foot flat on the floor, bend the right knee, support all of your weight on the right, and then straighten the right leg. Your left leg should remain relaxed. Leave the ball of your left foot on the floor as your left heel rises. You should again find yourself in that final position.

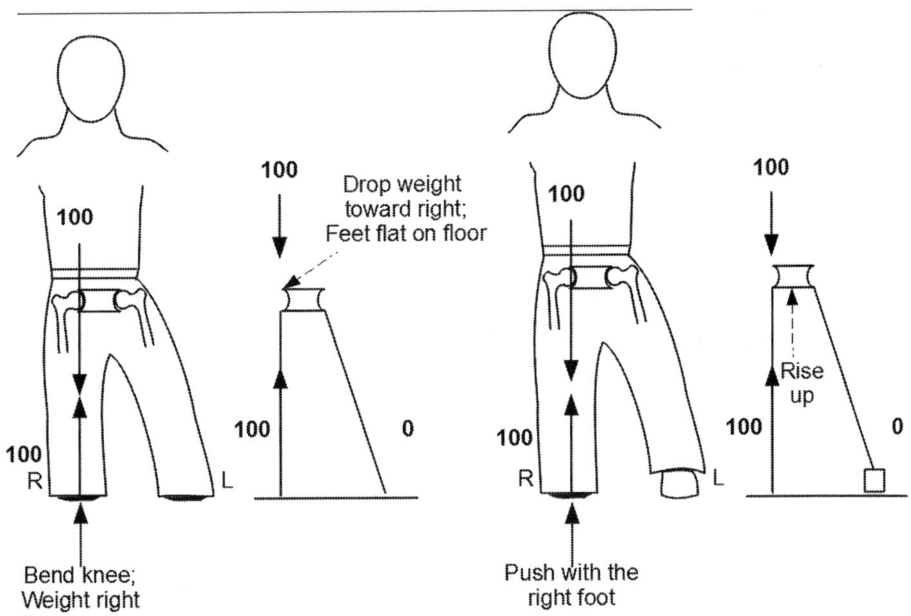

Bend right knee, support all your weight on right, and straighten right leg

The right leg (the forward foot in relation to the direction we are traveling) did all the work. Relaxing the right leg allowed the weight to sink onto the right leg. Flexing the right leg allowed you to rise upward. The pelvis lifted the left leg enough that your left heel came off the ground.

We ended up in exactly the same place, but by an entirely different action.

Relaxing on the right allowed gravity to do the work. We dropped onto our forward support. In rear-wheel drive, the left calf did all the work. We jumped onto our forward support.

It is much easier to stop someone from jumping than it is to catch them as they drop.

Are you still in that final position? Great. Now, keep the left leg relaxed and flex the ankle such that you lift the ball of the left foot off the floor. Your left leg should have swung or dropped and brought your feet together. That is the finish of the Aiki step. This action is why it feels as though we are dragging our left leg.

I like to practice getting back to the starting, neutral position by using the drop portion of the Aiki step. In other words, to get back to the beginning pose, I like to perform the Aiki step sideways.

Want to take this a bit further? How about we turn this into a hip-wheel turn?

Turning the drill into a hip-wheel turn (pun intended) is as simple as turning the torso as you perform the rise-up.

Start in the neutral position.

To move right (look left), bend the right leg and get fully weighted right. In lieu of simply pushing upward with the right leg to get into the last position, rotate your hips slightly and allow your right Kua to open. Keeping the ball of your left foot on the ground, the left heel should spin a bit and you should find yourself in a cat stance.

Move back to the neutral position by uncoiling your hip and allowing your left foot to twist on the ball. Shift your weight back to the middle.

Try the same action toward the left, return to neutral, shift right, return to neutral.

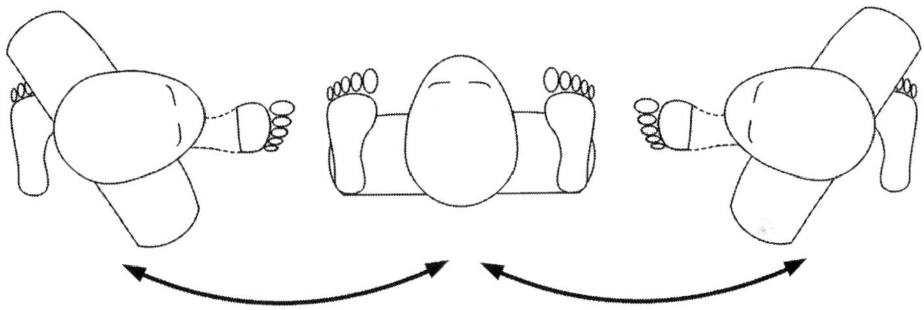

Hip-wheel turn drill

Do not be confused by the above diagram. The balls of the feet stay in the same place the whole time. It was an eyesore to draw it that way.

Tired yet?

Want to take it just a bit further?

You have learned how to use front-wheel drive to move laterally. We need to learn how to do this forward and backward.

Practice the Aiki step drill again, but this time, position your feet in front of each other. Step to the corner (shown as 2 below), and then practice forward and backward (shown as 3 below).

Feel for the front-wheel drive in all of the steps.

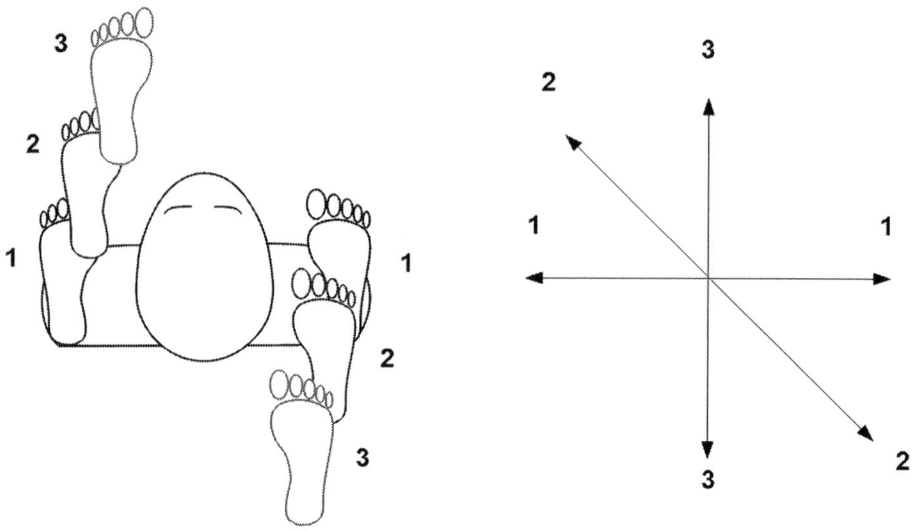

Change the position of the feet as you practice the Aiki step drill; side-to-side, corners, and front-back

The S and C

The S and C describe the shape of our torso as we apply this precept (as viewed from the side).

The cam forms the lower curves (base) of the S and C. A forward cam curves our lower half forward and the reverse cam curves it backward.

The rest of the S and C are formed by lining up your spine and shoulders with the pelvis.

We can create two Cs and two Ss by combining the curve in our hips with curves in our shoulders.

Let us take a quick look at the four shapes before we detail their value in Aiki.

The forward C

Relax your shoulders and keep them dropped as you spread your shoulder blades apart. Can you feel the bear shoulders effect? The top half of your spine should curve forward similarly to doing a crunch sit-up. Spreading your shoulder blades apart has the same effect on the top half of your spine as the forward cam has on the lower back and hips.

When you combine the forward cam and spread your shoulder blades, you create the forward C. The forward C is best for directing energy forward. Use it with the forward step. Useful in nearly every punching type movement (Shomenate #1, Aigamaeate #2, and Gyakugamaeate #3 to name just a few).

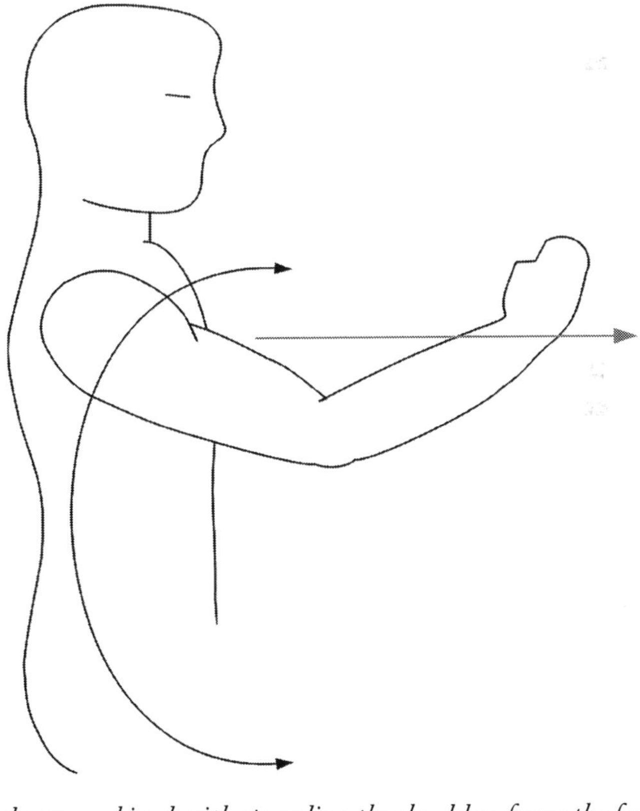

Forward cam combined with spreading the shoulders forms the forward C

You will be using this forward C in the soon to be explained forward push drills.

The backward C

You probably already figured this out, but let us go through the motions shall we? Bring your shoulder blades close together as you keep the shoulders down and relaxed. Did you feel the top half of your spine (even up into your neck) start curving backward?

Combine closing your shoulder blades with the reverse cam and you get the backward C. Obviously, you should be using this with a back step (Hikiotoshi #17).

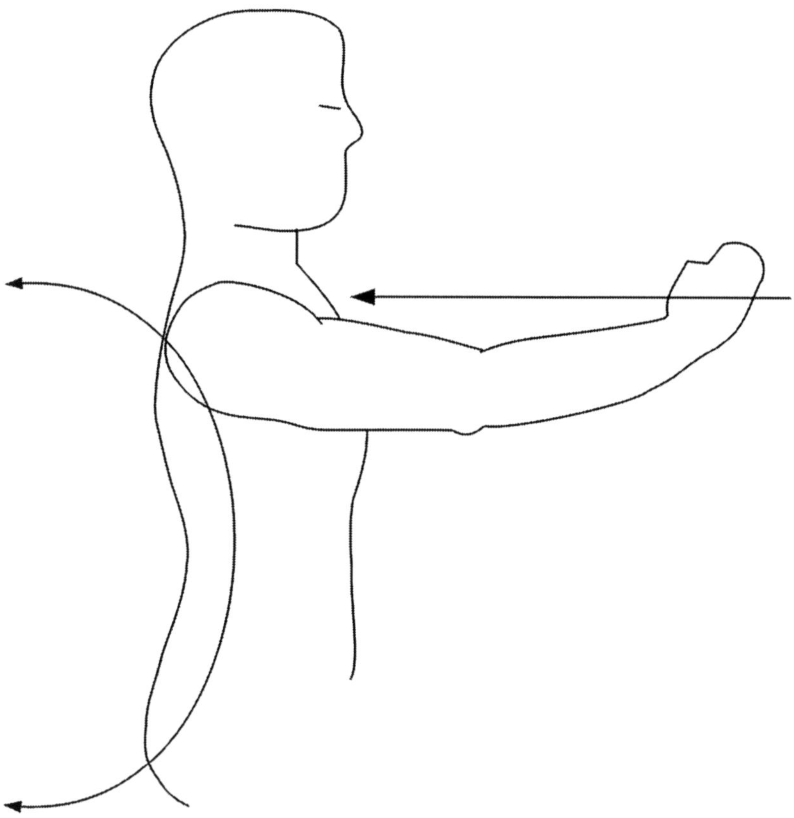

Backward cam combined with closing the shoulders forms the backward C

The forward S

I use the cam to determine the direction of the S and C. In this case, combine the forward cam with bringing your shoulder blades together and you get the forward S.

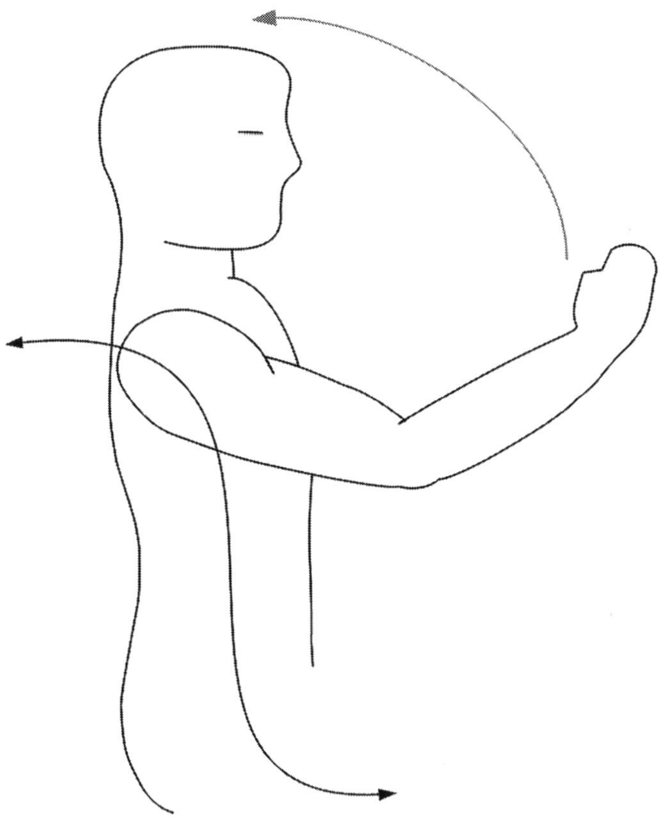

Forward cam combined with closing the shoulders forms the forward S

This is useful in Tenkai Kotehineri #13.

The backward S

For backward cam, spread the shoulders. Use with a back step.

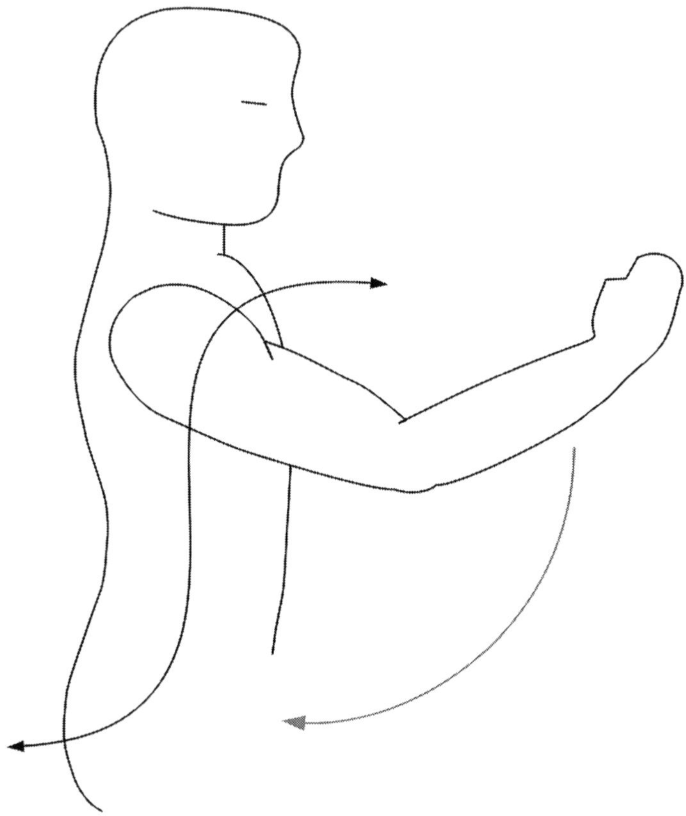

Backward cam combined with spreading the shoulders forms the backward S

This backward S is useful in Hikitaoshi #8.

How about some detail on why we make these distinctions? Why not use a quick Q&A to drive home the point?

Here is the setup:

The value of the cam is that it forms your hips into the bottom of a scoop. I like to describe it as the bottom of a front-end loader or snowplow. Using the cam and Aiki drop step, you literally uproot Uke as you move through him.

The bottom of the scoop (cam) does not meet force with force; it gets under and ricochets the object in a new direction. In effect, it is a curved incline plane.

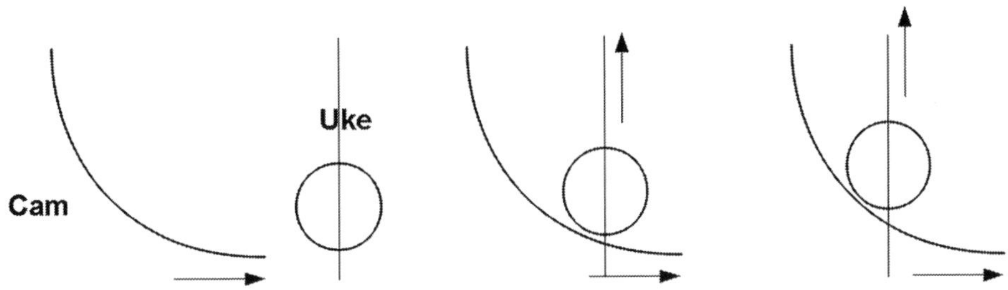

The cam acting as a scoop (curved inclined plane)

It works in the reverse direction as well. Using some form of attachment to Uke (he grabs, you grab, or both), you can use the reverse cam to uproot Uke.

Problems arise when the shoulders are not in position to continue directing Uke.

Here is the quiz:

What shape is the snowplow?

Forward C.

Why?

The plow uproots and folds the snow over in the same direction the plow is moving.

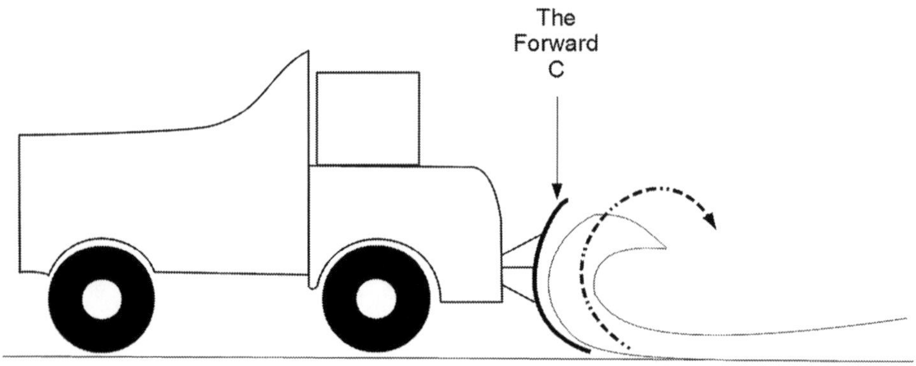

Forward C Snowplow uproots the snow and throws it back in the direction the plow is traveling

What would happen if the snowplow were shaped like a forward S?

> The plow would lift the snow up and over the top of the plow. Not so effective for a snowplow. If the plow lifts the snow over itself, the snow would fall behind the plow in practically the same place it started. Hmm. We can use that kind of behavior in Aikido though, correct?

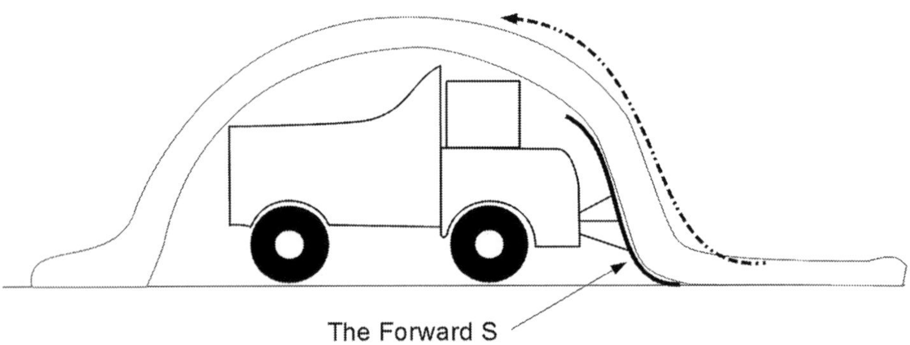

Forward S snowplow uproots the snow and lets snow pass over the plow

Getting the point?

If you are trying to strike in the forward direction, you want the forward C. If you want to uproot him and then let him drop on the other side of you as you pass underneath (as in Shihonage #14 or Tenkai Kotehineri #13), use a forward S. If you want to draw Uke out of his stance as you move away from him, use the reverse C (Hikiotoshi #17). When you want to drop him down as you back away, play with the reverse S (Hikitaoshi #8 or Tenkan version of Oshitaoshi #6).

This might seem like basics, but I have seen plenty of occasions where someone was completely frustrated with a technique because they lost sight of which direction they were trying to move and how to generate force in that direction. An S will not fit when a C is required and vice versa. Hips, spine, and shoulders must align with the technique. (Do not believe me? Try performing Shihonage #14 and keep your shoulder blades as far apart as possible the entire time. Do not laugh. I have seen it attempted.)

Analyze the position of your hips and shoulder blades in all you do.

As you advance in skill using this precept, use the movements of the pelvis and shoulder blades to breathe you. In other words, rolling your hips and shoulders from neutral to forward/backward will help regulate the pressure in your lungs. Your torso can reinforce the action of the diaphragm.

Integrating your breath with these motions is what I translate as Kokyu. Breathe your technique.

Apply the logic to a one-inch punch. Fa-jing is in here somewhere.

I still owe you a drill.

The S and C drill

So, how do we train the S and C? We technically only drill the forward and backward C. The S is not as common and is practiced outside of a drill.

For the backward C, practice helping someone out of a chair. Have Uke sit in a chair and hold his arms outward like they were giving someone a bear hug. Stand in front of Uke, rest your hands on their arms and use the backward C to effortlessly (and hopefully not too quickly) provide the force needed for Uke to stand upward. (Uke may have to dig his toes into the floor a bit or may suffer sliding off the chair and onto his rear.)

For contrast, try lifting Uke out of the chair using the other three shapes (forward S, backward S, and forward C). You might even try using neutral positions in your hips and shoulders.

For the forward cam, we use the push drill.

It is very simple. Stand facing Uke in a reverse punch stance. (In this explanation, we will use right hand and left foot forward.) Square your hips and connect to each other by touching the base of your palms together. Now use the forward C (forward cam and shoulder blades apart) and left foot Aiki step to push your partner backward across the floor.

Your partner can use the forward C to add resistance. You should learn very quickly that he with the lowest center of balance uproots the other.

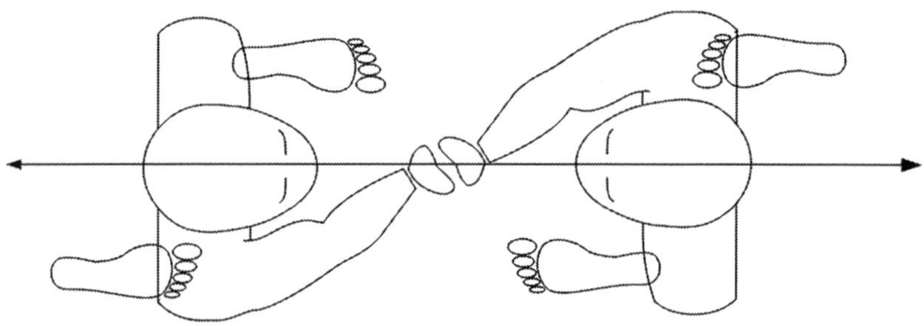

Lining up for the push drill

Here are a couple of thoughts to make the drill more interesting.

- The reverse punch stance makes it easier to stay in line with each other as you move. Less shoulder strength and skill is required. This does not mean you cannot change the stance. Experiment.
- Work toward making the drill one continued walk versus a step, by step, broken motion. It will help create a constant flow of pushing Uke

across the floor if you complete each step by placing the right foot even with, or just a bit past, your left foot.

- You alter the drill to practice at backward C by grasping each other's wrists and stepping backward.

Precept 4: The sagittal plane (the first belt hoop)

To understand the sagittal plane is to know where your center is and what it means to use it.

The sagittal plane is where you stand in this world, where your weight is supported.

If you have read the Basic Terms section on this topic, you know the basics of where it is.

We will begin by analyzing your center as a singular point. We are going to reveal the behavior of the center by relating it to a fulcrum. We will apply the analogies to our body as we explore how the center behaves. This should illuminate where the center is in a static situation. The next step will be moving the center around to see the effects. Then we will wrap it up with an understanding of how we move the center. If we can control where the center moves, the rest is up to your imagination.

We have a few drills that will give a very direct experience and awareness of working with your center. Take heed when we describe a few of the common issues that can arise when we are not fully aware of where the center is. Knowing what not to do is just as helpful as what we should do.

There are linear, rotational, and even spherical aspects to understand.

Do not underestimate the power of this Precept. We have two higher-tier Precepts to cover yet, but this is the lesson that made me feel like maybe I was not a beginner any more. The more I analyze Moe, Chris, and anyone else for that matter, the more it all comes back to this Precept. I hope I do it justice. (Excited? I am.)

Introduction to the Center of Balance (COB)

Some may argue that what we are describing is the center of mass. They are likely correct, but I do not want to argue names. More people seem to relate to center of balance versus center of mass. Since we are (re)defining many of the words in this document to suit our needs, I see no point in stopping now. For the purposes of this book, and so we can speak on common ground, we are describing the center of balance or COB. Know that it might be called center of mass in a different book.

We are going to use the words center or center of balance (COB) to describe the point in space that our mass/weight is condensed (gathered) around.

This COB is a single point of control. You only have one. Any force you generate will, in some way, be connected to this point.

Here is the trick: by knowing where the COB is and how it behaves, we increase our ability to align the rest of our body and, in conjunction with the COB, make something happen (work).

How the COB behaves

The COB is a fulcrum. The COB is the true middle of your physical self. It is a three-dimensional fulcrum.

The truth is that the COB behaves exactly like a ball. In almost every sense, it acts like a pool cue ball or even a bowling ball. The skin and bones that surround the COB add function, but it also hides the COB's nature.

I know that when I said fulcrum, it brought to mind a triangle sitting under a bar. That is a two-dimensional fulcrum, but two-dimensional fulcrums are a great place to start.

Vertically, your COB does act a good deal like a traditional first class lever (triangle and a bar). Horizontally, it acts like a turnstile.

We will work with these two-dimensional fulcrum (levers) on first the horizontal and then vertical planes. The last step is to combine the horizontal with the vertical and, in effect, round off the corners to make a ball.

Let us set up some scenarios and make some observations (like giving the answers, then showing the work).

In order that you can come to the same conclusions that I have, I am going to give you the conclusions up front and then work through the scenarios. The scenarios will explain everything.

COB as a fulcrum on the horizontal plane

A fulcrum is a support. The fulcrum is the immovable object that a plank (rigid object) rests against as the plank applies or accepts force.

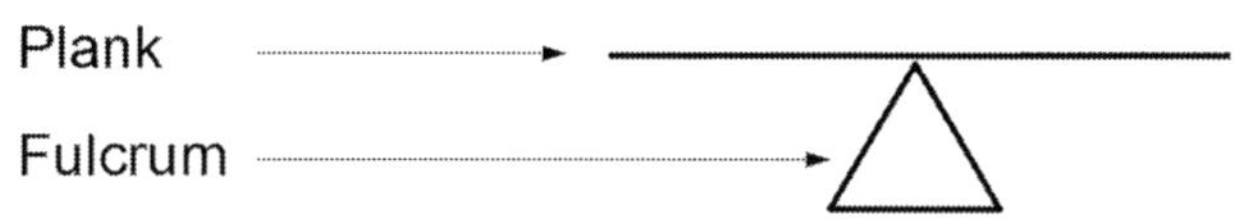

The two parts of our lever analogy; the plank supported by our fulcrum

Let us visit how our COB acts as a fulcrum on the horizontal plane.

Conclusions answer key, horizontally speaking:

Indirect pressure on the COB

- Horizontal indirect pressure will cause the COB to spin on the horizontal plane.
- The COB can move without moving. (It spins like a turnstile.)
- The indirect pressure can be applied to the COB via any rigid extremity attached to that center (e.g., arm, shoulder, hip) or at the sides of the COB itself.

Direct pressure on the COB

- Given adequate horizontal support, the COB is fixed and immovable. Direct pressure does not move it. Direct pressure does not spin the COB

- Direct pressure equates to something trying to move through your center. The object will bump or hit into the COB and create maximum impact.
- Uke moving toward your center or your center moving toward Uke is relative.

Limbs play a role

- Soft or loose limbs do not have effect on the center until they are stretched.
- We can attempt to stop the COB from rotating, but the rigid extremities have the effect of a breaker bar and add leverage to moving the COB. The COB is at a disadvantage.

The Brake

- The COB is a lever. The COB is in the middle of a pushing match between a brake and the external object.
- If the object comes in contact with the COB while the COB is spinning, the object must absorb the inertia of the arms and anything moving with the arms.

Horizontal scenario 1: what happens when someone walks through the arms of a turnstile? (Turnstile equals in this case a four-arm lever.)

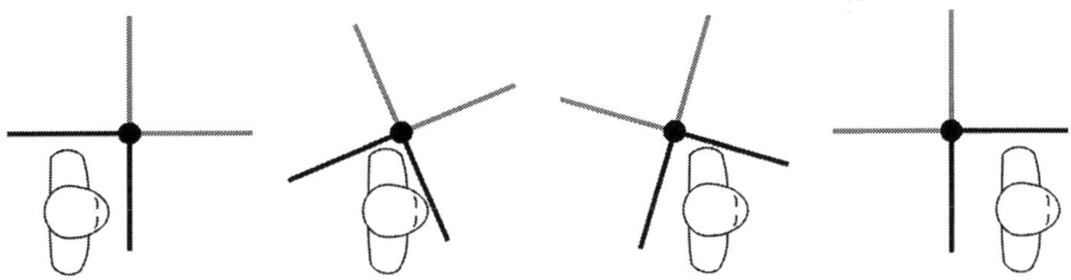

Person walking through a turnstile

Q&A

Where is the fulcrum in the turnstile?

That circle in the middle.

How did the fulcrum move?

It stayed stationary from an X/Y planar perspective, but it did move—it rotated!

Which had more effect on the other: the fulcrum or the person walking through the turnstile?

The person was unaffected, the fulcrum moved.

Did the person touch the fulcrum?

No.

Through what medium did the person affect force on the fulcrum?

The "arm" of the turnstile.

Can we say that the person "touched" the fulcrum indirectly?

Yes, awkward to say it that way, but sure.

Can we (do we) ever behave like the turnstile?

Of course!

Do all the same observations apply?

Of course! But in this case the person moved our shoulder instead of an arm.

Our body as a turnstile

Supported conclusions:

Indirect pressure on the COB

- Indirect pressure will cause the COB to spin.
- The COB moves without moving. It spins (like a turnstile).
- The indirect pressure can be applied to the COB via any rigid extremity attached to that center (e.g., arm, shoulder, hip).

Horizontal scenario 2: what happens when this person is not looking and tries to walk through the "pole" at the middle of the turnstile? (Assume the turnstile is bolted to the floor.)

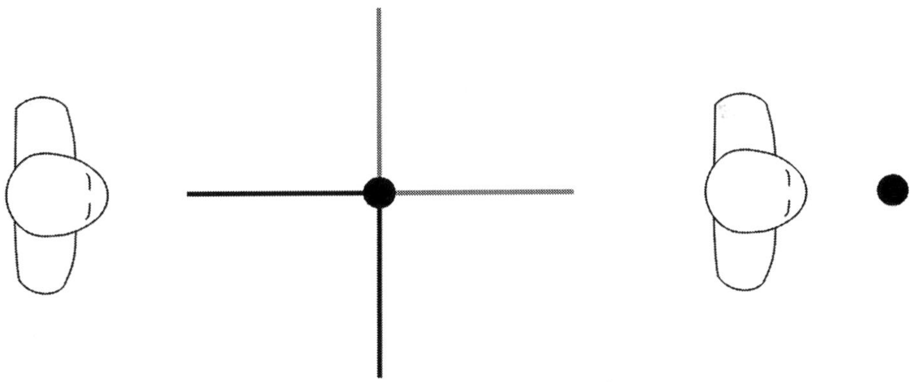

Person walking into the middle of the turnstile

Q&A

Could the person walk through the center of the turnstile?
No.

Why?
The person met an unmovable object and two objects cannot occupy the same space at the same time.

What value did the "arm" of the turnstile have in this case?
It extended the range at which the person had to stop.

Why?

The arm of the turnstile is unbendable and was directly between the person and the center of the turnstile. He may as well have walked directly into the pole at the center of the turnstile.

Could the turnstile have done the moving and run into the person?

Not in this scenario, not when it is bolted to the floor. If we bend the rules of reality a bit, the scenario would be the same. The turnstile would not spin should it somehow move across the floor and directly into the person.

Do we agree that the quicker the objects move, the harder the hit.

Yes, I would rather walk into a wall than run into one.

Can we (do we) ever behave like the turnstile?

Of course!

Do all the same observations apply?

Of course! We have arms. Technically, our arm is attached to our shoulder. So, to keep the COB from spinning, we use both arms to duplicate the action of the turnstile arm. Of course, it is a little harder for us to be immovable when we cannot bolt ourselves into the floor.

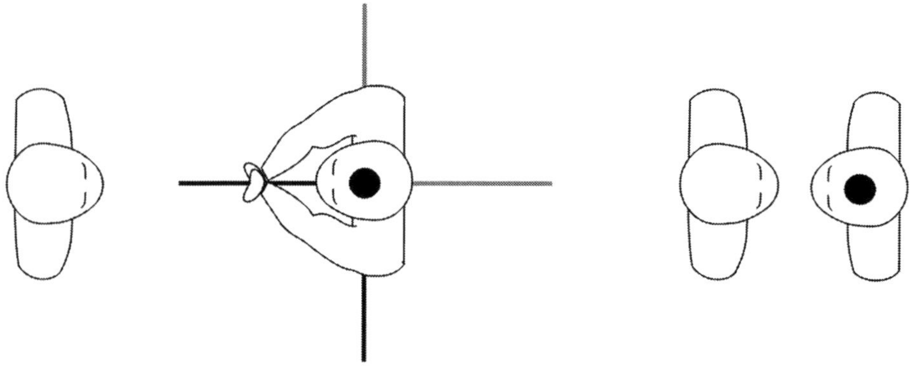

Person walking into the middle of us

Supported Conclusions:

Direct pressure on the COB

- Given adequate horizontal support, the COB is fixed and immovable. Direct pressure does not move it. Direct pressure does not spin the COB.
- Direct pressure equates to something trying to move through your center. The object will bump or hit into the COB and create maximum impact.
- Uke moving toward your center or your center moving toward Uke is relative.

Horizontal scenario 3: What happens if the arm of the turnstile is flexible?

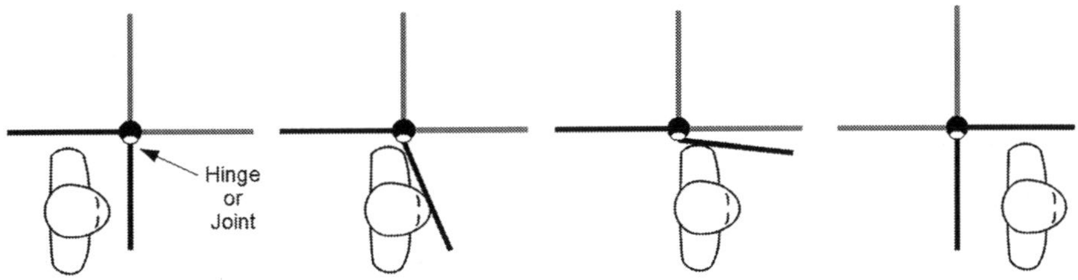

Flexible arm on the turnstile

Q&A

Which had more effect on the other: the fulcrum or the person walking through the turnstile?

Neither. The person was unaffected. The fulcrum did not spin.

Did the arm have a center?

Technically, yes. The arm seemed to be attached to the turnstile via a hinge. The hinge seemed to be the center of the arm. The hinge allowed the arm to move, but it had no effect on the turnstile to which it was attached.

What happens if the person pulled on the arm in a direction directly away from the hub of the turnstile and tries to walk through?

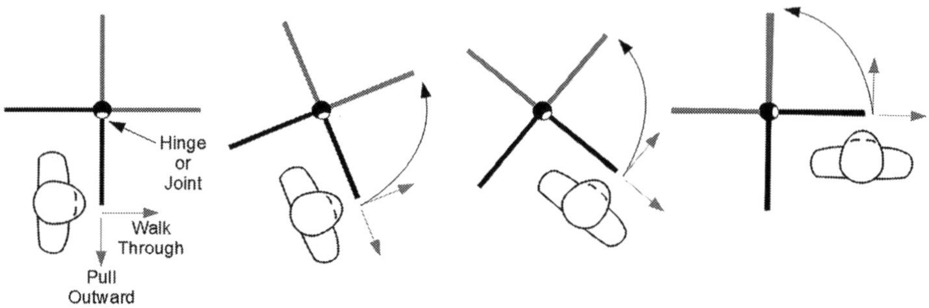

Person pulls on arm as he moves through

Which has more effect on the other: the fulcrum or the person walking through the turnstile?

They affect each other similarly. The fulcrum spins and the person is forced to orbit the turnstile in order to keep the pressure on the arm.

Does the person touch the fulcrum?

No.

Through what medium did the person affect force on the fulcrum?

The arm of the turnstile.

Was the hinge a factor?

No.

What if the person tried to simply hold onto the loose arm as the turnstile turned?

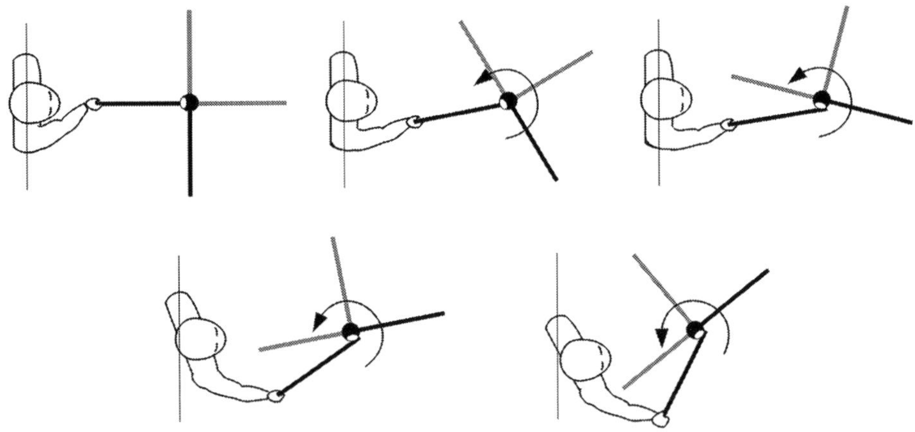

Person tries to hold onto the loose arm, which is wrapping around the center

The person tries to hold onto the loose arm as the center begins to rotate. What happens?

Eventually, the loose arm reaches a point at which the hinge can go no further and the arm begins coiling around the center. This is the equivalent of stretching the arm outward from the center. The person holding the turnstile arm is then pulled or coiled around the center.

What if the turnstile arm was completely loose, like a rope?

The person would feel the effects similarly to the hinged turnstile arm as the rope coils around the center of the turnstile.

What would the effect be if we keep the rigid turnstile arm, but remove the hinge?

The arc of the pull is larger and the person would feel the effects immediately.

Supported Conclusions:

Limbs play a role

- Soft or loose limbs do not have any effect on the center until they are stretched.

Horizontal scenario 4: What happens if we keep the turnstile arms rigid but we put a brake on the turnstile?

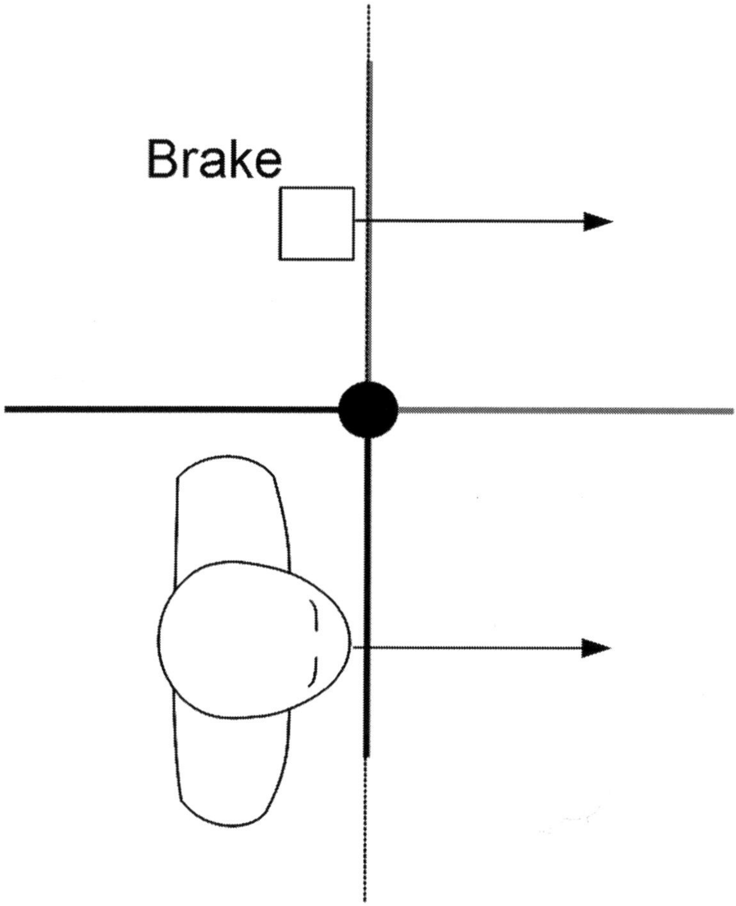

Brake on the turnstile

Q&A

Will the turnstile spin?
No.

Did it seem like a stalemate?
Yes.

If we do not accept a stalemate, what are the likely events?
Well…see below.

If the arm is not strong enough; the arm will break.

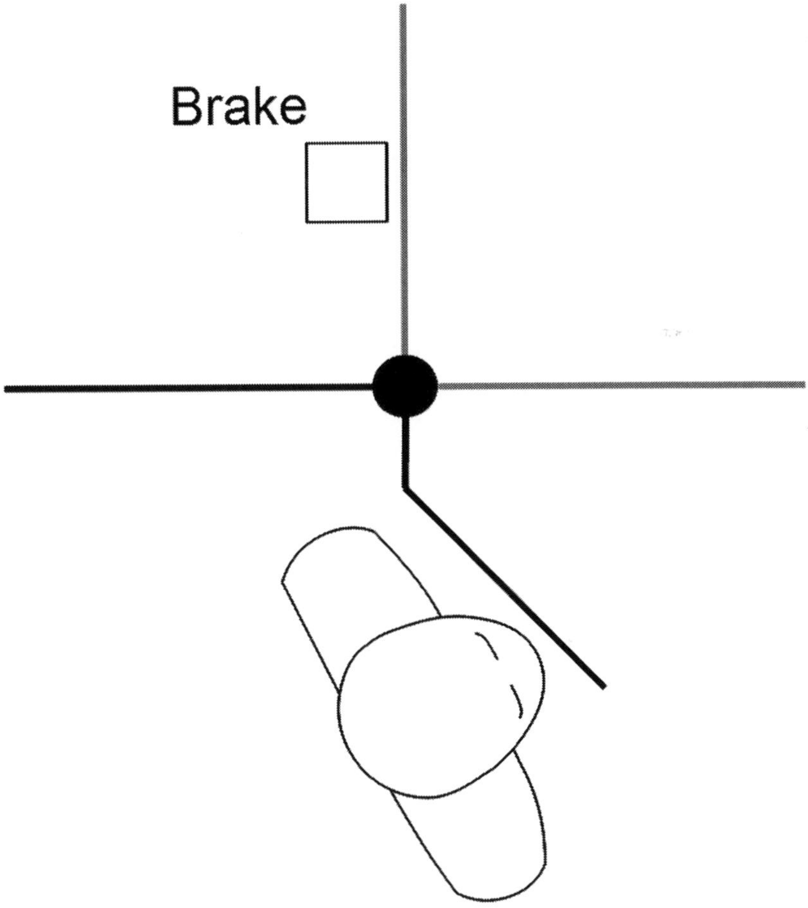

Arm might break

If the brake is weak or slips; the turnstile will spin as if there was no brake.

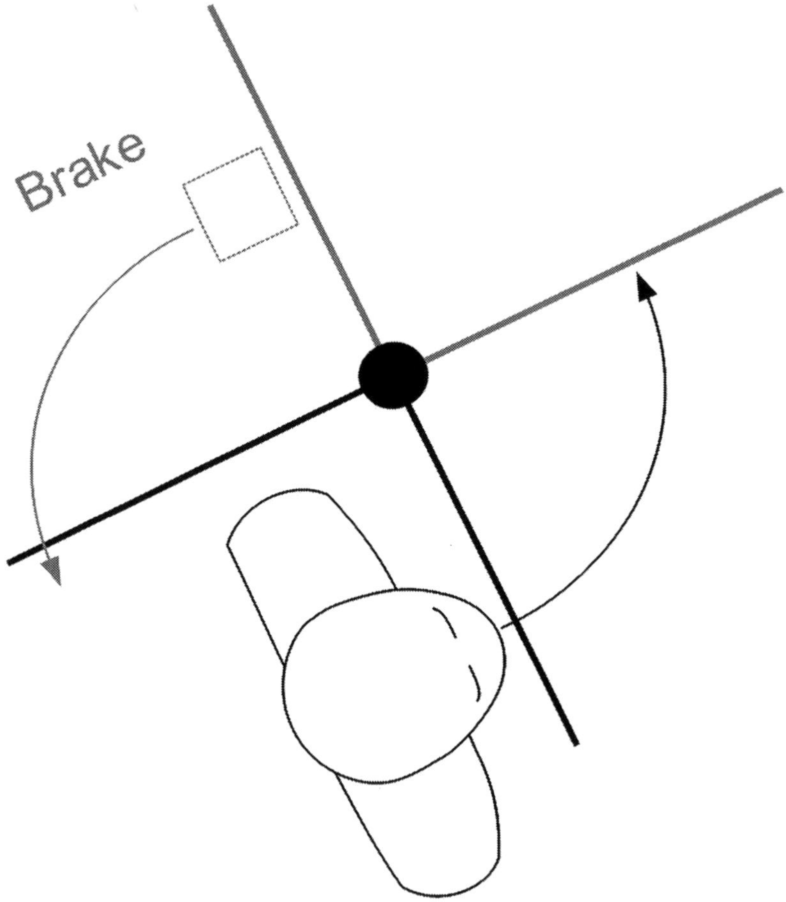

Brake slips

If the brake and the arms are strong, the center will have to move. Since the COB is no longer immobile, it ceases to be the COB. The brake will become the new fulcrum/center.

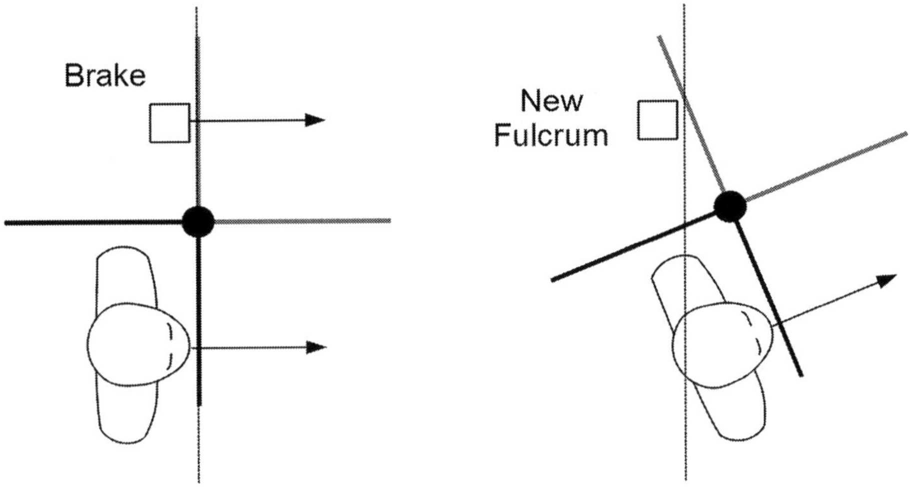

Brake becomes the new fulcrum/center

If we put ourselves in place of the turnstile, how do we map the parts of the turnstile to our body?

The arm is my arm(s), the center of the turnstile is my COB, and the brake is my stance.

Anything special we should notice about their relationship?

The arm and the brake are both in direct contact with the COB, but on opposite sides. Either the brake or Uke has greater leverage on the COB depending on the stance and where Uke is pushing on the arm.

What then is the most likely event?

It seems most likely that Uke pushing against my arm will overcome the pressure provided by my stance [brake].

Can you describe what it will look like when the brake gives way?

The brake is my stance. If my stance gives way, I have to step or fall. Either way, given that the COB is part of me, the COB will move with me.

Supported Conclusions:

Limbs play a role

- We can attempt to stop the COB from rotating, but the rigid extremities have the effect of a breaker bar and deploy with leverage. The COB is at a disadvantage.
- The COB is a lever. The COB is in the middle of a pushing match between a brake and the external object.

Horizontal scenario 5: The turnstile is already in motion when the person gets in the way of the motion of the arms.

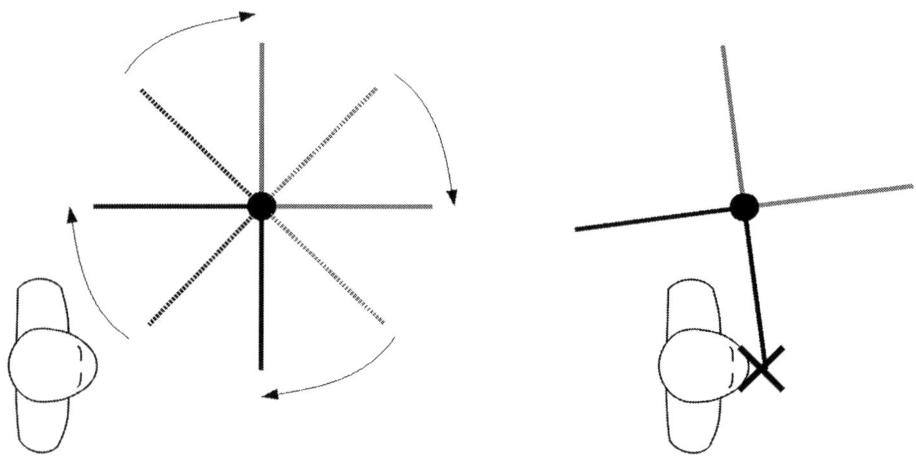

Person walks into a spinning turnstile

Q&A

The turnstile arms should be flying off into space. What is causing the turnstile arms to move in the direction they are headed?

Their attachment to the hub causes them to stay in orbit around the center.

Assuming that no other external forces exist, what is going to happen to the person?

The person gets hit with the inertia of the arms.

Does the mass of the hub have any effect here?

Technically yes, but let us set up the conditions such that the hub's effects are negligible. For our purposes, let us suggest the hub is infinitesimally small and made of ultra light material. The arms will be made of solid metal. In this way, the hub [fulcrum/COB], although spinning, does not add to the mass that hits Uke. The hub solely provides the centripetal force that keeps the arms in orbit.

Can you give an example to clarify?

Yes. It works like a teeter-totter. If you stood under the elevated side of the teeter-totter board as someone lifted the lowered half, you would get hit with the inertia of the board and nothing more. The composition [weight] of the fulcrum would have no bearing on how hard you were hit. The fulcrum could be made of steel or plastic. The only part the fulcrum plays here is to stay immobile and assist in the transfer of energy.

So the COB is weightless?

Yes, it is just a point that the rest of our physical being is centered around.

When does the mass of the COB play a part in imparting force into the person?

Never actually. The COB is just a point in space; it has no mass. When we use direct pressure, i.e., hit with the COB, we are simply trying to make the COB occupy the same space as another object.

So what does the hitting?

The rest of our body. It is the rest of the body that is trying to drive the COB through the object.

So, how does this information apply when we replace the turnstile with our body?

Just like a turnstile, we have arms and a COB. Spin our COB and let the arms deliver the strike.

Do you mean pulling back one arm as you extend the other?

Yes and no. If you want to engage all of the mass concentrated around your COB, your legs provide the motive force that spins your COB. It will appear as though one arm is moving toward Uke as the other moves back or away from Uke. The reality is that both sides are simply orbiting the COB without regard to Uke. Many times, people try to create the illusion of using their entire body by bending the joints in their arms, e.g., keeping the torso square while extending one arm and retracting the other. Solely extending/flexing arm joints is not the same thing. Your COB must be spinning if you hope to add your weight behind the punch.

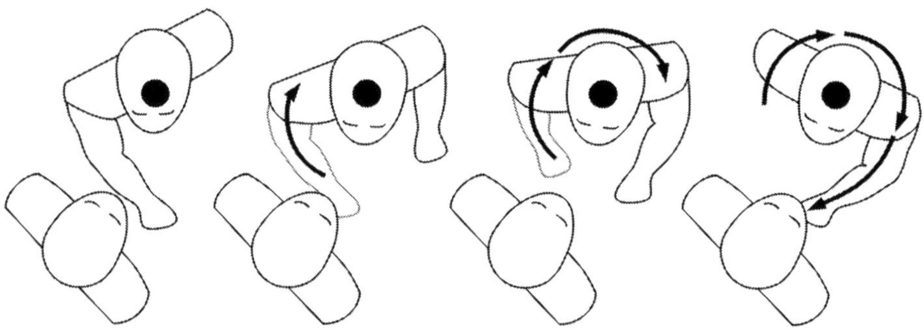

Moving the torso around the COB adds the entire body mass to the punch

Do you mean to say that a person who is not moving their hips when they are punching is not maximizing the impact?

Yes, but you have to accept that maximizing the impact is not always the appropriate way to punch. It might not be the most powerful punch, but they may be considering other factors.

Like what?

Loss of balance, follow up attack, multiple attackers, they do not need any more force than they are applying, etc. There is no right or wrong, only levels of appropriateness. The striker might have trimmed down the motion to such a subtlety that you are not aware that he is driving the entire mass behind the punch at the last second. They use minimum motion with maximum effectiveness.

Are there any other options to make the punch more effective?

Of course, but I have told you all that I feel is relevant for this book. Seek a master of the striking arts for more detail.

Let us make it real

That was a lot of detail on how the COB behaves on the horizontal plane, but it boils down to a few statements: pushing directly into the center of the COB is an attempt to collide with the COB. This direct touch does not spin the COB. Touching the COB in any other way will, in some way, try to spin the COB. The touches that cause the COB to spin are called indirect.

Want an instant epiphany? Use a heavy bag.

You do not actually have to punch. Simply make contact with the bag using an open hand. Now push directly into the middle of the bag. The bag should swing away from you, without spinning. That is direct pressure on the heavy bag's COB. Now, try pushing in any other direction through the bag, it will spin. That is indirect pressure on the COB.

Let us nurture some body awareness.

How to use the COB on the horizontal plane

We have seen the key behaviors of the COB from a horizontal, top-down, X/Y perspective. What can we derive from this analysis?

The key elements within us are the COB, our stance (brake), and the body (arms of the turnstile).

The center is passive and is moved by direct and indirect forces. We move our center horizontally by stepping (direct) or by turning our body (spinning around the center, indirect).

Forces outside our body move our center in the similarly way. Uke tries to push through our center (direct) or tries to turn us (indirect).

Let us try some drills.

Direct force

The interaction of the COB on the horizontal plane is very apparent in the "push drill" we learned in the third precept.

Let us take a second to analyze what is happening in this drill. Let us find some of the "difficulties" in the practice. We will again use a right-hand and left-foot forward stance (exactly as we described it in the Cam)

Where is your center at the start of the drill?

You probably squared up with even weight on your feet. If so, the COB would be in the center of your body.

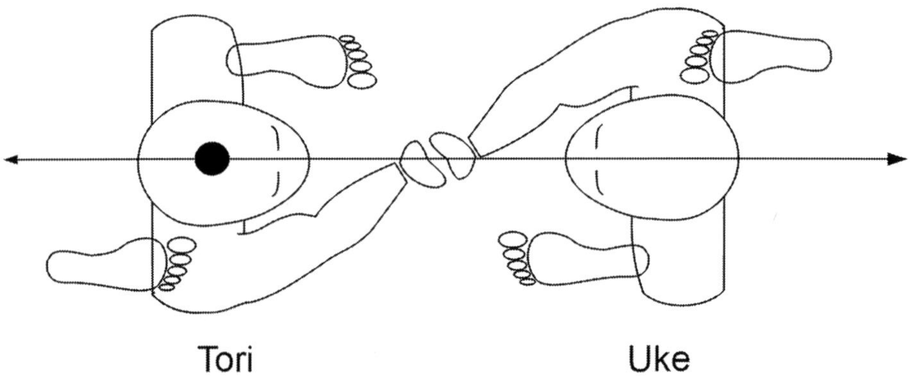

Lining up for the push drill Tori is double-weighted

Did you leave your center in the middle of your body as you tried to move forward? If you did, something like this likely happened.

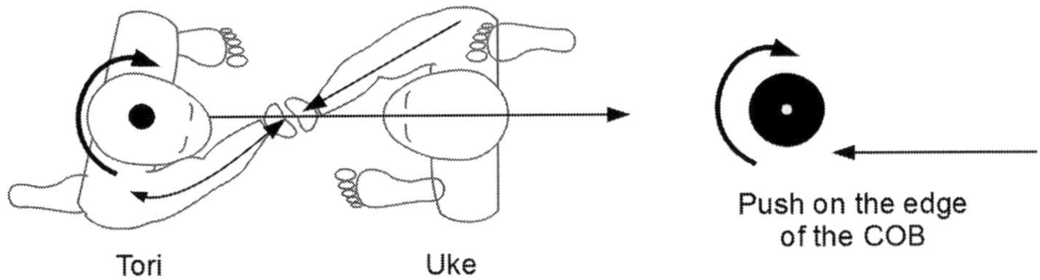

Tori's center is not on the line of force;
Uke pushes on the edge of the COB (via the arms);
Indirect pressure is applied, Tori's center rotates.

What you discovered is the effect of indirect force on your COB. Uke's resistance spun your center as you tried to move forward. (Even with a perfect forward C and front-wheel drive.)

If you want to push Uke along the floor, you are going to need some direct force. To create direct force, your COB has to be on the line of the force.

Try squaring the hips, weighting yourself on the right side, and driving from the right hip (dropping downward and forward in a forward C, wedging your torso between your hip and Uke). Remember front-wheel drive as you come back up!

Weighting on the right has the effect of shifting the COB onto the line of force, which in turn facilitates a direct force.

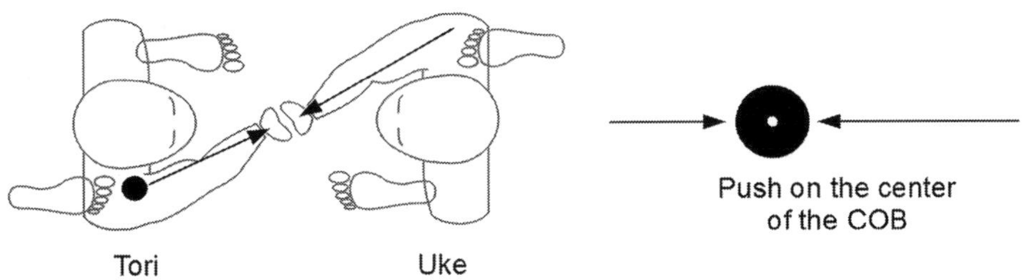

Tori's center is on the line of the force; direct pressure is applied

If you applied a forward C, you were able to uproot Uke and start him backward. (The C is the vertical aspect of the drill.)

At least it started out that way. For some, this little bit clears up the issue, but others find they could start the motion but were thrown backward shortly into the step. What happened to them?

One likely reason, they let their C turn into an S, but an even more likely issue: they did not adjust the line of force as their COB shifted from right to left side. What does that mean?

From the kinesthetic, feeling in your body sense, the COB follows your weighted-ness. You shift your COB from one hip joint to the other as you step.

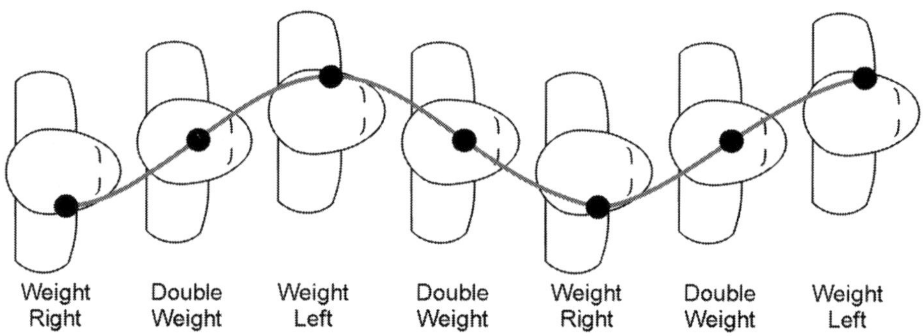

How the COB moves as we step; the COB follows the weighted-ness

In the case where we are lose the ability to drive through Uke before we finish the step, we are starting with a direct force on our COB and then, as we shift our weight, the COB moves and we shift into indirect pressure.

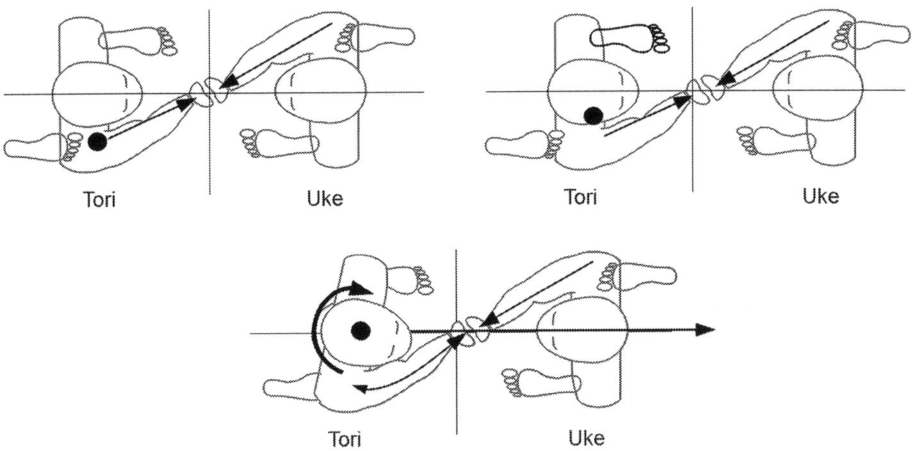

Tori moves forward with direct force on his COB, but the step shifts the COB off the line of attack

Maintain direct force on Uke's center by keeping your arm between Uke's and your COB.

The shift from direct to indirect force on the COB issues arise on both sides of this drill. Uke is just as susceptible to this COB shift. It is Uke's job to attempt keep his center in the way of your progress. (This can be a very important concept. Just ask any offensive lineman!)

Uke can do his best to stay in your way, but some of you may have even figured out that you have to apply direct force on Uke's COB, or you will spin Uke versus drive him backward.

If you are having issues, continue to ask yourself, "Where is my COB?" or "Where is my weight?" and then, "Is the hand I am pushing with between Uke's and my COB?"

Keep playing with this drill. You will get it.

Indirect force

There is no good or bad, only levels of appropriateness. In other words, direct force is not always the most appropriate answer.

Where have we encountered indirect force spinning Uke's COB?

We saw the spin in Uke when we covered Parallelism, in the sense of sliding Uke. We detailed how the spin controlled Uke's hip joint and weakened his stance (made Uke less stable).

These sagittal plane lessons will help expand awareness of how to apply force to Uke, but the focus of the second tier precepts is us.

Is there strength in permitting ourselves to spin? Of course!

Indirect force on our COB has multiple uses. The most typical use is during our entry. The turning step (tenkan-ashi) entry is an example of where we control the indirect force on our COB.

Uke is gunning for a direct impact. We shift our COB enough to change that direct impact into an indirect pressure (as we rotate around the COB). This is how we slip the punch.

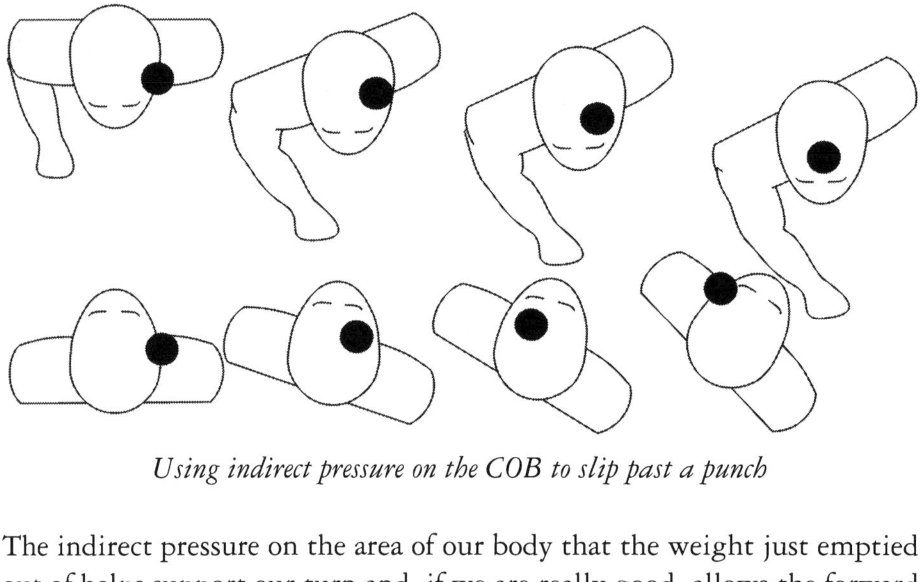

Using indirect pressure on the COB to slip past a punch

The indirect pressure on the area of our body that the weight just emptied out of helps support our turn and, if we are really good, allows the forward empty side of our lever to strike. (I will bet you thought I was going to say "full" instead of "empty." We will have to discuss that sometime. I maintain both sides of the lever are empty, only the fulcrum is full.)

We can control the effects of Uke's force as long as we have control of where we place the fulcrum (our COB).

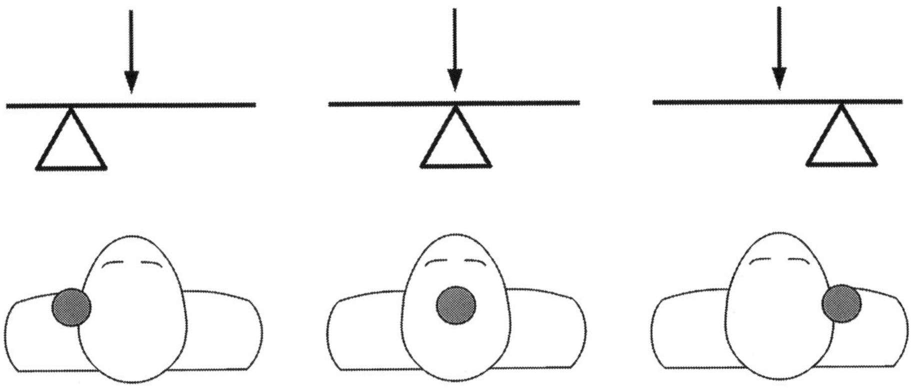

Three different COB positions; each affects the identical incoming force differently

We used the push-drill to get a feel for direct force. We use the hip-wheel turn drill to begin to feel how we move the COB and apply/absorb indirect force. Yes, the same drill we use to teach front-wheel drive. Here is how:

Line up face to face with Uke. Get into a comfortable horse stance, legs just slightly further than the shoulders. Uke will place his hand on your chest (or middle-line of the body) and attempt to push straight into you (along your no-line). Your task is to use front-wheel-drive to shift your COB to either side and allow Uke's push to pass through you.

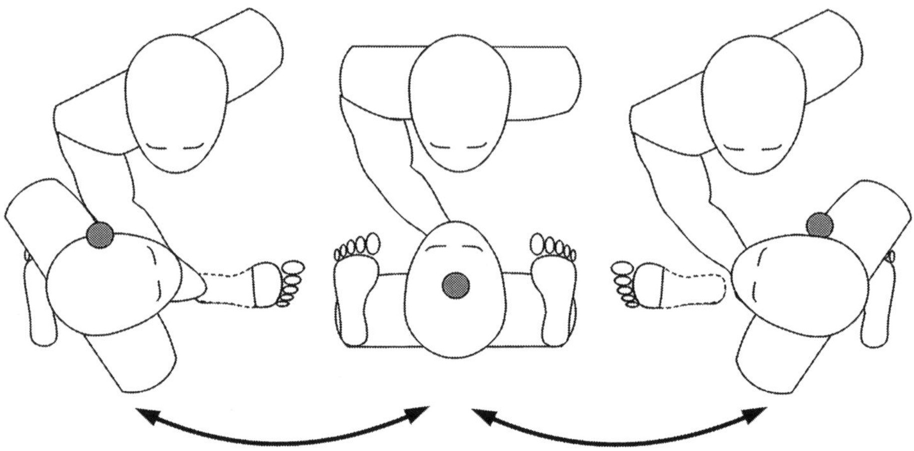

Hip-wheel turn drill modified to teach horizontal control of COB

We perform this drill to both sides, each time returning to the starting point. Do not miss the opportunity to track Uke's fist as he retracts it. Follow Uke's hand as you move back toward the starting position. Keep the Aiki drop step (front-wheel drive) intact at all times.

We started this drill with a direct contact to the chest. Taking it a step further, back up a step and begin this drill wrist-to-wrist with Uke (in lieu of his hand on your chest). Focus on allowing Uke's force push to spin you out of harm's way. Basically, turn this into a simple push hands drill.

If you are comfortable with the previous step, explore the opportunities for striking with your free hand. Be certain to practice on both sides. For the Tomiki style players, find Gyakugamaeate #3 and Aigamaeate #2. For those with a more traditional karate background, seek inspiration from the Na-Hanchi kata.

Cheat a little. Make it easier for yourself by starting in a forward-foot stance. You will have to consistently move toward the side with the forward foot.

Striking with the COB on the horizontal plane
From the horizontal perspective, we have two options when trying to "hit" something.

This first is to drive our center through the object, by direct contact (e.g., striking with the hip where the COB resides) or by proxy (arm, leg, head, etc., between your COB and the object). We call that direct force. Consider this linear striking.

The second hitting option is to deliver our energy (inertia) by rotating our body around the COB. Rotational striking leverages the COB as a fulcrum and, by striking with our hip or other body part, impart our indirect force. It is much like the description of walking into the arms of a rotating turnstile.

In most cases, simply due to the construction of our bodies, we are combining these options.

COB as a fulcrum on the vertical plane

We introduced a lot of information about the horizontal aspects of the COB. The good news is most of what we need to know about the COB in the vertical plane is similar information.

Let us put the answer key up front, and again, run through scenarios, make some observations.

Answer Key, Vertically Speaking:

General vertical aspects of the COB

- The COB concentrates the downward force of your body.
- Your COB is a fulcrum, but vertically, it is not a support.
- The COB needs to be supported or it will find the ground.
- Your legs support your center of balance with three exceptions:
    1) You have upward momentum (e.g., jumping)
    2) You are supporting yourself on something (e.g., leaning on something)
    3) There is nothing keeping your COB from the ground (e.g., falling).

- The COB acts like a plate resting on top of a table. The plate slides from one side of the table to the other (e.g., COB moves from hip to hip as we walk).

Indirect vertical pressure on the COB
- Indirect vertical pressure will cause the COB plate to tilt.
- The indirect pressure can be applied to the COB by adding weight to the torso or simply tipping the torso (e.g., by resting on and arm, shoulder, hip).
- In many ways, your vertebrae act like a stack of plates.

Direct vertical pressure on the COB
- Direct pressure equates to something trying to move through your center. The object will bump or hit into the COB.
- Direct vertical pressure on the COB does not create tilt. The pressure rests at the center of the COB plate.
- The COB adjusts for the newly offered weight by adding it to the existing weight. If the legs are strong enough, the primary effect is a change in inertia.
- The strength of your legs determines how much direct vertical pressure you can withstand.

Limbs play a role
- Soft or loose arms do not have effect on the center until they are stretched
- We can attempt to stop the COB from tilting, but the further the stack of plates leans over the bottom plate (COB), the more torque that gets applied to the COB. The COB is at a disadvantage.

The brake
- When standing, if the COB tilts, the supporting leg's foot or other leg will attempt to resist the tilt.

Vertical scenario 1: Standing single and double-weighted.

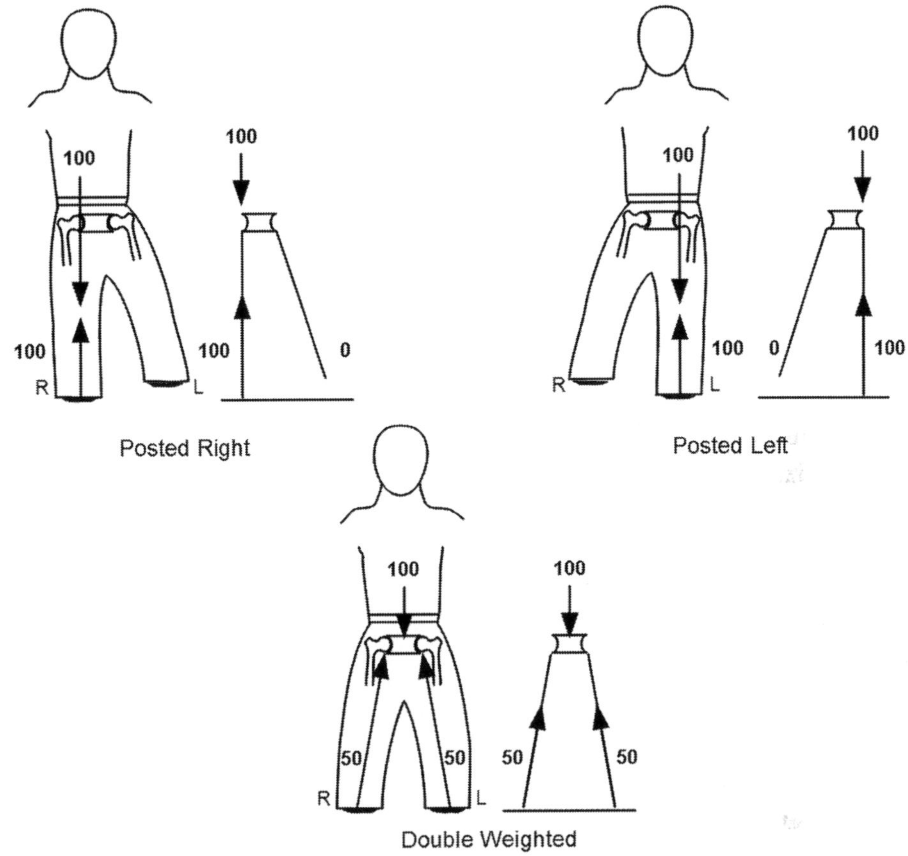

Three simple positions: Single-weighted on right and left, double-weighted

Why must you hold yourself up?
    Gravity is pulling me downward.

What holds you up?
    Unless I am leaning on something, my legs hold me up.

In a single-weighted stance, what is your leg holding up?
    The grounded or weighted leg is supporting the rest of my body.

Including the other leg?

Yes.

Your entire body does not sit above that leg, how is your leg holding you up?

The COB concentrates all of the weight of my body. The leg need only support the COB.

So, your weighted leg is in direct contact with the COB?

Exactly correct. The leg applies a direct upward pressure onto the COB.

In which direction is gravity pulling your COB?

Gravity is pulling downward through the middle of my COB. Said differently, gravity applies direct downward pressure on the COB.

What would happen if your leg were not there to support you?

I would fall.

What supports us when we jump?

Nothing supports us when we jump. We have disconnected from the ground by overcoming gravity for a short time.

Are legs the only things that can hold us up?

No, you may lean on something to hold yourself up, e.g., sit on a chair, lean on a wall, a crutch, or someone else.

Supported conclusions

- The COB concentrates the downward force of your body.
- Your COB is a fulcrum, but vertically, it is not a support.
- The COB needs to be supported or it will find the ground.
- Your legs support your center of balance with three exceptions:
  1) There is nothing keeping your COB from the ground (i.e., falling).
  2) You have upward momentum (e.g., jumping).
  3) You are supporting yourself on something (e.g., leaning on something).

Vertical scenario 2: Standing and shifting our weight; Tilting our hips

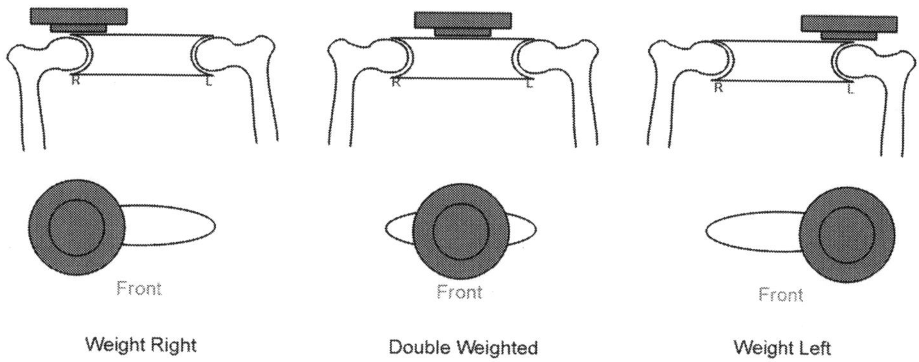

Position of the COB plate as we shift our weight from right to left leg

Where is your center of balance when standing even-weighted on two feet?
The COB sits in the middle of my pelvis.

So the COB is not directly over a leg bone?
No, the pelvis acts like a "board" between the two supports.

What holds up your pelvis?
Unless I am leaning on something, my two legs share the work of holding up the pelvis.

"Legs and a board across them" sounds like a description of a table. Can we use that description?
Yes, especially when you relate the two feet at the bottom as replacing the other two legs you find on a typical four-legged table.

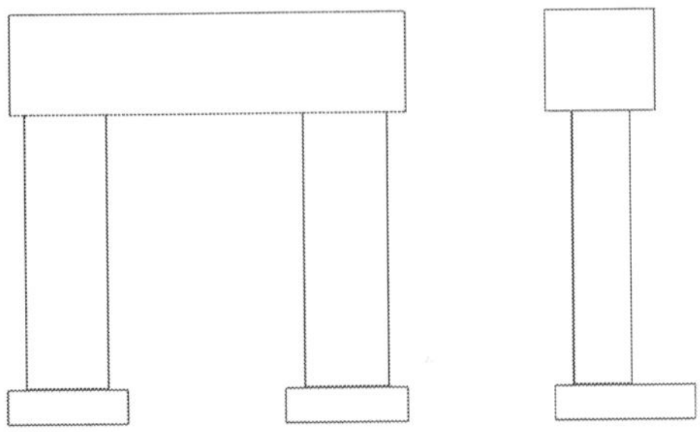

Your base (pelvis, legs, and feet) depicted roughly as a table; front, and side view

What happens when you pick up one of your legs?

The COB has to be directly above the grounded, weighted leg, or you fall. The COB slides to the weighted leg. Sliding the COB might make more sense if you imagine a plate that slides from one side of the table to the other due to one side of the table being raised or lowered.

What happens when I shift and pick up the other leg?

The COB plate slides across the table to the other support, just like the effect a boat rocking back and forth has on any object that is not tied down.

Can the plate slide off the end of the table?

Yes.

What happens?

You fall, just like a plate that fell off the side of the table.

What happens if the table tilts on its long axis backward and forward instead of tilting from leg to leg?

It is a shorter trip to sliding off the table and you fall.

Supported Conclusion:

- The COB acts like a dinner plate that slides across the top of a narrow table. The COB is the plate; the narrow table is your hips.

Vertical scenario 3: Carrying the weight

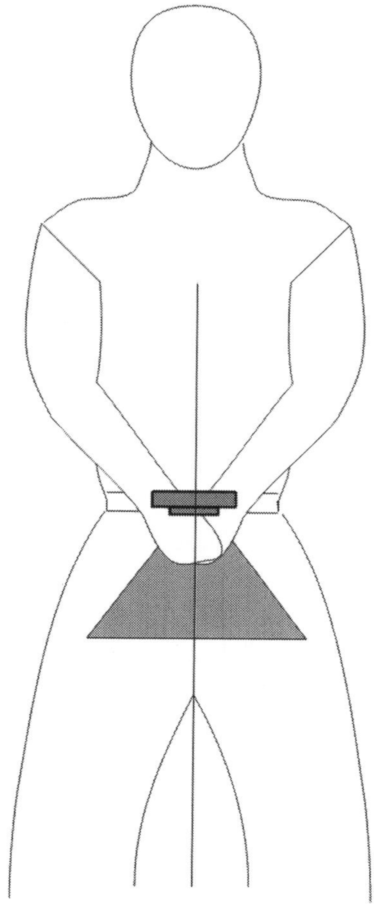

Double-weighted stance; holding a heavy object

What happens when someone knocks the legs out from under the COB?
It is called a sweep or a trip, and we fall.

Can someone attack the COB instead of the parts that make up the table?
Yes. They can apply their weight to the plate.

How does someone add weight to our COB?

They add weight simply by leaning on us.

Does that mean they are borrowing the support of our legs?

Yes.

This seems to give Uke a good bit of control over us. How do we keep ourselves from falling over?

Uke adding weight to our frame is not much different than when we carry something. When we carry something, we add the weight to our overall mass and rebalance it through the direct center of our COB. Sometimes Sensei will use fancy words and call it "channeling the energy into the floor."

When do I do these things?

Ever catch a ball? The effect of a baseball might be too subtle to notice. Imagine catching something heavier, like a medicine ball. No matter the weight of the object, you are effectively channeling that weight into the floor both horizontally and vertically. If you did not channel it directly, you would be knocked over or at least spin around.

Direct vertical pressure on my COB seems like a burden for me. What is the benefit of having Uke's weight applying direct vertical pressure on my COB?

Two good things happen when direct vertical pressure is applied on the COB. The first benefit is that the weight is added to ours and passed directly to the leg or legs. It is easy to contend with the additional weight. Your legs are much stronger than you might be aware.

What is the second benefit of Uke putting direct vertical pressure on our COB?

We become one of Uke's legs. So if we shift or move our COB, Uke comes with us. This is the essence of yin connection.

How much of Uke's weight is necessary for us to have influence on his center?

That is an excellent question! Glad I thought of it! Our control of Uke increases as more of his weight is applied. You could get to the point that you are carrying Uke, but the reality is, you really only need a small amount of Uke's weight. You will need less and less of Uke's weight as you advance in skill.

Will I eventually be able to control Uke simply by having his arm rest on me?

No, not solely by his arm resting on you. Remember, loose limbs have their own COB at the hinge/joint that attaches them to the rest of the torso. Uke could burden you with his arm, but controlling Uke requires his true COB to rest on you. Uke leaning on you is a reference to his COB. A bridge forms between the true COB's when someone leans on the other. A loose limb does not make a bridge.

What happens if the legs are not strong enough to support all of the applied weight?

We fall.

Is it safe to conclude that we slow down a bit as we support Uke?

Yes. It is the same as carrying something. Your ability to move will vary with the amount of additional weight you support. So too does your influence on Uke's balance.

Show me an example of direct vertical pressure on the COB.

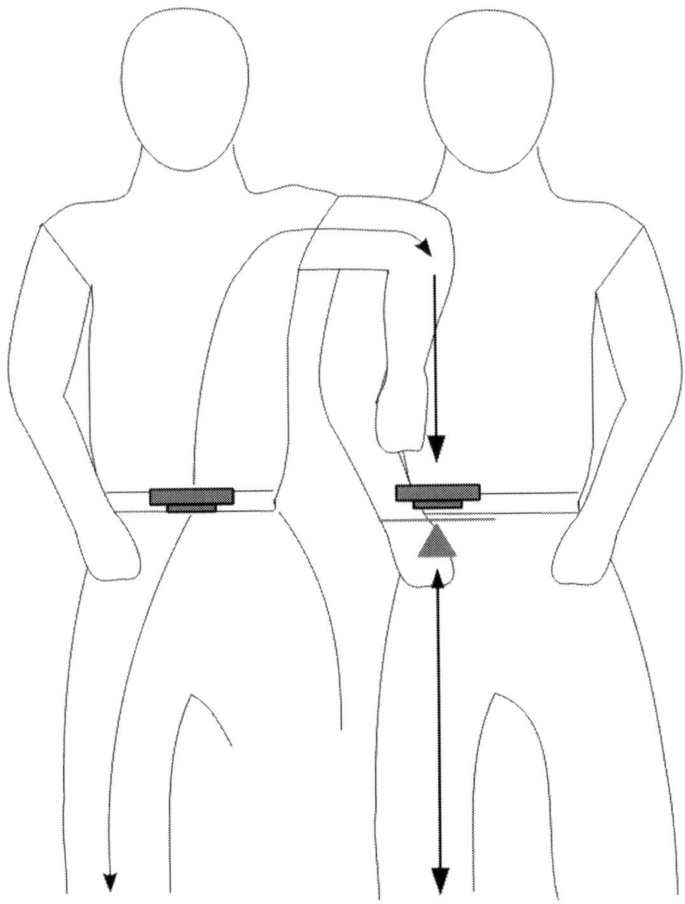

Post right stance; Uke applying direct vertical pressure directly over our COB

Here Uke is leaning on the shoulder directly above our COB and leg. The weight is added to the overall weight of our body and kept off the floor.

Supported Conclusions

Direct vertical pressure on the COB

- Direct vertical pressure equates to something trying to move through your center. The object will bump or hit into the COB.
- Direct vertical pressure on the COB does not create tilt. The pressure rests at the center of the COB plate.
- The COB adjusts for the newly offered weight by adding it to the existing weight. If the legs are strong enough, the primary effect is a change in inertia.
- The strength of your legs determines how much direct vertical pressure you can withstand.

Vertical scenario 4: Getting some help tilting our hips

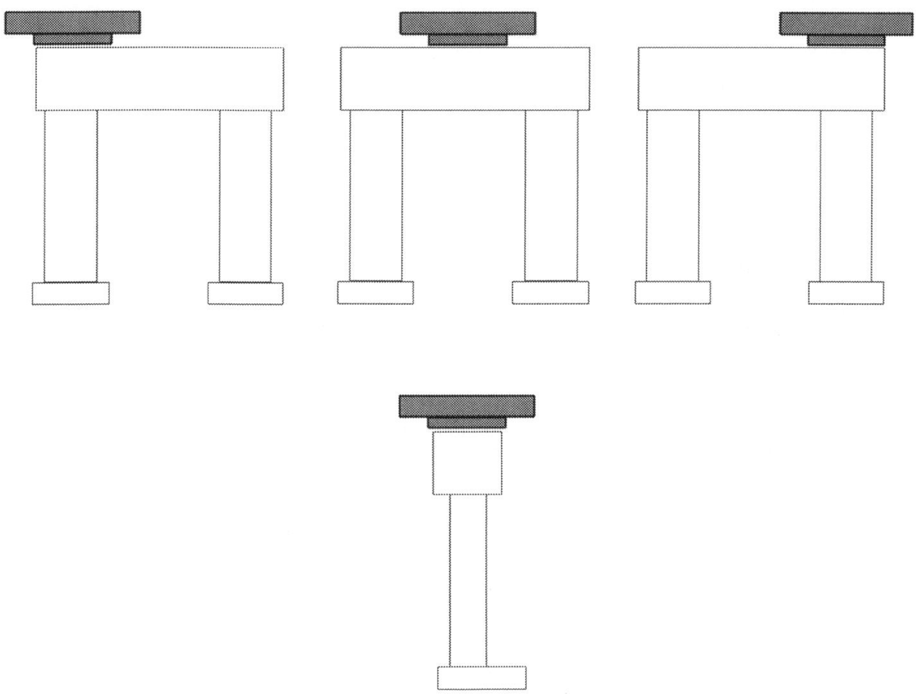

The COB plate and position atop the pelvic table

What happens when weight is applied to the edges of the COB plate?

It depends on which edge of the plate is receiving the weight. If we put weight on an edge that sits above the table top of the pelvis, the plate will be supported. [See middle picture below.] Although a bit unwieldy, we have opportunity to slide the plate and get the weight off the edge of the table and onto the middle once again.

What if the weight is on an edge of the plate that hangs over the table?

The indirect pressure of the additional weight will cause the COB to tilt. [See side pictures below.]

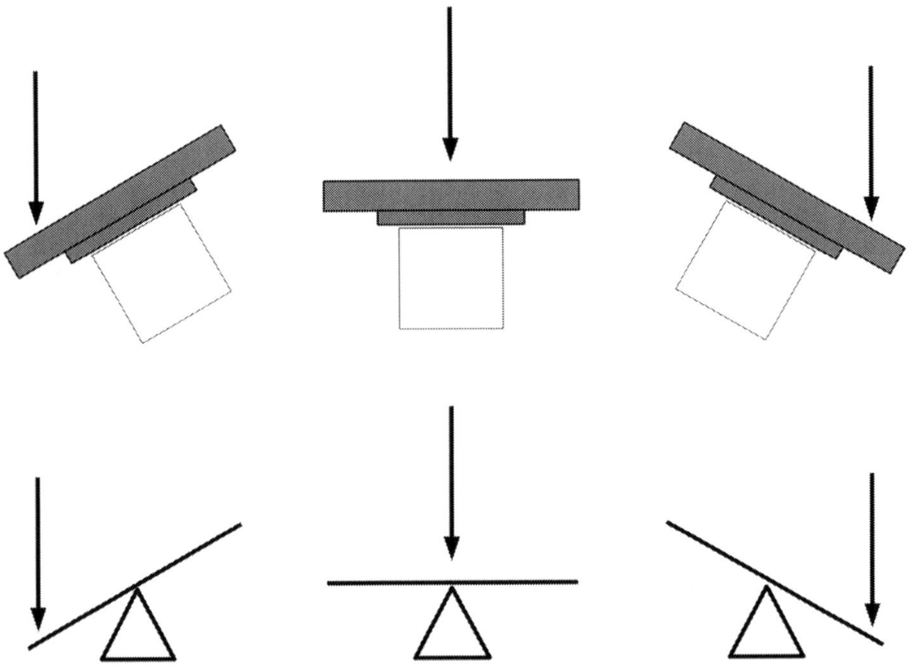

Force applied directly (middle picture) and indirectly (sides) on the COB plate

What happens next?

The plate will eventually fall off the table and, subsequently, we fall to the floor.

Show me an example of indirect vertical pressure on the COB and what happens.

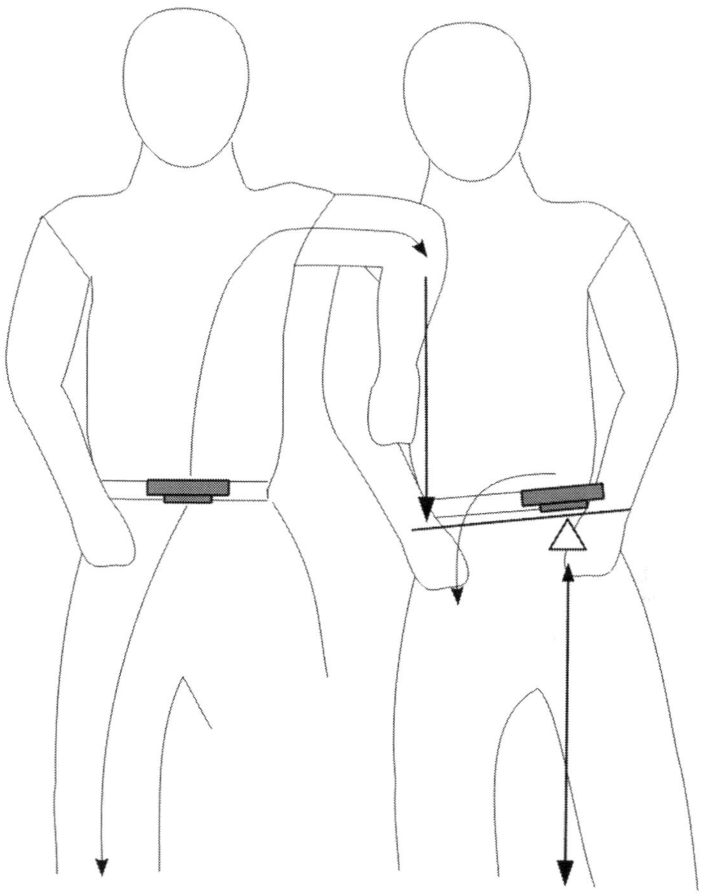

Post-left stance; Uke applying indirect vertical pressure to our COB

In this picture Uke leans on the shoulder opposite of where our COB sits. This should resemble having someone lean on the end of a teeter-totter. The COB acts as the fulcrum and you will experience the vertical lever action of the COB as you are made to tip. Your body recognizes the off-balance condition and will slide the COB plate under the force as quickly as possible.

Supported Conclusions

Indirect vertical pressure on the COB

- Indirect vertical pressure will cause the COB plate to tilt.
- The indirect pressure can be applied to the COB by adding weight to the torso or simply tipping the torso (e.g., by resting on and arm, shoulder, hip, COB, etc.).

Vertical scenario 5: Advanced ways to add weight

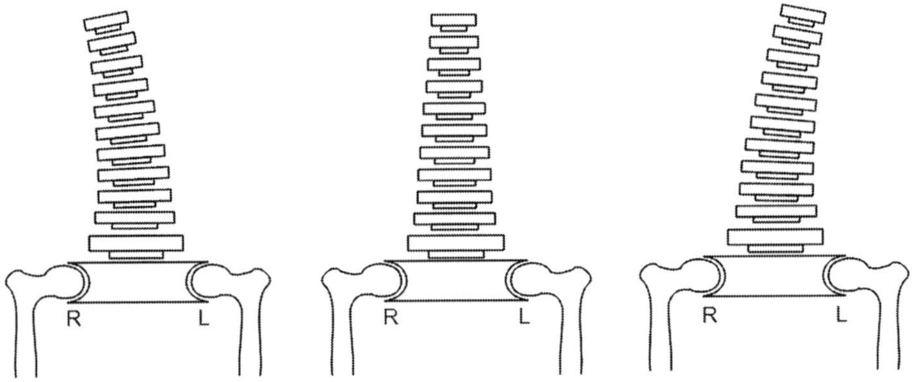

Spine as a wobbly stack of plates

It is easy to understand that a rigid arm, neck, or torso will add indirect pressure to my COB plate.

What happens when they try to add weight to a loose arm?

As in the horizontal COB lesson, loose appendages have their own center of balance (the joint that attaches them to the body becomes a hinge) and do not affect the COB vertically unless they are stretched, fully compressed, or joint locked.

The spine is flexible and allows my upper torso to lean over unsupported areas. Is that an issue?

Your spine is a lot like a stack of plates. Your base (legs, pelvis, and feet) are working overtime to stay underneath and support that wobbly stack. If you lean too far, your spine acts like a slinky. Hopefully, as the top of the stack begins to topple, you are aware enough to use your arms to do a cartwheel or controlled Ukemi.

What are my feet doing this whole time?

Most tables come with four legs. Since you only come equipped with two legs, your feet are doing their best to add the brake to your rotating hips.

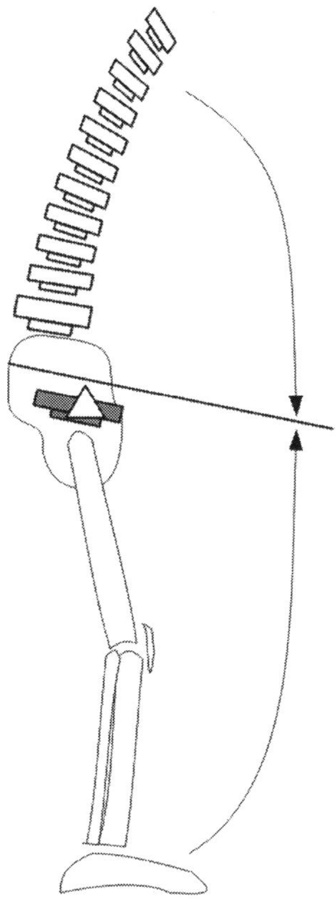

Feet provide a brake to keep the COB from tipping

Is that why it seems easier to spin Uke's hips backward than forward?

Yes. The heel presents some amount of resistance, but the ball of the foot offers a wider base. The wider base delivers more resistance and additional room to move. This is important because our spine can bend forward much further than it can backward or sideways.

Supported Conclusions

Limbs play a role

- Soft or loose arms do not have effect on the center until they are stretched.
- In many ways, your vertebrae act like a stack of plates.
- We can attempt to stop the COB from tilting, but the further the stack of plates leans over the bottom plate (COB), the more torque gets applied to the COB. The COB is at a disadvantage.

The brake

- If the COB tilts, the supporting leg's foot or other leg will attempt to resist the tilt.

I hope this gives insight to the vertical aspect of your COB. Let us look at what we can do with that knowledge.

How to use the COB on the vertical plane

I did not mention it until now, but you may have noticed that the base of our bodies will naturally do all it can to keep the COB from falling.

The brain will sacrifice the body to protect itself. Sometime around the age of one we learn that sudden stopping can hurt, and that lesson seems to stick with us the rest of our lives. Your hip's insatiable desire to keep you upright is actually your brain's way of saying, "Keep me off the floor." You may argue with your brain, "Hey, I am in the middle of an attack," but the brain has a prime objective: avoid sudden stops! The subconscious impulse to protect our brain will override any and all other actions.

One more idea to be clear on before we progress. You may have noticed that we have only described the effect of loose limbs and their need to be stretched. A joint lock will create a rigid limb. Let us use joint locks as a generic term for actions like kote-gaeshi, kote-mawashi, arm bars, etc. A fully or partially extended arm is technically not joint locked and behaves like a loose limb until we make it rigid by locking one or all of these joints in this particular order: shoulder, elbow, and wrist. (I guess you could include the fingers if you want to get nasty.) Locking the shoulder is the most important and is the typical measure of using Aiki.

Let us get back to the action.

It is very uncomfortable or downright off-balancing to have indirect vertical pressure on your COB. Your body is not designed to support weight in this manner. Indirect pressure on your COB is an easy method to lose balance, or even worse, throwing out your back or damaging the joints in your base. We should consciously avoid indirect vertical pressure as much as possible. (Your subconscious already knows this.)

So we know we have the "what" and "why" of how to keep ourselves safe. The "what" is to use as much direct vertical pressure as possible. The "why" is to avoid loss of balance or injury.

What is the secret of "how"? Keep the pressure of our COB over one of our supports!

<u>Sensing the vertical aspect of the COB</u>

Play with these next drills, but be careful to limit the weight. Technically, you could learn these lessons with absolutely no weight, but it may make it easier to use something. Start with something around one pound and only add weight if you cannot get a sense of being burdened. Any more than twenty pounds seems outrageously too heavy.

Double-weight yourself (e.g., horse stance). Pick up any moderately heavy but compact object with both hands, and let your arms extend fully. (For example, a half-gallon of milk, a cooking pan, most ladies' purses, etc.) The object should be hanging down at the middle of your body with your arms in a "V" pattern.

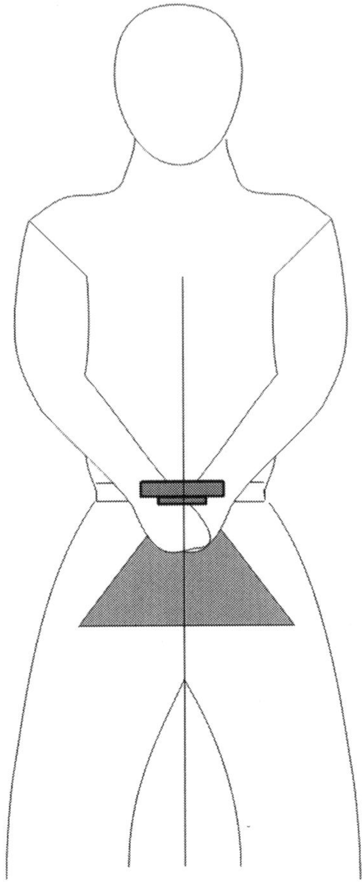

Start this exercise with a moderately weighted object at your center

Now, let go with the left hand, let the right arm move over and hang to your side. You should be able to sense your COB has slid to the right slightly. The COB is not exactly in the middle of your body any longer. Your right leg is carrying more of the weight than the left.

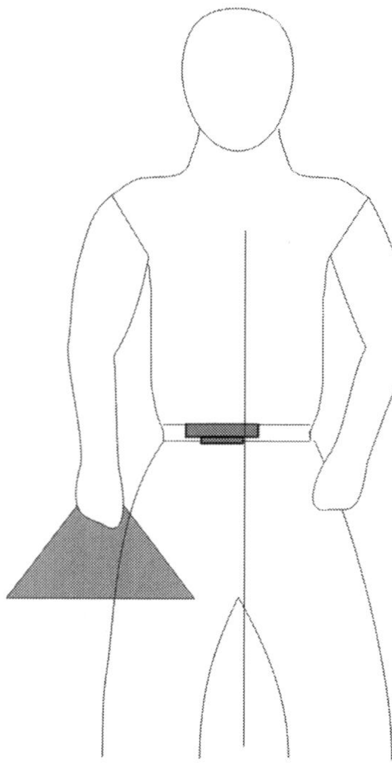

Letting go with left hand; body slightly weighted right

While keeping the object on the outside of your body (on your upper leg/ hip), complete the shift of your body to the right side. In other words, shift your weight so that you are standing on your right leg only (single-weighted on the right side, while keeping the object on the side of your upper leg/hip). This completes the COB slide. I like to call this "posted right" or "post right" because it feels like your right leg is a post stuck into the ground.

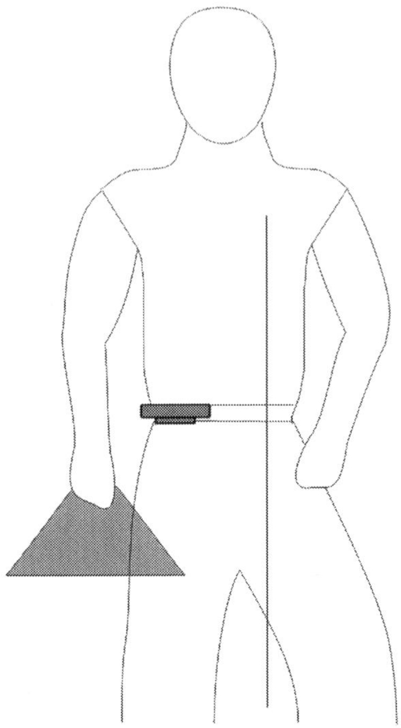

Completing the slide to the right by shifting to one-legged stance

This should give the awareness that shifting your weight is the same as sliding the COB. You have balanced your weight and the weight of an additional object onto your COB and supported it with a leg.

Let us go a bit further. Where are we most comfortable?

Still in that post-right pose with the object on your side? Bring your right arm in front of your body such that your hand or wrist area is directly in front of your first belt hoop. (Or kua, inguinal crease; however you would like to term it.) What should you be feeling? You should feel that the additional weight of the object rests more comfortably onto your frame. This position puts the object as close as the object can be to your COB. This moderate amount of weight will likely not be as dramatic as a one hundred plus pound object (Uke!), but you should be able to get a feel for where you would rather wear the additional weight provided by the object.

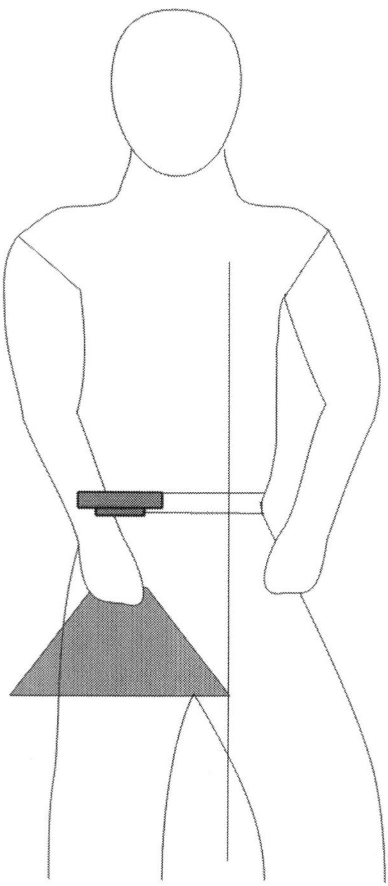

Wearing the additional weight as close to the COB as you can

Further yet! How does my foot factor in?

Get back into the post right position. This time, extend the right arm, with object in hand, directly outward and to the side. You should feel the need to counter-balance that weight by extending your left leg further to the left. Take note:

- You should be sensing the COB as the fulcrum between these two masses: your leg and the object.
- Your leg is heavy. It did not take a lot of leg motion to counter the weight of the object held outward.

- Your body naturally prefers to use the left leg as opposed to your left arm to counter balance the weight. Not only is your leg is in a better position to apply leverage on the COB in this case, but your body is smart enough to know that your pelvis and leg bones are most comfortable when the belt-line is parallel to the floor.

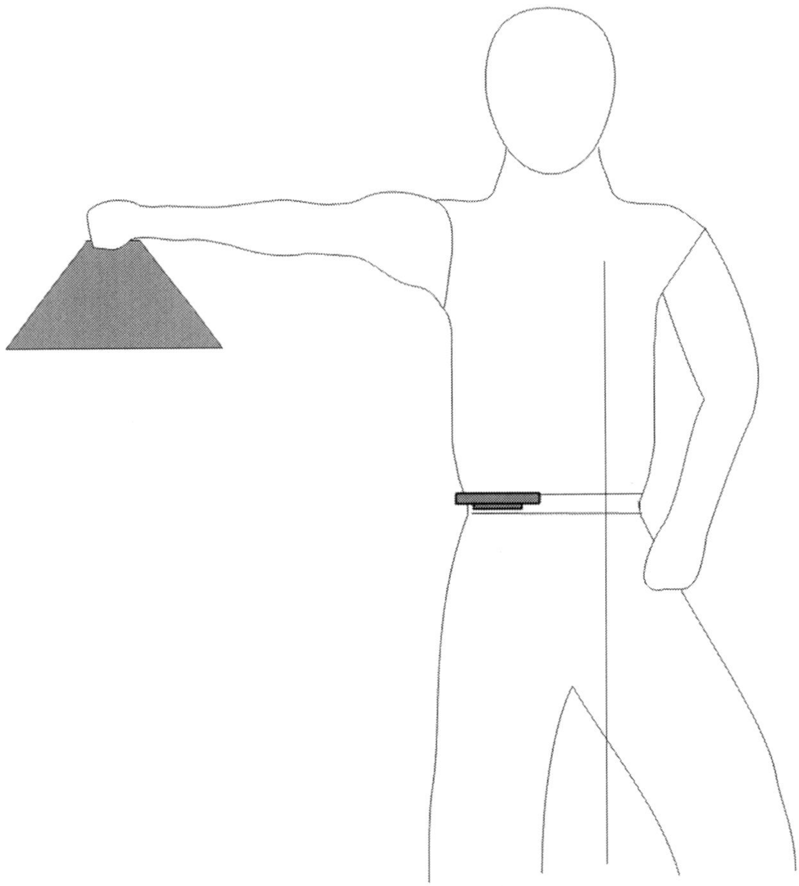

Place the additional weight as far from the COB as you can; counter-balance with leg

Take a second to notice something about your unweighted, left leg. You are using that left leg to counter-balance the weight. Leaving the weight to your side, test how easily can you move that left leg in front or behind you. You should find it is rather difficult. This is because your body is using that leg to apply a brake to the force of the object falling. Your left leg is occupied. Can we free that left leg so it can do other things for us? Let us see.

Get back into the post right position and extend your right arm, with object in hand, directly forward in front of your first belt hoop. You should feel that your right foot has made a quick adjustment. The foot is providing the brake that keeps your hips/COB from tilting forward. You likely did not notice any adjustment in your left leg, but your left leg is now free to swing behind yourself.

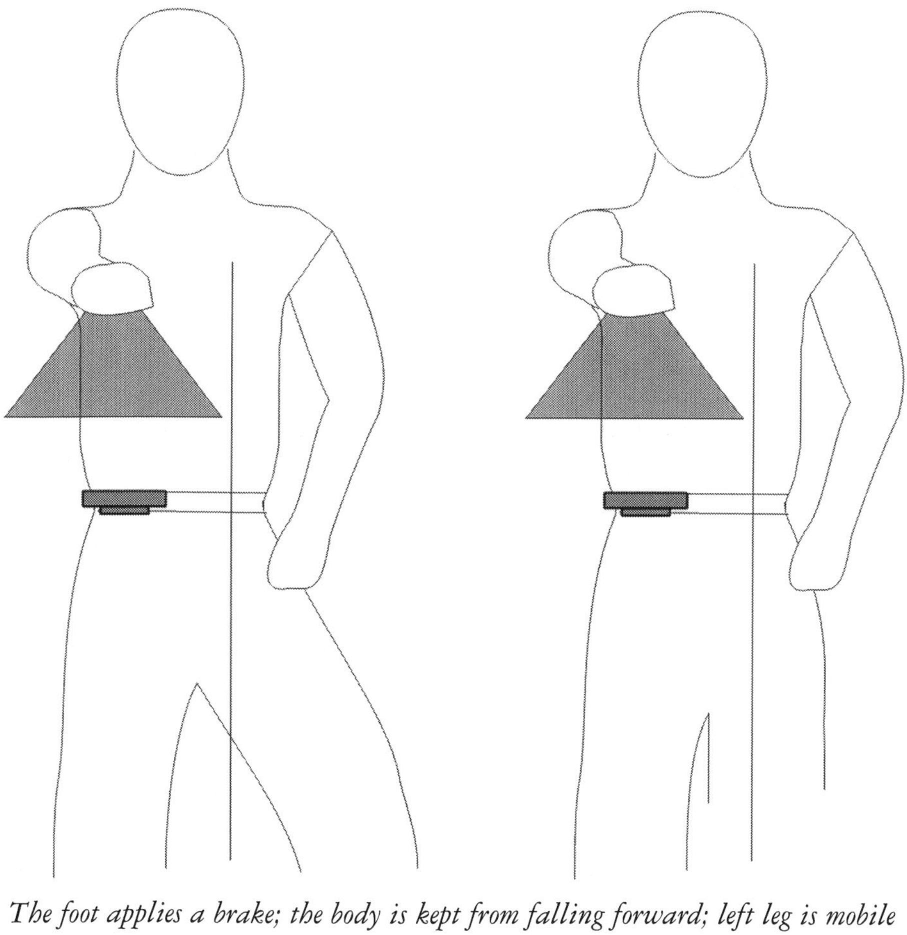

The foot applies a brake; the body is kept from falling forward; left leg is mobile

Keeping the additional weight on this forward plane (e.g., the forward space directly in front of your COB, high or low) maintains independence for your left leg. You may use your left leg to begin influencing the object. How? Stay balanced on the right and use your hip to swing your left leg in an orbit around your COB. You should feel the reciprocal action of your leg swing imposed upon the object. If your leg is moving counterclockwise, so too is the object. You should be sensing the horizontal turnstile and how generating indirect horizontal force is intertwined with correct vertical alignment.

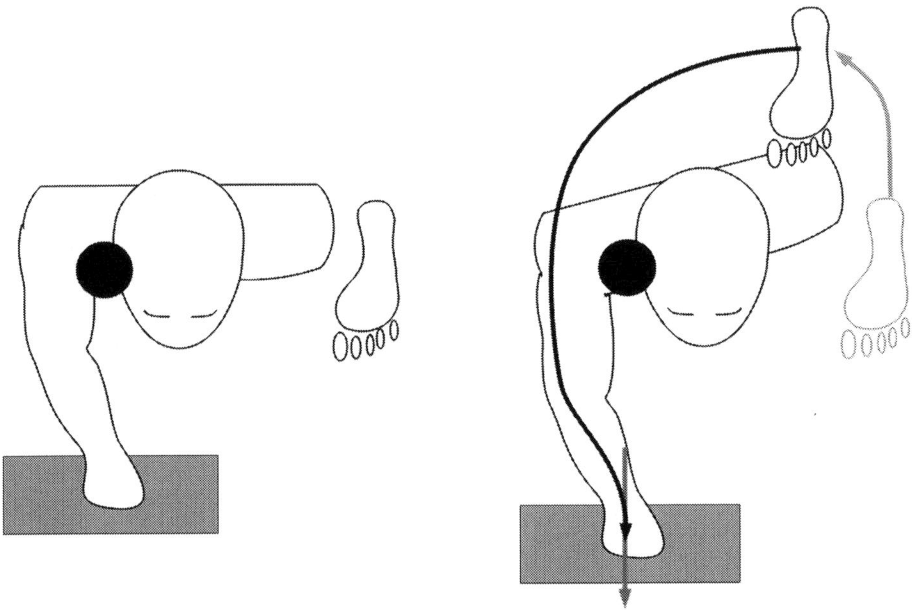

Swinging the dragon's tail; left leg is mobile; mass of the leg is added to the rotation

I have heard using the unweighted leg in this manner called "using your left leg as a rudder" or "swinging the dragon's tail." I am not certain I like those descriptions, but they are valid. The reason I am reluctant to use these terms is they seem to imply the left leg (in this case) is performing the action. It is the weighted kua (right kua in this case) that should be causing the action. The swinging leg helps support the rotation. Keep your front-wheel drive in mind and be certain the twist that performs the swinging of the appendages is driven from your weighted kua. Open the right side kua and allow the arm to extend.

Investigate further by starting in a horse stance with the weight hanging in the middle of the body. Begin rocking from side to side using Aiki stepping (front-wheel drive). Support the weight with one hand, both hands, or switch off as you move. I will give you the hint that you will find it easiest to keep the object moving from one side's first belt hoop to the other.

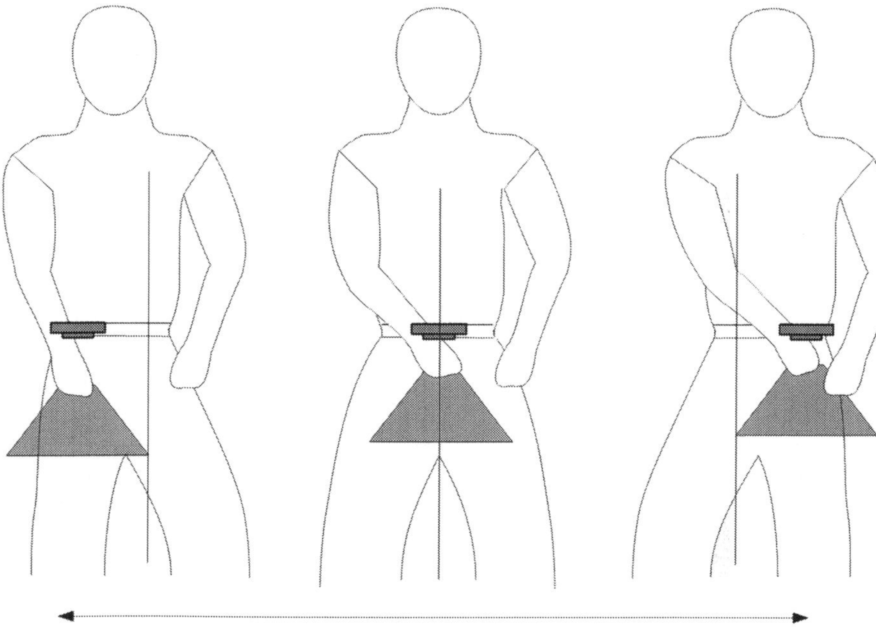

Practicing the front-wheel drive drill with the weight

Learn some contrast! What is not so efficient?

Get into the post right position with the object and right arm in the pocket of your right-side first belt hoop. This time, as you shift your weight to the left, let the weight and arm stay in your right-side first belt hoop. You should be able to post left, but it will feel insanely more awkward than when we shift the object to the left as well. This is due to the indirect vertical pressure being applied to your COB. The indirect pressure is pushing downward and into the hips, but it is not a strong position to be in. The weight you are holding is on the same side as the unweighted leg. You have to counterbalance the additional weight, but do not have many options. You should find you are leaning and may have to kick your head to the side. This situation gets worse when you trade this rather light object for Uke. Avoid indirect vertical pressure on your COB as much as you can.

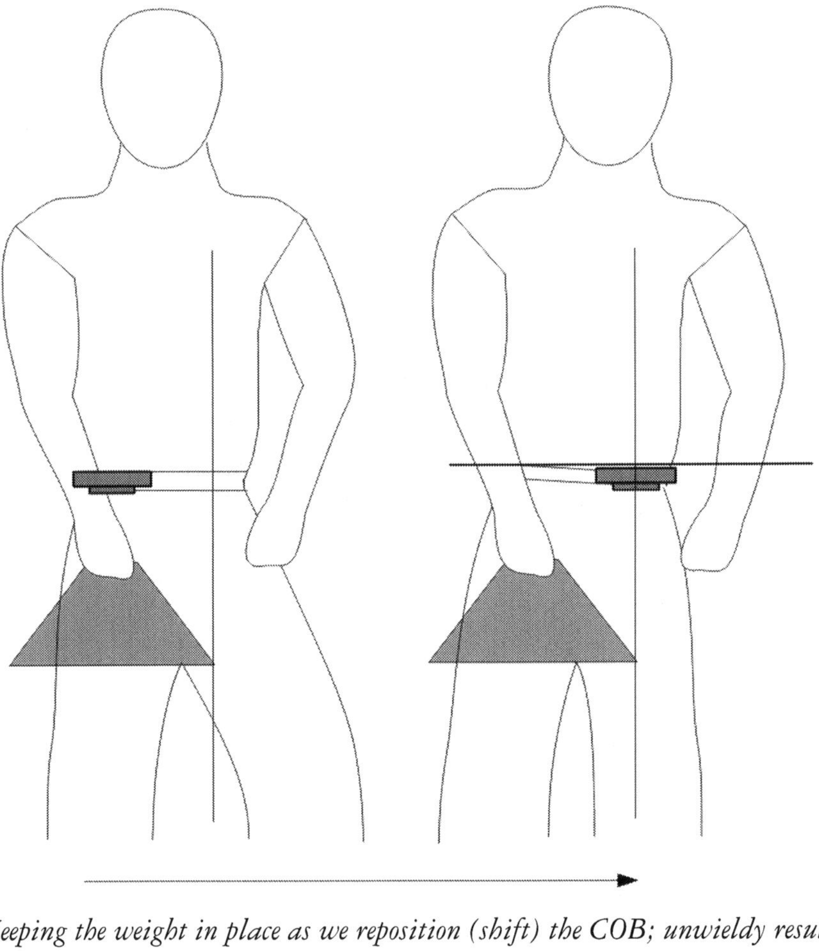

Keeping the weight in place as we reposition (shift) the COB; unwieldy result

Now if we only had a drill that included Uke to increase our awareness of what it means to keep the pressure of our COB over our support(s). Oh yeah! We do.

The elephant arms drill

This is exactly like the investigation we just did with the moderately weighted object, but with Uke!

Face Uke in a double-weighted stance (horse stance). Bring your hands to the middle and overlap them (I suggest you avoid interleaving your fingers, but whatever makes you comfortable). For those with kids, you might recognize this position as part of the elephant dance. The arms represent the elephant trunk, and they swing them from side to side as they walk like an elephant. We are going to do almost the same thing. Have Uke put his hand or hands into yours and apply some (not all) of his weight by leaning onto your hands.

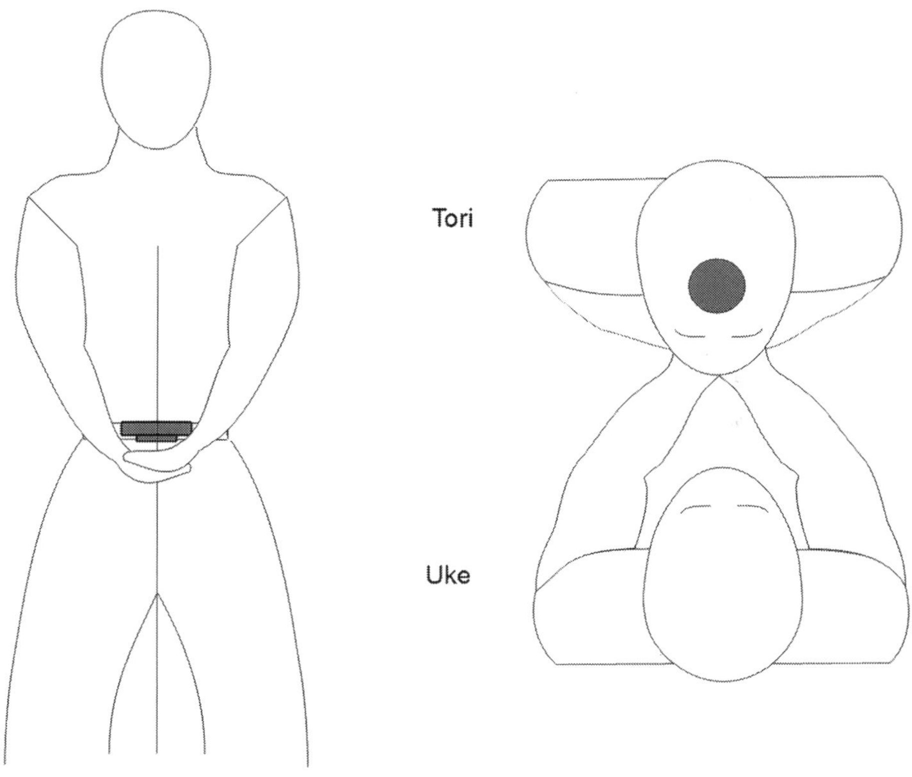

Center your weight and crossing hands; Tori and Uke lined up for elephant arms drill

Begin the drill by replicating the earlier experiment of shifting from side to side, bringing along your hands, and stopping at the weighted side's first belt hoop. All the same observations apply.

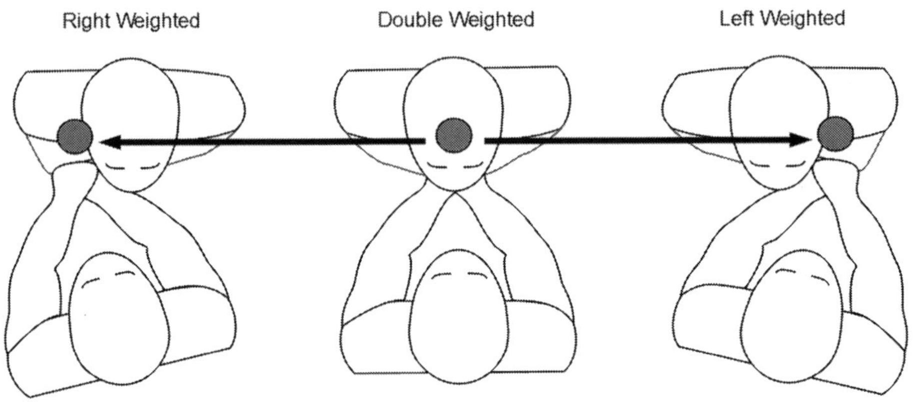

Elephant arms drill; shifting the COB left and right and taking Uke's weight with you

Be careful to keep the hands in front of your COB. If you are doing this correctly, you should not feel much strain. I like to describe it as Uke feels rather light. The effect on our bodies seems to be but a tenth of the actual weight applied.

Another key element to watch for is Uke not following you. If you are doing your part correctly, this means Uke is not getting into the spirit of this drill and is not actually leaning on you. All Uke has to do is truly lean on your hands and keep up.

There is yet another secret to this drill.

You may have noticed that Uke has a good bit of inertia if you rest at the first belt hoop positions. Uke becomes stationary. You might even get stuck in the double-weighted position in the middle of your shift (at your transition from the drop to the front-wheel drive in the Aiki step.) The trick to overcoming Uke's inertia is to give Uke a reason to move in the direction you wish to go. How? Tilt your hands!

If you have been keeping the hands parallel to the floor, Uke is being supported by a direct upward vertical pressure. Change it! Deflect him! If you are posted right, start by dipping your left shoulder a bit and let Uke slide toward your left in much the same way you are about to slide your COB to the left side. Reverse this on your way to the right side. Pay some attention to the timing of when you dip the hands and when begin sliding your COB.

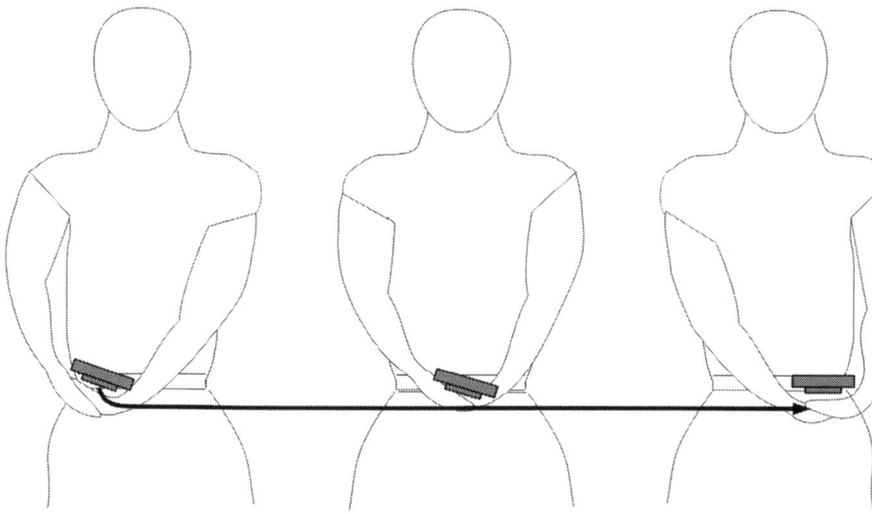

Tilting your hands to influence Uke to fall in the direction you want to go

There is a subtlety in the hands here. Using the right-to-left shift depicted above, which tilting method is easier: lifting our right hand or dropping the left? Hint: dropping the left is easier. This is front-wheel drive with your hands. Your COB should be doing the same thing. The method of relaxing and offering Uke a place to drop is called "creating voids."

What does the tilt do? It creates an inclined plane that allows Uke to fall off of your hands in the direction you want to go. The pressure applied to Uke's arm is awkward to Uke. Uke's shoulder, elbow, and wrist joint combo prefer to accept the pressure perpendicularly (straight into the palm). Your tilt pushes harder on one side of his hand versus the other. Aside from the obvious deflection of Uke's force, your tilt will trigger Uke's reflex action to even out the pressure on his hand.

In this version of the drill, the tilt you create works best when applied against Uke's pinky. When applied to Uke's pinky, the pressure on Uke's pinky is like a cross-between a kote-hineri and a gooseneck type joint lock.

Pushing on the sides of the body, in lieu of directly into it, is something we will see again, often.

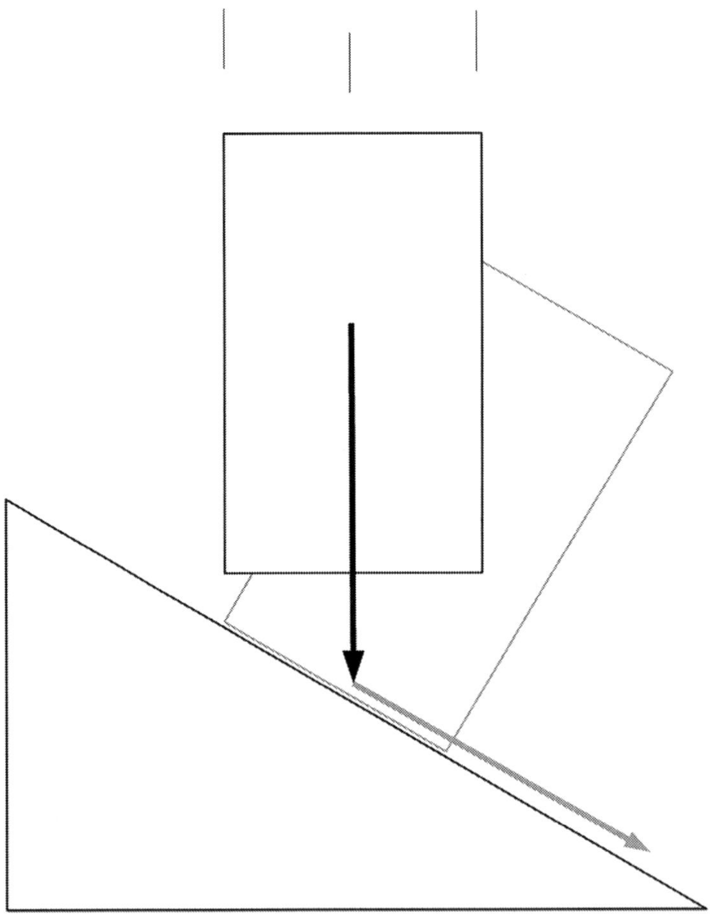

The effect your tilted hands are having on Uke; depicted using basic shapes

Having fun? Never thought moving Uke could be so easy huh? Well, it gets better!

So far, we have only directed Uke left and right. Walk like an elephant in any direction you wish. Deflect Uke with your hands and move in that direction. Not too quickly, because Uke is relying on your COB to stand. Uke will have some trouble keeping up. Next, put a bit of twist to your steps (swing the tail of the dragon if you please) and see what it does to Uke.

The trick here is to keep Uke leaning on you at all times. Be wary that you are not putting him back on his stance by giving his weight back to him. One key to Aiki is to keep Uke relying on us for support, e.g., leaning on us. Otherwise we break the connection and become two freely moving objects again. We want to maintain the one body condition that this drill sets up for us. Hopefully you are starting to get a feel for what ittaika means.

One more change to the drill before we leave this lesson.

The Ryu

This tweak is named the Ryu. The longer name for the Ryu is Tomoe across the center-line. That longer name will make more sense in a short few more pages.

Post right, put Uke in your right side, but before you begin tilting your hands and sliding the COB (and Uke) to your left, close your right kua and bring your left belt hoop to the point of contact. Now, put your left leg outward to the side and slide Uke across to the left, all the while keeping Uke on your left belt hoop.

It may take a second to realize how to keep your hands in synch with your COB.

"So what?" you say. The Ryu makes much more sense when we get to spooling. In a short preview, the Ryu puts a slight rotation into your COB as you draw Uke across in the elephant arms drill. This trick of closing the kua to join the unweighted first belt hoop to the object before we slide Uke across ourselves can open new opportunities in follow up attacks.

As above, so below; elephant arms with the hands turned over
I did promise the other key to Aiki. Here it is: The elephant arms drill works the same way when we lean on Uke (yang connection).

This time as we try the elephant arms drill, instead of cupping your hands to allow Uke to rest on them, turn your hands over (palm down) and press your weight onto Uke's hands.

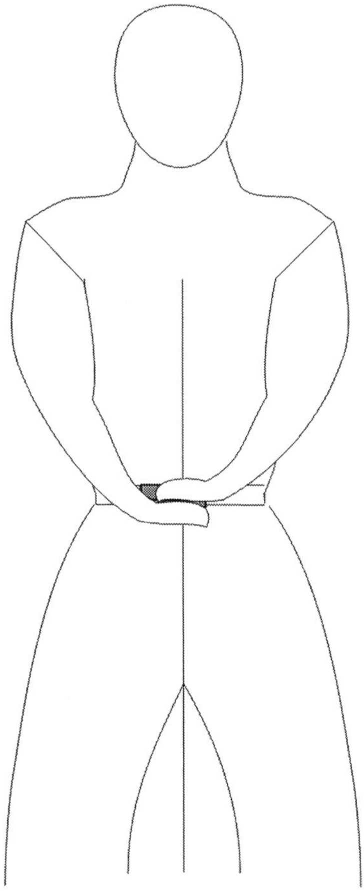

Elephant arms drill with your hands palm down and resting on Uke

All of the same experiences apply (e.g., Uke should stay in front of your COB at all times, tilt your hands, the Ryu, etc.). Everything should feel the same with the exception that you are resting on Uke.

It really is that simple. You should be able to experiment with leaning on Uke on your own, but in any version of the elephant arms drill, watch that you do not allow Uke to take over with his center.

Aiki has two strategies. The first is to keep Uke falling or resting on our COB (yin connection). The second strategy is to keep Uke supporting our weight in ways that keep him off balance (yang connection).

Maintain an indirect pressure on Uke's center at all times, especially in this palm down version of the drill. (You might have experienced that using direct pressure on Uke's center allowed him to grab your center and Uke took over. In effect, Uke was able to lead you into the palm up version of the drill with him in control)

The elephant arms drill is a great way to understand how we gain and lose Aiki (e.g., Uke typically takes over once your hands cross the "middle" of the distance between you. Greater success lies close to Uke or to yourself.).

Now that we have covered the COB horizontally and vertically, let us bring this back to the beginning and take the time to explain how to combine the perspectives and view our COB as a three-dimensional fulcrum.

The Cob as a three-dimensional fulcrum

We have spent a good deal of time describing the COB's behavior in the horizontal (forward and backward, left and right) and vertical (up and down) planes.

We combine these perspectives to understand the COB as a three-dimensional fulcrum.

The short version, the COB is a ball (an orb!).

Indirect pressure

By studying the indirect pressure behaviors, we learn that we can lever against the COB forward/backward, up/down, and left/right. In other words, we are free to spin in any direction around a particular point in space. (Put yourself in mind of the acrobatics performed by skydivers.) That particular point in space is where our weight is equal in all dimensions (forward/backward, up/down, and left/right). You could say that point is where we are balanced in all dimensions.

It should be obvious that a point in space is nothing more than a ball, but for the sake of discussion...

If we can move around this point in any direction with equal resistance, we should conclude that the object we are moving around has no corners. In other words, all paths around the object are equal in length. Can you think of an object that has no corners and all paths around are equal length? (Hint: a ball.)

The COB behaves exactly like a ball when it meets with indirect pressure. Imagine an inflatable beach ball floating on top of the water. Indirect pressure can be applied in any direction and the ball will spin but not necessarily move in any direction.

The only path to make contact with this COB is our bodies. The softness of our bodies, the flexibility of our joints, and the overall irregularity of our shape all complicate the methods to applying indirect pressure on the COB. Flesh, bone, and stance get in the way of the COB behaving exactly like that inflatable ball on the water. The body adds textures and nuances to the COB behavior. The body obscures the ability to notice that what hides inside us is a ball.

Direct pressure

No two objects can occupy the same space at the same time.

The result of two objects colliding (direct pressure between two objects) depends greatly upon the composition of those objects.

Again we find the body that surrounds the COB that complicates the behavior.

Since all objects have a center of balance, we have to remove the variables introduced by the object's body so that we can observe the behavior of the COB.

As we remove the coverings and strip the object down to just the COB, we should again recognize that the COB is nothing more than a point in space. What is a three-dimensional point in space look like? It is a ball!

Let us describe the COB as a cue ball.

How does the analogy of a pool cue ball help? Watch a pool shark work magic on the pool table. How many different directions do they use to spin the cue ball and what is the net effect when the cue ball hits the target ball? This interaction between the cue ball and the rest of the balls on the table is exactly what is going on inside us and Uke as we interact.

The question to ask is, "How is a ball a fulcrum?" The answer comes in the similarities between a ball and a teeter totter.

The first similarity is, "Direct pressure on a ball is like landing on the middle of a teeter-totter. There is no rise or fall, just deflection." If the board of the teeter-totter is horizontal, it is like landing on the ground that supports the fulcrum. In the sense of pool balls, it resembles a pool cue hitting another ball head on.

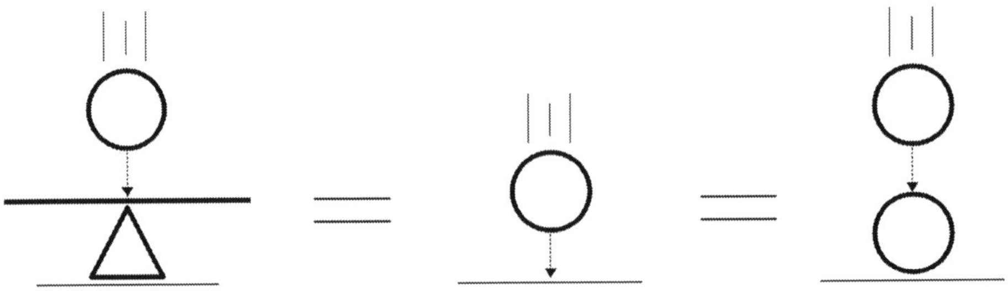

Landing on the fulcrum is exactly the same as landing on the center of a sphere

Conversely, if the teeter-totter board is inclined in either direction, it is like falling on a ramp. You can liken it to the cue ball hitting another ball slightly off center, but it is better expressed as rolling off of a log. (In the rolling off of the log analogy, the COB stays in its place and spins.) If you do not like the log analogy because the log is not shaped like a ball, imagine trying to land on giant beach ball on the water.

Object striking off center is re-directed; similarity between lever and a ball

Another striking similarity: the surface of the ball is like the ends of the teeter-totter. When the teeter-totter board is balanced, putting weight on one side will cause one side to fall and the opposite side to rise. Both sides will reciprocally rise or fall the same distance. The outside of a ball offers the same effect. In effect, the perimeter of a ball is a curved plank.

Consider a ball as a three-dimensional wheel or better yet, a three-dimensional pulley.

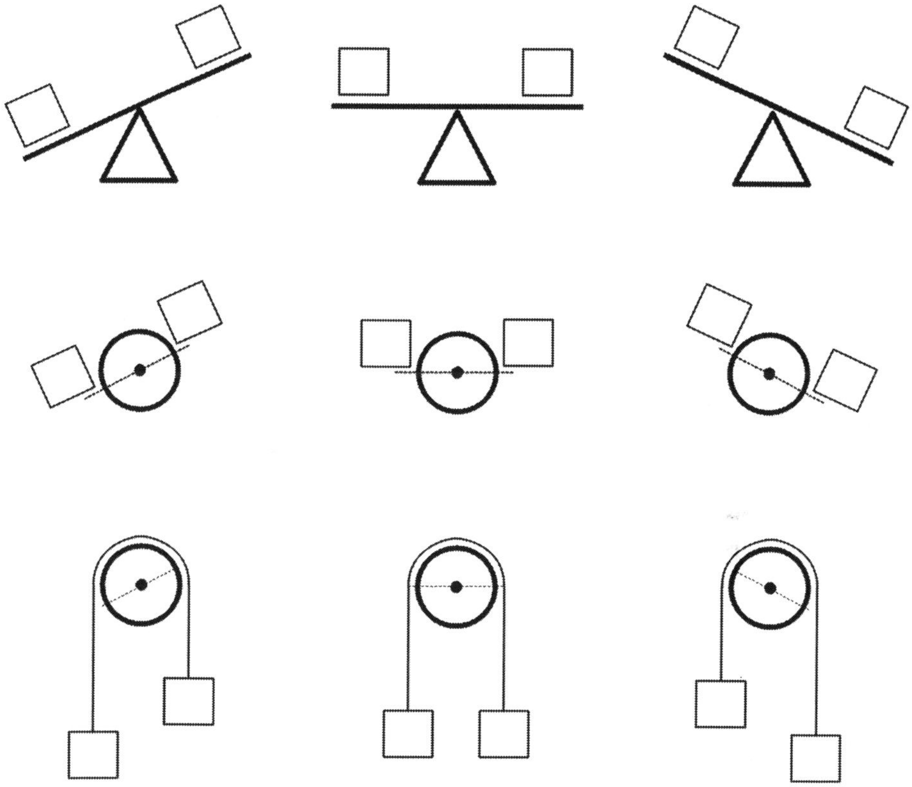

Juxtaposition of second class lever; a ball with a lip; and a pulley

A ball is a three-dimensional fulcrum. By viewing the COB as a ball, we can better predict the effect the COB will have on other objects and vice-versa.

COB and sagittal plane summary

We are going to close Precept Four: the sagittal plane (the first belt hoop) with a quick summary.

What did we learn?

- The center of balance" probably should have been described as the center of mass, but COB is a friendlier phrase.

- We learned how the COB behaves horizontally and vertically by revealing the COB as the fulcrum of a lever.
- The direct and indirect pressures applied to the COB create predictable results.
- The COB relies on our base or stance to provide support and stability. The rest of our body becomes that rigid object (plank) that leverages this fixed, immobile position.
- Driving our center through Uke or Uke impaling himself on our center is the same with one exception: the intent. Both situations have the same effect, but different motivation.
- We move the COB by shifting our weight.
- The COB does not move far. It pretty much stays in an area shaped like the top of a table that sits between our hip sockets. There are three basic positions for our COB to rest in. When we are double-weighted, it sits in the middle. When we shift to one side or the other, the COB comes to rest at our first belt hoop (or kua).
- We are strongest in that area in front of our COB. Any height will do. We perform best when we keep the focus of our efforts in that sagittal plane that divides us in half.

Using the drills, we gain a deeper awareness of our center and can begin the task of consciously putting our COB to use.

Here is food for thought, because pictures sometimes say more than words:

The COB in three dimensions

Tier 2 Advanced

There is one more concept I feel I must share before we close out Tier 2. The concept is called spooling. Spooling relies on another concept we call the belts.

We have explored the effects of sliding Uke. That we should spin Uke's center as we move him along the path(s) he is least able to resist (no-line, 20, or the combination of these two {footballs}).

Early on, I realized that Sensei was using the weak lines in my stance. I tried using these lines, but something was always missing. It was not until much later on that I became aware of the COB. That awareness opened the door to noticing the spin. At that point, I understood that Sensei was spinning me as he guided my center. The question then became, "What is Sensei doing to create the spin?"

In short, Sensei was wrapping me around his COB. I called this action spooling, but I still did not know how it was creating the spin in my COB.

At first, I likened spooling to wrapping fishing line around a reel. (To be specific, like putting line on one of the deep sea, horizontal fishing reels {not the flip caster type}.) Something was still not correct.

Spooling was vague until it evolved from threading line onto a reel into the analogy of a serpentine belt on the engine of a car. Spooling is a pulley system!

This pulley system consists of two wheels and a belt. The wheels are the three-dimensional wheels we call the COB, and for now, the belt is our arms.

Spooling is represented by three special belts: the oval, the eight, and the tomoe.

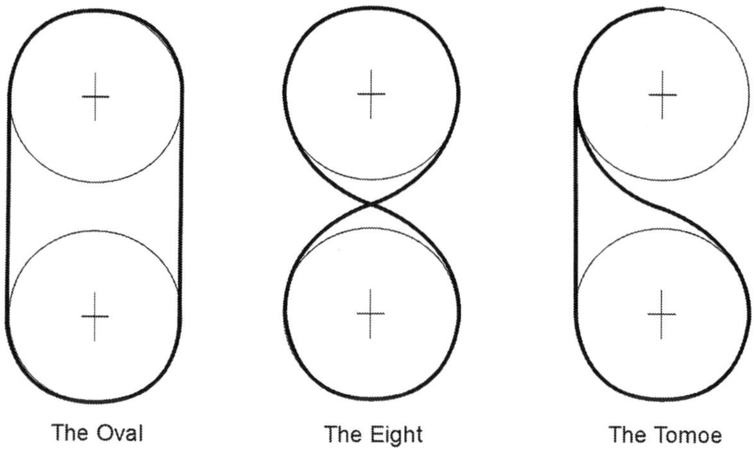

The three belt configurations that make up spooling

A revealing way to approach the belts is:
The oval = mirror-hand grab
The eight = cross-hand grab
The tomoe = two-hand grab

All three-belt drills are an exercise in guiding Uke's center by controlling our COB.

I am only going to describe this in two dimensions. Pay attention so you can go the rest of the way to three dimensions on your own (or wait for the next book). We are about to play a version of Aiki push hands.

The oval

The oval is the most obvious of the belts. It starts with two mirror hand grabs.

Line up face to face with Uke. Begin in the horse stance. Reach outward and grasp each other's wrists.

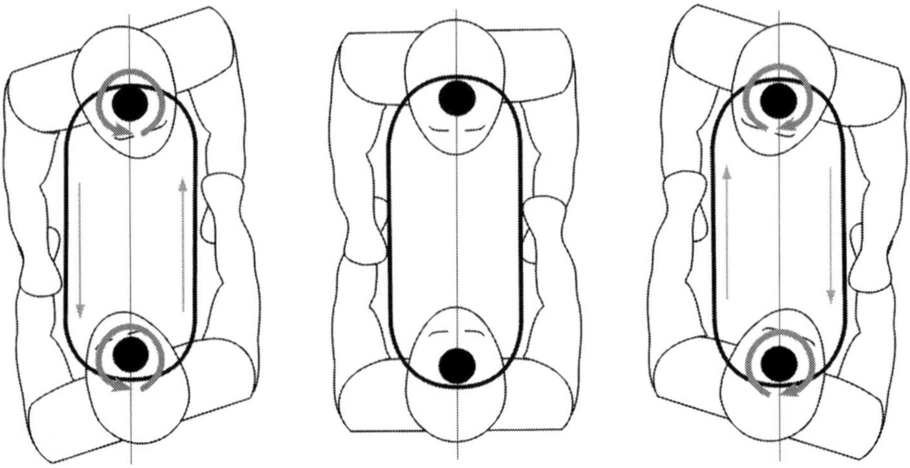

The oval; both COB's rotate in the same direction

The goal is to spin Uke's COB by spinning our own COB. Also known as: use your hips, not your arms!

You might get a sense of rotating Uke by pulling with one arm, and pushing with the other, but that is not connected to the power of our COB. You might even get by just using your arms as long as you are bigger and stronger than Uke, but remember, there is always a bigger Uke.

To do this drill correctly, relax the arms and begin opening and closing your kua. In other words, relax your arms and start feeling the simultaneous push forward and the push backward generated in your hips. Yup, you read that correctly, no mistake. They are both pushes!

Now, I know it sounds strange, but both of your hands should be pushing. Your forward moving arm pushes indirectly on the outside of Uke's COB and your backward moving arm pushes Uke away from your center as you spool Uke around your COB. The backward moving arm pushes, it does not pull.

You can liken the action of the backward moving arm to the edges of a gear. Think of the gear connected to the pedals of a bicycle (chain wheel that attaches to the crank/pedals). The edges of the gear push outward, away from the center, keeping the chain away from the center as it moves around the gear. Allow the rotation of the COB to draw Uke toward you, but never pull. Your bicep does not flex. You continually push on Uke's wrist to keep his trajectory from collapsing onto your COB. All push and no pull is a very important concept. It applies to all of the belts.

In the beginning, you may additionally need to adjust the distance between you and Uke to remove slack in your arms (i.e., begin the practice such that both Uke and Tori have fully extended arms.) You can increase the challenge by lining up closer than extended arm-length to each other and learn how to hang your arms to remove the slack. The weight of your arms stretches Uke's and offers the same effect as arms straight outward.

Leave both COB's in place as you cause them to spin. Neither side should feel any cause to step. (Spinning Uke while making him want to step is called sliding. We are isolating the spin portion so we can improve our ability to slide Uke.)

Take this drill further by using alternate stances. Be certain to mix up the starting position of your and Uke's COB (e.g., Uke or your COB start posted left, right, and in the middle).

Do not limit yourself to simply grabbing attacks. Realize that the oval is there in a block and punch as well.

Begin feeling the oval in your techniques. We find the oval in Shomenate #1. Of course, apply a vertical aspect and begin playing with Tenchinage (heaven and earth throws).

Notice that both COB's will rotate in the same direction at the same time (clockwise or counterclockwise). This distinguishes the oval from the eight.

The eight

You might have noticed the figure eight described by this belt. The rules of the eight drill are just as obvious as the oval. The eight causes the COB's to spin in opposite directions. Uke will spin clockwise while you spin counterclockwise and vice versa.

Line up as we did for the oval. This time, one of you crosses their arms and grabs the opposite side wrists. We call these cross-hand grabs (e.g., right hand grabs Uke's right, left hand grabs Uke's left).

Remember to relax and push with the arms; use the hips to generate the movement. Do not pull with the arms! (All push, no pull!)

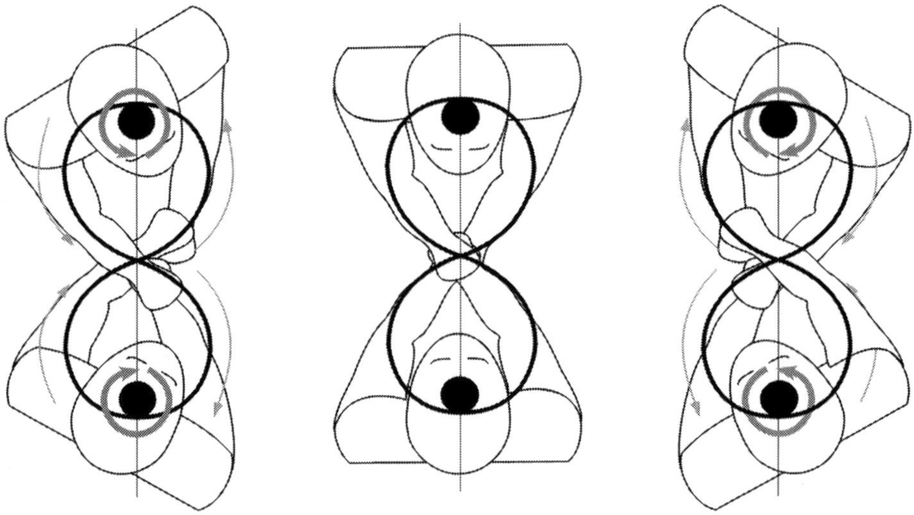

The eight; COB's rotate in opposite direction

Again, do not limit yourself to simply grabbing attacks. Realize that the eight is there in a block and punch as well.

From a technique perspective, we see the eight in Gyakugamaeate #3.

Enough said about the oval and the eight? Good, because the next belt gets a bit trickier.

The tomoe

This one looks suspiciously like half of the tai chi symbol, because it is.

The tomoe is a hybrid of the oval and the eight, but the tomoe is very unique from the other two belts in that it lacks a control on both sides of Uke's torso.

The oval and the eight use a reciprocal action, where one side our body moves away as the other one moves closer. We can compensate on one side or the other if either is deficient at controlling Uke's center. In these first two belts, Uke spins as quickly as we do.

In the tomoe, we spin Uke's COB by approaching Uke from only one side. The tomoe is more like entering with two arms in a wedge formation, almost exactly like holding a sword. (There is a deep significance in that statement. Most of Aikido is built upon sword work.)

Our entire body moves as a unit around Uke. Uke spins and we do not, or at least, Uke spins much faster than we do. We seem to move in an orbit around Uke's center.

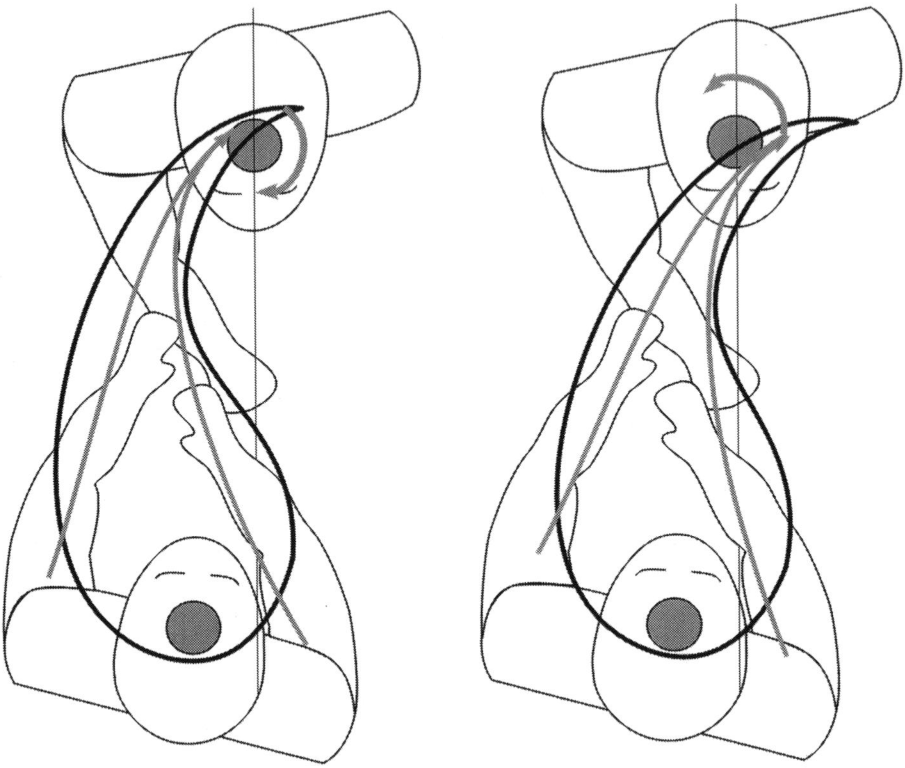

The tomoe slips behind or in front of Uke and spins him accordingly

The left-most picture depicts the Tomoe moving behind Uke's center and is sometimes used in Oshitaoshi #6. The right-most picture shows the Tomoe moving in front of Uke's center and is expressed in Maeotoshi #15.

We most commonly see the tomoe applied in a two-hand grab (although it can be done with only one hand). The tomoe is defined by how our centers are moving, not by the number of hands involved.

When moving toward Uke, the tomoe is often described as a push cut. When moving away from Uke, I have heard the Tomoe described as sheathing the sword.

The lack of control on both sides of Uke's COB can present complication.

Most persons can easily lead Uke away from his center by stretching his arm, but find difficulty in moving inward. This is primarily due to Uke's arm being flexible. How do we move toward Uke and affect his COB if his arm is flexible? The answer is: we cannot. We need to make Uke want to stiffen his arm, but how?

Well, we have not investigated daito hands yet. Daito Hands/lever arms will make the tomoe easier to perform. So too would joint locks, but those techniques are crutches. Let us learn a more Aiki way to apply the tomoe (i.e., the daito hands/lever arms and joint locks are icing on the cake; let us first learn to bake before we decorate).

Here is a short aside to understand touching Uke's center. Touching Uke's center removes the need for joint locks and daito hands because touching Uke's center will cause Uke to stiffen his arm and offer us the structure we need to spin Uke's center.

Touching Uke's center

Uke's soft body hides his COB and complicates the control of Uke's COB.

Uke's flesh and muscles are contributors to the issue, but nothing is quite as perplexing as the effects of his joints. The more joints involved, the trickier things become. This implies that working with Uke's arms is one of the most complicated ways to attempt a manipulation of his COB.

Uke's flexible arm presents a sizable challenge toward spinning Uke's center when we move toward Uke using a tomoe (two-hand grab). You simply cannot push a rope down the road and you cannot manipulate Uke's COB if his arm is limp. We need a way to create structure in Uke's arm, some manner of connecting it to his center.

We have three options that connect Uke's arm to his center, three ways to make Uke's arm rigid.

The first is a joint lock or putting torsion into the arm. Let us leave this option out for now, not that this is not effective, but we are here to lean Aiki, not joint locks.

The second is stretching the arm. It means that we are keeping the momentum of the arm moving away from the center, keeping the slack out of the arm. This is a simple concept, and we apply this method as we move away from Uke and draw him into the tomoe. With just a few exceptions, this method does not apply when we move toward Uke.

The third option is to have Uke stiffen his appendage for us. In this way, we can move toward Uke and compress his arm. We want Uke to maintain resistance to our entry similar to Uke trying to lift weights (e.g., bench press, flies, bicep curls, etc.). To put it simply, we want Uke to block.

In order for Uke to block, and I mean really block, we have to present a threat.

Great! Another "What," but "How" do we present a threat?

Eat lots of onions before practice! Okay, maybe that was bad humor (but it works for me!).

A much more viable martial method to present a threat is to understand what Uke holds most dear and advance on it.

What does Uke hold most dear? Ask yourself a couple of quick questions. "Why do I instinctively hold my head in between my hands when someone is about to throw a rock?" "Why do I cover my head when I hear a loud noise?" "What do I fear the most about falling?" "Why do persons put their hands out to catch themselves when falling?"

Did you figure it out yet? (And no, the answer I am looking for to, "Why do persons put their hands out to catch themselves when falling" is not, "Because they do not know how to do proper Ukemi.")

The answer to "What does Uke hold most dear?" is: Uke's brain is his most prized possession. The brain will sacrifice the body to protect itself. Your brain would gladly let your arms suffer before allowing any harm to come to your head. It is our most primal self-preservation instinct.

Your brain knows about projectiles. If you see an object coming your way, your brain will force you to avoid getting hit in the head by ducking and covering. The key words there are "covering" and "see." (The word "sense" would be a good substitute, too.)

Your brain also remembers suddenly stopping at the end of a fall. It does not like the effects that sudden stopping has on any part of your body, and since the time you were learning to walk, the brain has been actively monitoring and adjusting your body to maintain stability and balance.

The brain instinctively protects your stability and balance secondary only to avoiding direct contact to your head.

We trigger this instinct in Uke when we directly attack his eyes or COB, preferably both at the same time.

Safety first! Pointing at Uke's chest is likely enough to make Uke react. If you are careful, attacking Uke's eyes should be pretty straightforward. Even at a distance, simply pointing your fingers toward Uke's eyes will do the trick. Uke will understand that you are on a trajectory toward his most precious object.

Remember, some people are a bit too comfortable in class and will not react naturally because they have let their defenses down. (Is that not the most paradoxical situation? We go to class to learn self-defense, but forget to keep another person's hands out of our face? Silly, but it happens, especially with under-belts that trust you implicitly. You simply cannot assume that people will act in their own best interests.) Do not touch Uke's eyes. As Uke, protect yourself at all times. Appropriate Ukemi is Uke's victory.

Attacking Uke's COB means we project direct force on Uke's COB. (Read it again, direct pressure, not indirect. Indirect pressure on the COB is not instantly perceived as a threat to our balance.)

Applying direct pressure to Uke's COB can be abbreviated as touching Uke's center, but touching Uke's center makes no sense unless you understand one very important concept: you need to know where Uke's center is!

By now, you should have an excellent awareness of your COB. It is time to start watching Uke and building the awareness of where Uke's COB is.

Your instincts will sharpen to a much more granular awareness, but for purposes of introducing this concept to a new student, you can describe the COB (ours and Uke's) as having three positions: center, right, and left. I often describe the position of Uke's COB as a horizontal traffic light across the chest. (I realize that the COB is down in the hips, but people new to martial arts are not typically aware of anything below their eyes). I often ask which light is lit as an analogy of which position the center is in (middle, post left, or post right). I use that analogy on both Uke and Tori.

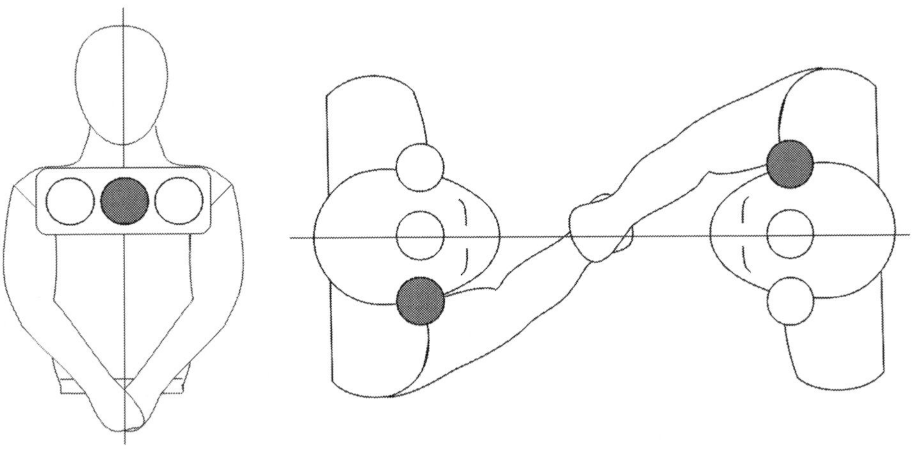

Three basic COB (light) positions; the COB exists where the light is lit; all three centered

Remember the push drill? The key objective is to keep our arm directly between ours and Uke's COB. Keeping the rigid arm directly between our

COB's equates to direct force on both Uke's and our bodies. No one spins! To keep our arm between our COB's, we have to keep our arm between the lights.

The trick is to begin sensing which lights are lit on both Uke and us. With the correct lights identified, we can begin to sense how to keep direct pressure between the COB's.

Why does Uke keep his arm rigid in the push drill? No, not because it is a drill, but because if he did not, you would crash into his COB. Our natural instinct is to hold at a distance any object coming toward our COB. This is called blocking. When Uke blocks, he offers us a rigid arm.

To put this into use; as Uke grabs your wrist, point your hand directly at his COB. Find which side he is balanced on (find which of the three positions is lit) and direct your COB toward Uke's keeping an unbendable arm in between. Uke should hit your structure and sense that he has to contend with it.

You can additionally begin pointing at Uke's head. (Carefully!)

Note that Uke will attempt to move your arm out of the way or will slide his COB out of the middle position to lessen the impact to the head.

Uke sliding his COB out of the middle position is a common reason why people miss the throws when they put their hand in Uke's face. We apply pressure on the chin and Uke simply bleeds the pressure off as he spins and shifts to the side. That shift and spin causes us to apply indirect pressure on Uke's COB. (Uke's head is in the middle but his COB is posted left or right.) We end up helping Uke spin and he walks out of the attack.

We practice this very same self-preservation technique in the hip-wheel turn drill. The hip-wheel turn drill teaches us how to slip a punch. Try the hip-wheel drill while pushing on the chin and you will know exactly what I am describing.

Indirect pressure on Uke's COB is not recognized as an attack because we are not trying to move through Uke's COB. In that sense, we are not contending for the same space. Uke's COB is secure in its position.

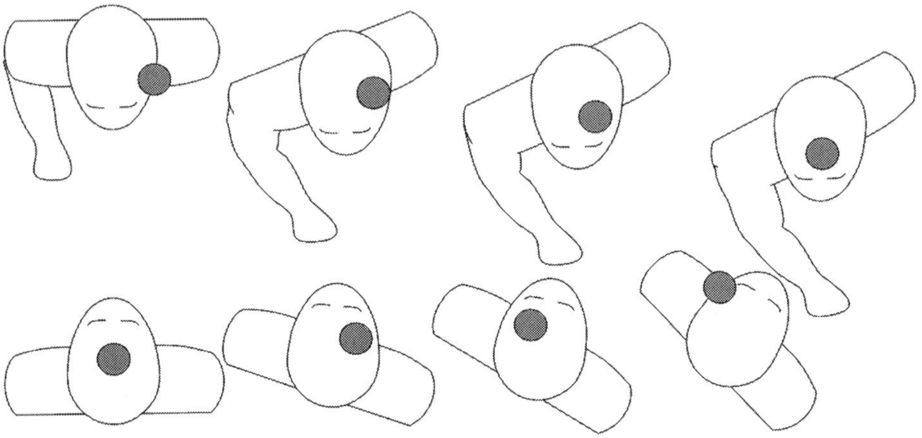

Slipping a punch keeps direct pressure off of the COB

Feel what it is like when you do not pose a threat. As Uke grabs your wrist (any hand, just pick one), point your hand at either of the unlit COB positions and direct your COB toward it keeping an unbendable arm in between. You should be able to sense that Uke is not being pressured to defend himself. Uke has slipped your attack.

Try again, as we first suggested, and point at the light. Got Uke on his guard? Great. Now experiment a little to find just how far off the line you can be before Uke stops sensing your action as a threat (e.g., point to the side of the light in ever so slightly increasing increments). I think you will notice that there is a very fine line between direct and indirect touch.

I urge you to take the time to perform this drill and build the awareness. A great deal of Aiki techniques rely upon toggling between indirect and direct touch. Most will start with direct pressure until Uke's COB is pushed up against the wall of his base, and then spin him using that almost direct, but definitively indirect touch. (We joke and call it "Mostly Direct" touch)

[Special note about the picture above. It is different than the one you saw earlier in this tier of precepts. This particular version implies that we start in a double-weighted stance. In order to leave that stance, the second picture from the left implies shifting the weight to the right foot before transitioning to the left. I do not recommend that as a standard stepping routine but wanted to address the issue. The similar picture used earlier in this tier depicts starting the motions weighted right and simply transitioning to the left.]

Back to the tomoe

That was a fairly long aside, but now you should have an idea of how to touch Uke's center. This is otherwise known as using Aiki to make Uke present a rigid arm.

We need this skill as we move inward, toward Uke in the tomoe.

There are four directions of travel in the tomoe.

Tomoe behind

The first is moving inward and forcing the point of the tomoe inward and behind Uke's center (tomoe behind).

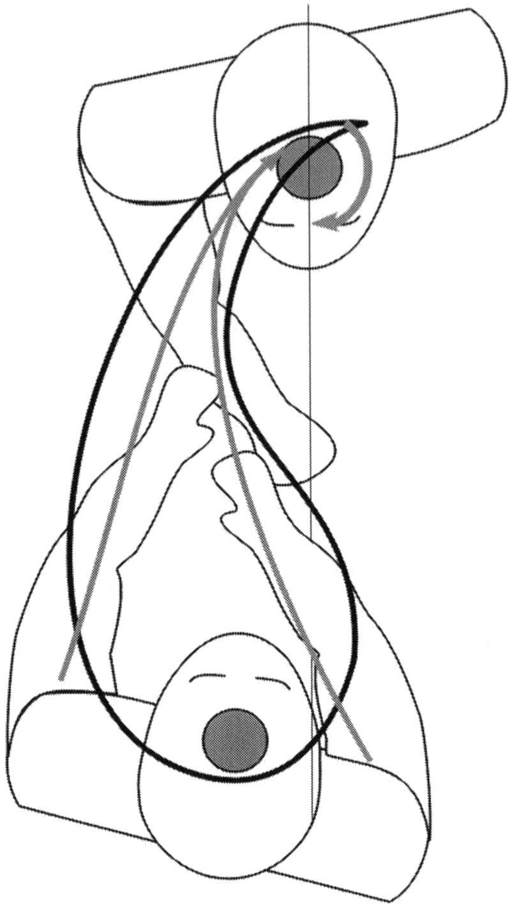

Driving the tomoe behind Uke's COB; in this example, spinning Uke clockwise

Note that the first step of this drill is actually to touch Uke's center and then allow the point of the tomoe to slip slightly off center. (Direct, then indirect touch!) The touch and roll causes Uke to stiffen his arm and offers you connection to his COB. The shift from direct to a blend of direct and indirect pressure stands him up and then spins him.

Be conscious not to go too wide as you slip off center. We do not want Uke to simply ward us off and attack with the other arm. We want to keep a good combination of direct and indirect pressure on Uke's COB. This is how we slide Uke along the footballs. The indirect pressure will spin Uke as the direct pressure moves him along the weak lines in his stance: the footballs. The spin will cause the hips to rotate, which will in turn open or close Uke's kua. Once Uke is in position, you can drop your arms to apply indirect vertical pressure on Uke's COB and he will fall.

The best drill to learn this skill is Oshitaoshi #6.

Tomoe to the front

The second tomoe direction involves driving the point of the tomoe in front of Uke's COB (tomoe to the front or tomoe in front).

Uke will spin in the opposite direction this time, but the rules are the same. We want that combination of direct and indirect pressures to guide Uke's body.

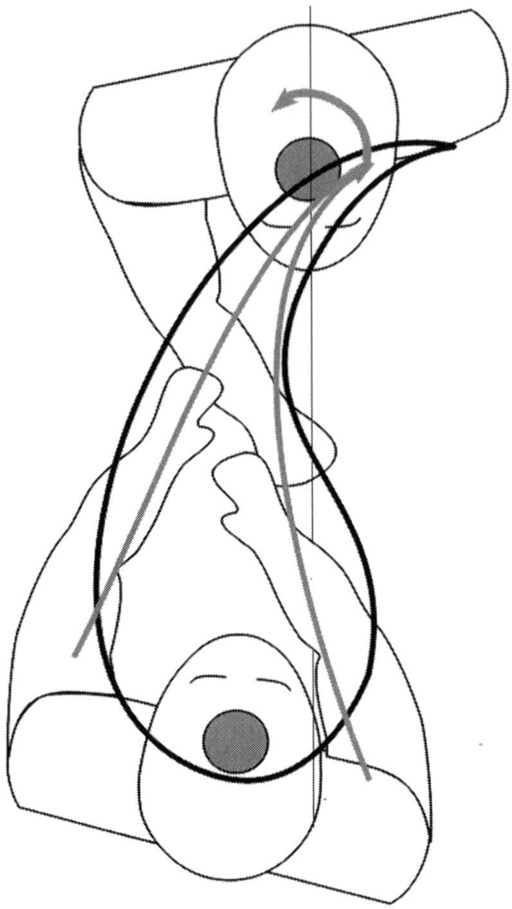

Driving the tomoe in front of Uke's COB; spinning Uke counter clockwise

Bringing the tomoe across Uke's front is best expressed as Maeotoshi #15. We take advantage of our move toward Uke by sliding our near-side arm under Uke's and affecting a throw. For now, call it success if you can make Uke turn away with little or no effort.

You could get fancy and try Gyakugamaeate #3 or even Oshitaoshi #6 with the tomoe to the front.

The final two tomoe directions are fairly obvious.

Tomoe across the center-line

We connect with Uke and draw him forward in a path across the center-line and around our COB. I call this one tomoe across the center-line.

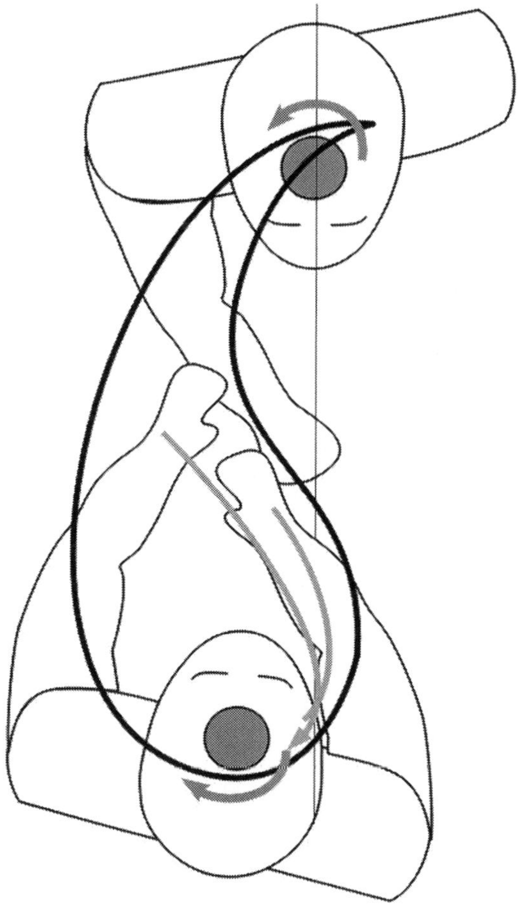

Tomoe across the center-line keeps you outside as it draws Uke around our COB

Tomoe across the center-line keeps us on the outside of Uke. (We are positioned outside Uke's arms, not between them.)

The common expression of tomoe across the center-line is the beginning of Shihonage #14. You could argue that the tomoe across the front was also

Shihonage, and you would be correct. I am merely stating that tomoe across the center-line is how Shihonage has most commonly been presented to me.

Be mindful that we want the force to be applied to the rear side of Uke's COB. We want Uke spinning counterclockwise in the above example in order to remove his other hand as a threat. Remember, we are only contacting one side, but the control must influence Uke's entire body.

A fortunate situation for us is that Uke is typically forward-weighted. Not many people fight on their heels. From the perspective of the coronal plane (that plane that divides us into front and back), the arm is connected near the middle of the body. The shoulder joint sits behind the COB when Uke is standing toward the balls of his feet. Extending Uke's arm then results in applying force to the rear of his COB.

There are more advanced ways to effect Tomoe across the center-line (e.g., Hikitaoshi #9), but my favorite expression of tomoe across the center-line is Sumiotoshi #16 as performed by Moe. It is a lot more circular than you will find in many Tomiki Aikido manuals. Moe connects with Uke as above (at three o'clock on the tomoe bubble), but instead of moving inward, toward Uke, he posts right at the initial contact, slides his center along the clockwise direction (bottom of the tomoe) and shifts to a post left position; all the while collecting Uke's joints (from elbow to the ankle) with a Hineri motion (daito hand). Having moved around the bottom of the clock (from three o'clock, through six o'clock and finally arriving at nine o'clock on the tomoe bubble), he clicks his heels together, shifts the weight to the right foot, steps with his left foot as he begins one of three (common to him) throws as he sees fit. It is quite a ride for Uke.

Tomoe on the inside

The final tomoe direction is called tomoe on the inside or inside tomoe. This move brings you directly in front of Uke. We consider the area between Uke's arms as the inside.

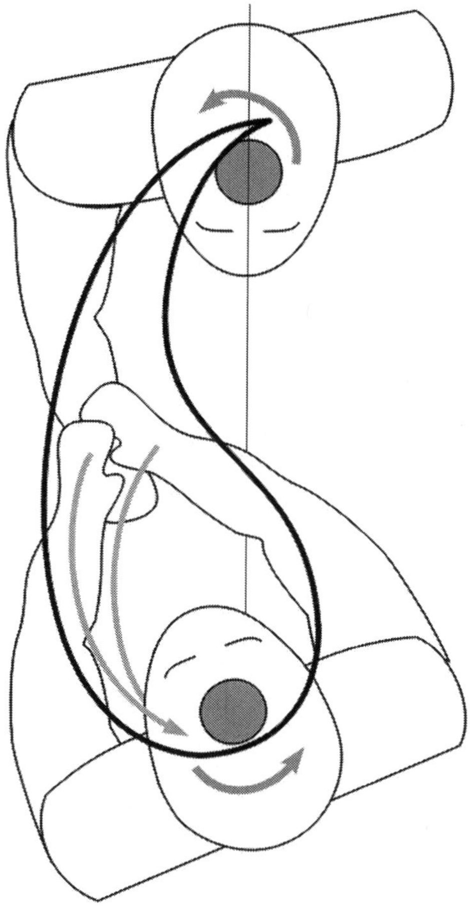

Tomoe on the inside or inside tomoe

You can express inside tomoe in Shomenate #1, but the best example is Hikiotoshi #17. Hikiotoshi draws Uke around your post-left COB as you step away from Uke.

Spooling and the belts wrap-up

Here are a couple of things to keep in mind when advancing your awareness of spooling:

- The use of the belts is a lesson in both direct and indirect pressure on the COB, Uke's and ours. We use the belts to impart force onto Uke's COB. In other words, we use the belts to spin the other person's COB.
- Take note of which direction the COB's are spinning.
- Do not get stuck thinking that we have to be the drive wheel. Yes, we can be the yang side that makes the belt move. We can also exploit the yin by allowing Uke to move his wheel and cause us to spin. All we need do is guide that force. I have full awareness now that, in very particular cases, Moe has been completely relaxing and allowed my fall to push the non-weighted half of his torso out of the way. In doing so, he used my efforts to fuel his evasion. Yin or yang, either way we are in control. Take turns driving.
- When posted right, open your senses to feel the COB. Recognize the right side of your body as the short side of the lever and the left side as the long side. Both sides of the lever are actually empty. You can lead Uke's right hand directly toward your left belt hoop and he will pass through you. The same is true if you lead Uke's left hand Uke to the empty space just outside or your right hip. This action teaches how to fight on one foot and move without stepping. Do not forget to swing the dragon's tail.
- Try again posted on the left. Take note of the short and long sides of the lever. Guide Uke through your empty right belt hoop, or just outside the left hip.
- Become the footballs. Match the edge of your pulley with the curve of Uke's football and spin. Uke is weakest here. This should start to feel like Uke is not even attached to you.
- Now that you can fight on one foot, begin shifting your weight from side to side using the Aiki step as you spin Uke.
- Go to three dimensions. Rise and fall as you spiral.

CONNECTION BUILDERS

Connection

Before we move to the last set of Precepts, we should take some time to add some additional background to the word connection. (I am going to assume you have taken the time to read the basic terms section defining connection.)

Connection is the closest western word equivalent to the eastern word Aiki.

Great! But what is connection (Aiki)?

In the martial sense, connection is direct access to Uke's balance and stability, the situation where we own the ability to guide or direct Uke's inertia.

We create connection by affixing two bodies together such that one is supporting the other.

Connection is characterized by relationship. No, not a romantic relationship, but a relationship built upon depending on one another to maintain balance. Never get into business with someone who has less to lose than you do, and never get into an Aikido technique with an Uke that is not supporting or leaning on you.

Co-mingling our balance with Uke's forms a vehicle to communicate our intent to Uke. Connecting our COB's in such a way that one is supporting the other creates a dependency inherent in all relationships. The dependency is the reason Uke is receptive to our cues on how Uke should move.

In the light of this definition, I expect you can reason that a strike can be a method to creating connection. You should also be able to reason that we can apply a joint lock in such a way as to create connection. In fact, all manner of martial arts techniques can be used to create connection, but more times than not, connection is not used (even by those supposedly practicing Aikido!).

To be blunt, connection is not a prerequisite for an effective martial technique.

Since you are reading this book, I will assume you would like to gain proficiency in creating connection. Let us get to some detail on how to build connection, and then you can decide where and when you wish to use it.

Two sides of connection/Aiki

There are the two sides to connection.

The first invites Uke to join with us by relying on our COB to maintain his balance (expressed in the elephant arms drill with Tori's palms up). In this way, Uke actively joins himself to us. In doing so, we lead Uke along by his volition. He depends on us. This is yin on our part. It is not the best analogy, but you can liken the yin side of connection to rolling a suitcase. The suitcase is relying on you to hold it in a tipped position and lead it around.

The alternate side of Aiki is also a drawing in or invitation to Uke to join with us. In this method, however, we project our center onto Uke's weaknesses (tipping his center) and we actively guide Uke (expressed in the elephant arms drill with palms down, resting on Uke). We are Uke's dependent, and he is doing all he can to support us. This expression of Aiki is yang from our perspective. Again, not the best of analogies, but you can liken the yang side of Aiki to riding a skateboard. We place our balance on the board and then push ourselves along.

Both sides of Aiki are an expression of leading, in the sense that someone is guiding or directing another's actions. The contradiction is that an Aiki technique is actually a control of ourselves and not Uke. You move, and Uke follows. It is vastly different than trying to move Uke; just move you. (Warning: Preachy comment coming: You are the only part of the equation that you actually have control over. You never actually have control of another person. Any other perspective denies our divinity and the divinity of others.)

How do I know when connection is established? What is the best way to sense when connection exists?

The primary indication is that Uke moves when you do (Captain Obvious to the rescue!) but since making Uke move when we do is also the goal, we should probably seek a more defined sense that we have established connection.

There are many indications that Uke is seeking assistance to maintain his balance (e.g., his toes grab the floor, his shoulders go back and belly goes out, he sticks his butt out, etc.), but the best indication you can use to sense connection is the pressure on the point of contact between you and Uke.

We call the spot where Uke and Tori meet the "conjunction point." In the case where Uke has grabbed our wrist, the conjunction point is the space between our wrist and Uke's hand. If we have our hand in Uke's face, the conjunction point is between our palm and Uke's face. If we are hip to hip with Uke (as in Gedanate #4), the conjunction point is between our hips. Etc.

This conjunction point is always part of the bridge we use to create connection. As such, if we have successfully created connection (one person leaning on the other), we should be sensing pressure on the conjunction point. The amount and direction of the pressure varies, but you should notice that you typically lose connection at the instant the pressure changes quickly or simply ceases.

The pressure on the conjunction point will often stretch the skin in this area. If the conjunction point is on the wrist, look for the skin to be twisted to either side. You might see the skin sliding upward as if you were rolling up your sleeves or downward as if you were rolling down your socks.

On Uke's side, connection feels like a constant attempt to regain stability. Connection dangles the carrot of stability in front of Uke, but never quite delivers.

How, you ask? Well then, I guess it is time to discuss the last two Precepts.

The purpose of the last two Precepts is to create connection.

There are many ways to create connection without involving our arms, but that is outside the scope of this book.

We will be describing the last two precepts by detailing how the hands play a role in creating connection.

Daito hands and lever arms will focus on what we do with our body; Aiki-Age and Aiki-Sage put the attention on what is happening to Uke's COB.

Precept 5: Lever arms and daito hands

The first four precepts explain the basics of how to use our legs and torso.

Frustration can arise if we do not correctly channel the energy created by our lower half into our hands.

Lever arms and daito hands are a way to apply the force generated by the body and to create connection.

No surprise, but both techniques represent a type of lever.

Lever arms is a forward and backward lever (e.g., along the line of the forearm bones) and daito hands is side to side (e.g. twisting the forearm).

The goal of both lever arms and daito hands is to create a semi-stable platform for Uke to rest on or press against. The trick to both techniques is to understand where to place the fulcrum in such a way that Uke finds structure but not stability.

Here is the progression of how we learn lever arms/daito hands: falling off a lever, falling off a fence, and then twist the bow.

Falling off a lever is an engineering explanation of why lever arms/daito hands works.

Falling off the lever then becomes a real-world concept when we morph it into falling off the fence.

Once we understand these basic mechanics, we focus upon yin connection and applying falling off the fence to daito hands and then lever arms.

We then flip over to the yang connection. We maintain continuity by revisiting falling off the fence, but quickly adopt a more digestible explanation called twisting the bow. Twisting the bow will be revealed as a method to creating heavy hands.

Hang in there. It is not as confusing as it may sound.

Falling off the lever

The best (two-dimensional) example of a semi-stable base is a teeter-totter, but not all teeter-totters (first-class levers) are created equal.

Earlier we explored how a first-class lever acts like an inclined plane at the point above the fulcrum. This is an important concept, because a lever provides both support and redirection at the point above the fulcrum. We need a little of both.

Let us start with support.

Since the lever itself provides no support out on the ends of the lever arm, we must support the object on the space above the fulcrum. The point above the fulcrum acts exactly like a table.

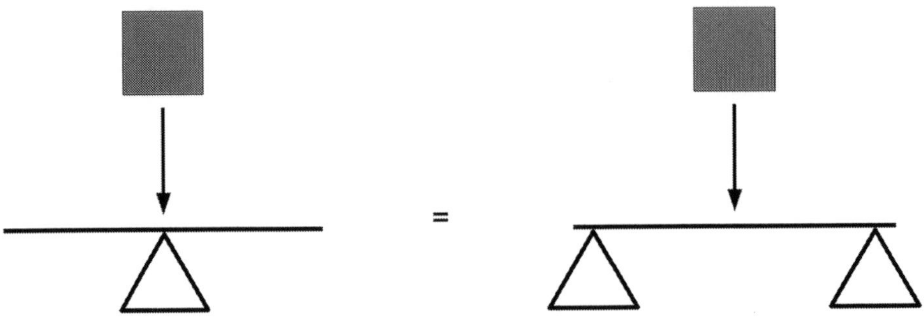

Falling directly on the fulcrum is, in effect, like falling on a table

Once the object is supported (balanced), we have two options for having that object fall off of the lever.

The first option is to wait for the object to simply throw itself off. When we map this analogy to martial arts, it is like waiting for Uke to throw himself. (Uke only throws himself in dojos. Waiting for Uke to throw himself does not work outside the dojo.)

Our second option is to get in there and help the object fall off. We accomplish this by tilting the lever arm. This is where the redirection begins.

This tilt (incline) converts the lever from a level table into a slope (inclined plane) for the object to fall off of.

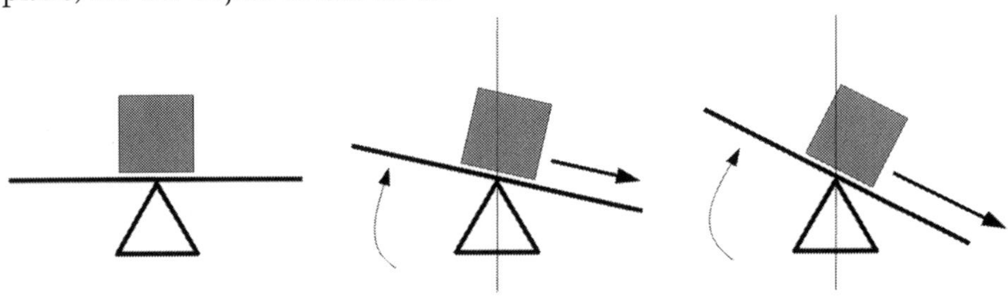

Tilt the arm of the lever and the object begins to slide or fall off

Gravity joins with us and helps drag the object downward. The object begins to fall as less and less of the object is above the fulcrum.

Fairly simple concept: we support an object directly above the fulcrum, offer a few seconds of stability, tilt the arm, and the object falls off. But wait! There is more!

Remember I mentioned that not all levers are created equal? Here is the part where most people go awry.

Take notice that the lever depicted above has a rather thin arm. Nothing is glaringly wrong, but we should be aware that this thin arm is rather inefficient at moving the supported object off of the fulcrum.

We want a small amount of motion in the arm to quickly move the object into the desired position (partially above the fulcrum, where the fulcrum is applying indirect vertical pressure on the object's COB).

How do we improve the lever's ability to move the supported object off of the fulcrum? We add width to the arm!

Take a look at this:

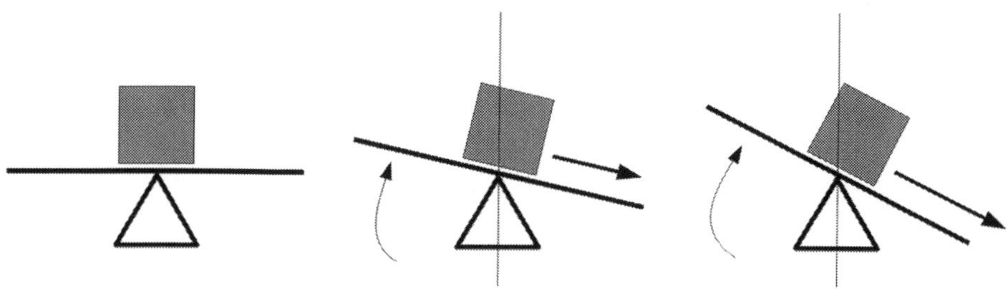

Effect on a supported object as we tilt the lever's arm to 27.29 degrees

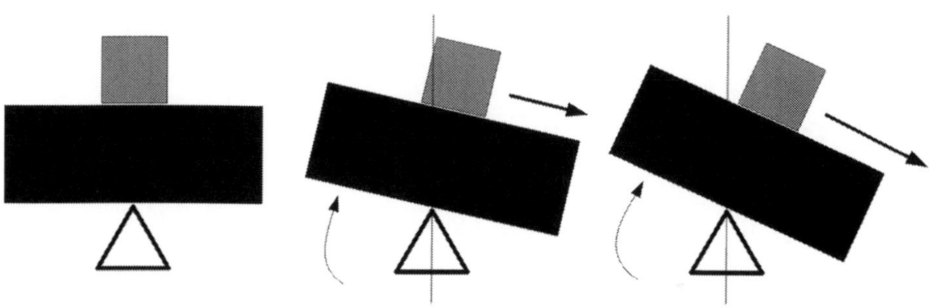

Effect on a supported object as we tilt the lever's arm to 24.59 degrees

First, yes I could tell the exact degree of rotation because the computer aided drafting tool tells you the exact angle. Second, I did not move the block (square) in relation to the arm of the lever. Better stated, I did not let the block slide along the arm of the lever. The picture above represents the block being glued in place onto the arm.

As you can see above, the lever with the thinner arm rotated slightly further than the lever with a thicker arm, but still did not move the block completely off of the fulcrum. (It will take nearly eighty degrees of rotation for the lever with the thinner arm to completely move the block off of the fulcrum.)

The lever with the thicker arm had to move only slightly (in comparison) to completely move the block off the fulcrum (support). Less motion, but more movement.

Falling off the lever seems childish and simple, but it is the engineering answer to how we become semi-supportive of Uke.

Let us simplify this concept even more, and apply it to our sense of Aiki.

Falling off the fence

Falling off the fence is a much simpler way to convert knowledge gained from falling off a lever into body awareness.

Ever walk across the top of a fence? If not, it is not hard to imagine.

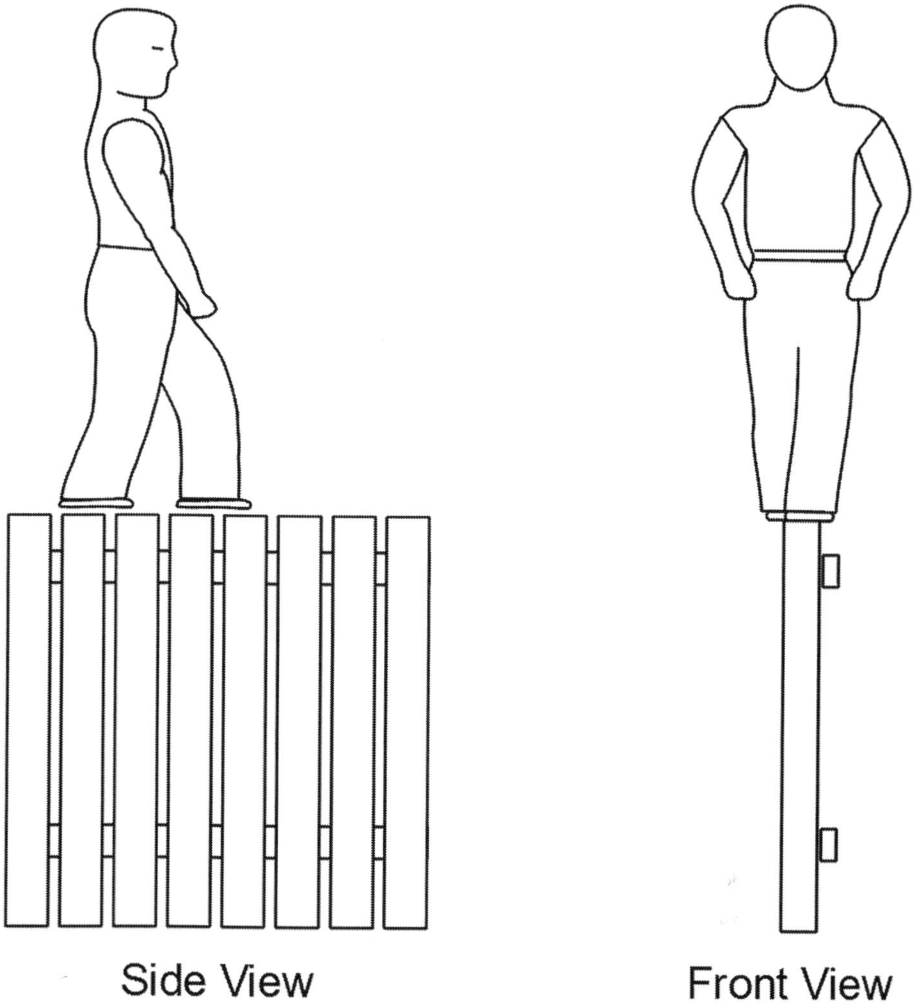

Walking along the top of a fence

If the fence stays intact and that guy on top of the fence loses his footing, he will fall, but that is not the action we are looking for. That story would be analogous to the supported object jumping off the lever. Instead, let us imagine what happens when the fence causes the action.

What would happen if the fence fell over?

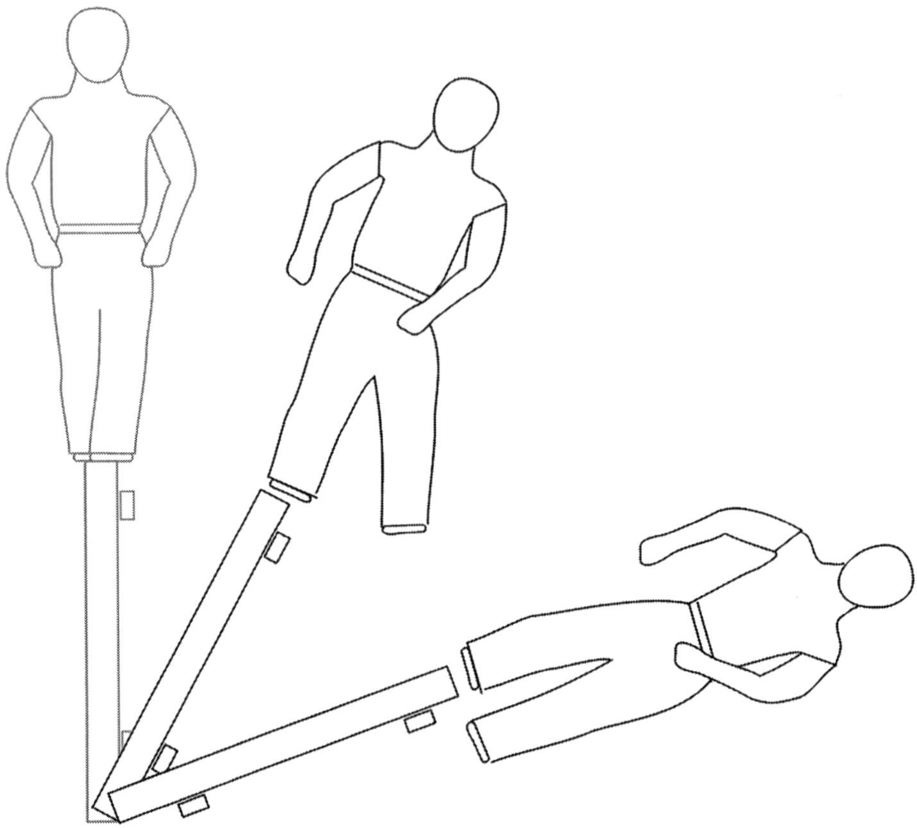

Fence collapses

The walker falls because the fence collapsed. Got it? Fence falls over, so does the guy standing on it. That is it! I told you it was simple.

Enough said about falling off the fence, but before we dive into building connection using daito hands, I am going to leave you with one picture as food for thought on how we make the jump from lever to fence. This is strictly extra credit. You need not worry if this makes no sense. Feel free to review it after you have read the rest of the chapter.

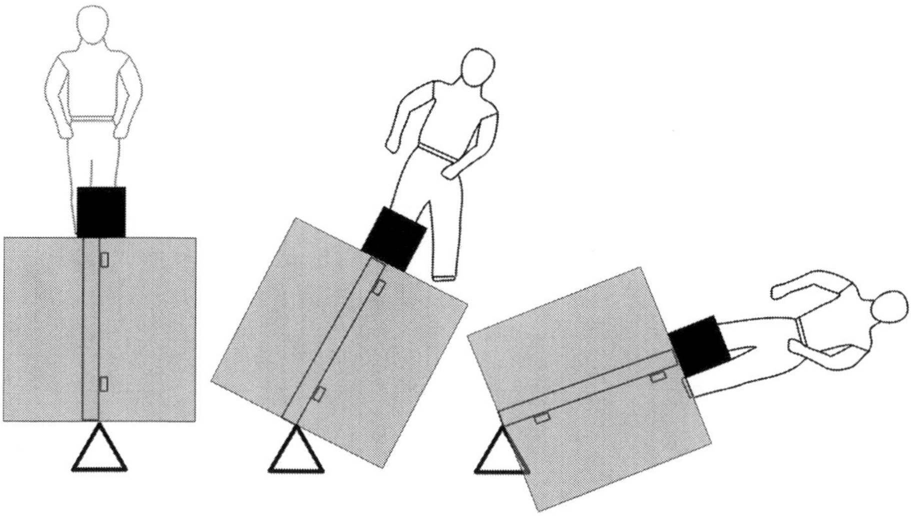

How the fence acts as a lever with wide arm

Daito hands and Yin Connection

At its simplest, daito hands is how we make use of twisting our forearm bones.

The twist in our forearms can become an effective lever. The secret lies in knowing where to put the fulcrum (pivot).

This is where falling off the fence comes in.

Let us first understand how our forearms relate to a fence.

Our forearm bones sit in a very similar position compared to the horizontal supports that keep the vertical slats of the fence together. The index finger and radius bone resemble the upper horizontal support. Our pinky finger and ulna resemble the bottom horizontal support.

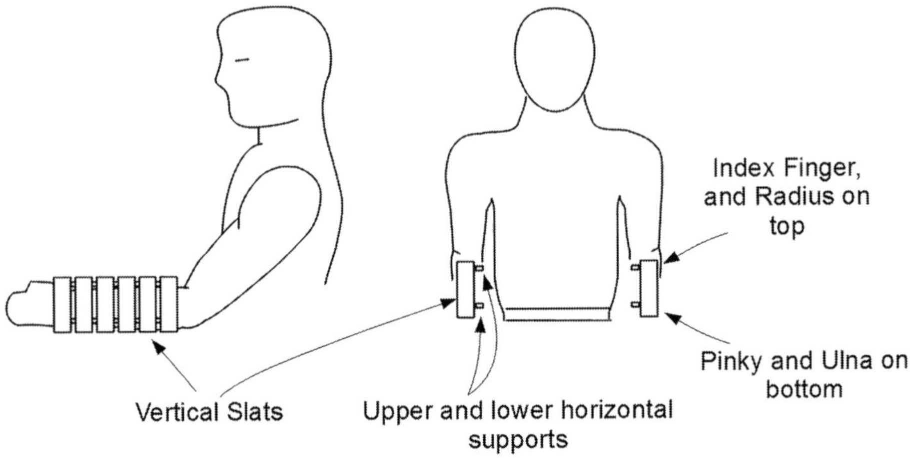

Imagining the forearm and hand combination as a fence

Now that our forearms are equivalent to a fence, we can use daito hands to collapse the fence.

We collapse the fence on the top or the bottom. This means we rotate our forearm around the horizontal supports: the index (top) or pinky (bottom).

We use the terms index pivot and pinky pivot to describe which horizontal support we are using as the pivot.

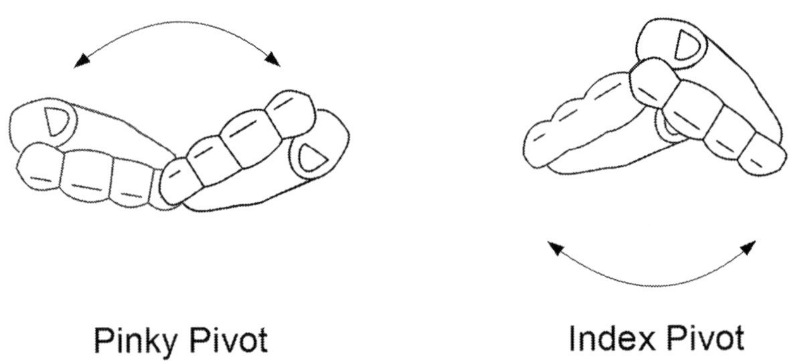

Right hand pinky and index pivot

We have a fence, we know how to collapse it. Now we need to get Uke to stand on our fence.

Let us start with Uke grabbing our left wrist.

The first thing we should notice is that it is rather difficult to twist our wrists once someone has grabbed them. Even the smallest of persons can effect enough force to lock our forearms in place if they are stable and supporting themselves.

Uke is touching us, but he is not using us for support. There is contact, but no "Connection" to Uke's COB. Relating this to our falling off the fence analogy, there is no gravity pulling Uke downward. You might say that Uke is not "resting on the fence." Let us fix that.

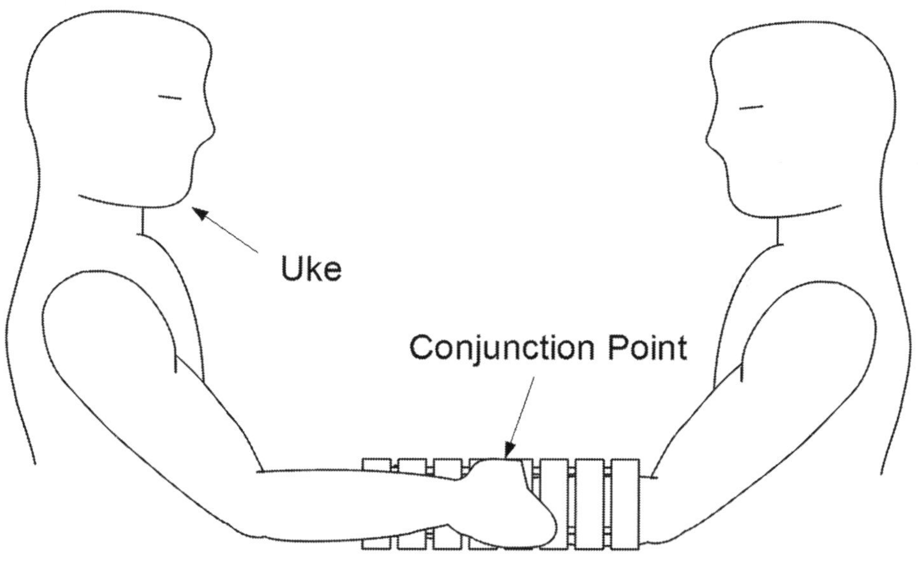

Uke has grabbed but is not leaning on us

We mimic the effect gravity had on the man walking the fence by touching Uke's center. The action of touching Uke's center compresses the space between our COB's and presents a threat to Uke's position. You might say we create the bridge and force the issue of Uke leaning (or pressing) on us. Effectively, we put Uke on top of the fence.

The setup is complete, but a quick word about creating the connection in this exercise.

Uke has three choices as we touch his center. Uke can let us invade, step out of there, or push against our progress. If Uke lets you invade, tickle him. It will not happen again. If Uke is stepping out of there, consider that you might be presenting too great of a threat. It is easy to be too aggressive if you are larger than Uke. Touching Uke's center can be subtle and still gain the desired effect. Too little a threat, and Uke just stands there mocking you. To get it just right, I suggest you put yourself in mind of the push drills. Cam your hips forward and get under Uke's strength. If you are doing this correctly, Uke will be doing all he can to keep you from entering into his structure.

Back to the daito hand lesson.

Let us assume that you are touching Uke's center correctly. Uke will feel our structure via the point on our wrist at which Uke has grabbed (the conjunction point). Uke should be pushing against your wrist in attempt to halt or redirect your hand. Uke is now resting on the top of the fence.

Just as Uke settles on the top of the fence, we pivot our wrists (turn the left wrist in-ward, pivoting at the pinky as depicted below) all the while maintaining the initial pressure and contact to Uke's COB. Uke finds himself falling off of the fence. You could say that we put the fence underneath him and then we toppled the fence.

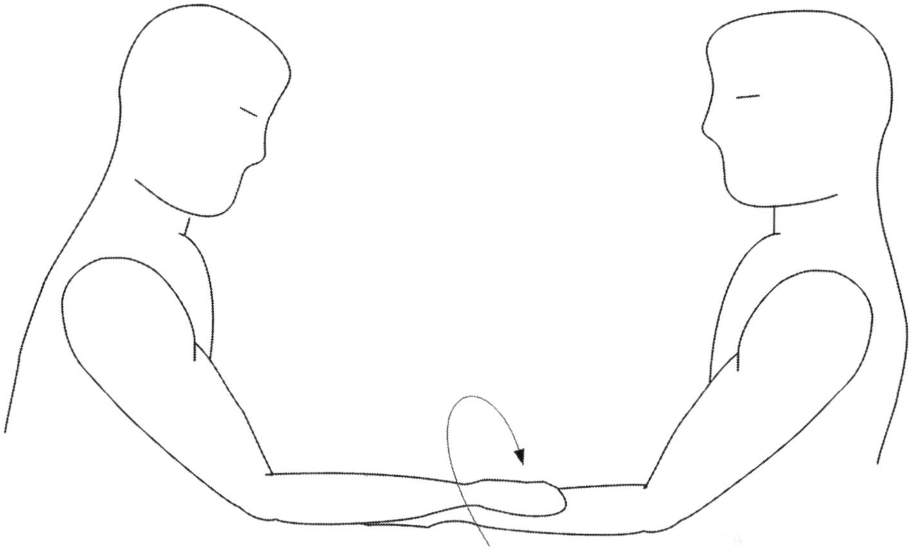

Inward, left hand pinky pivot; Uke falls off the fence

Relax into that twist, and Uke should find himself dropping into the void. Creating voids by relaxing is an extremely powerful way to create Aiki, and it requires almost no strength.

An important subtlety to be aware of is that there are times when an index or pinky pivot are most appropriate. An index pivot, in this scenario, would not have had as drastic an effect on Uke. (Try it.)

The simple rule is this: use the pivot furthest from the point of contact. In this example, Uke is leaning on the top of our arm, so the pinky pivot was the most effective answer. An index pivot would have been suitable if Uke grabbed the bottom of our wrist (had we presented our hand to Uke with the blade of our hand upward).

Why does this rule apply? The rule of using the pivot furthest from the point of contact creates the thicker lever arm. Consider this:

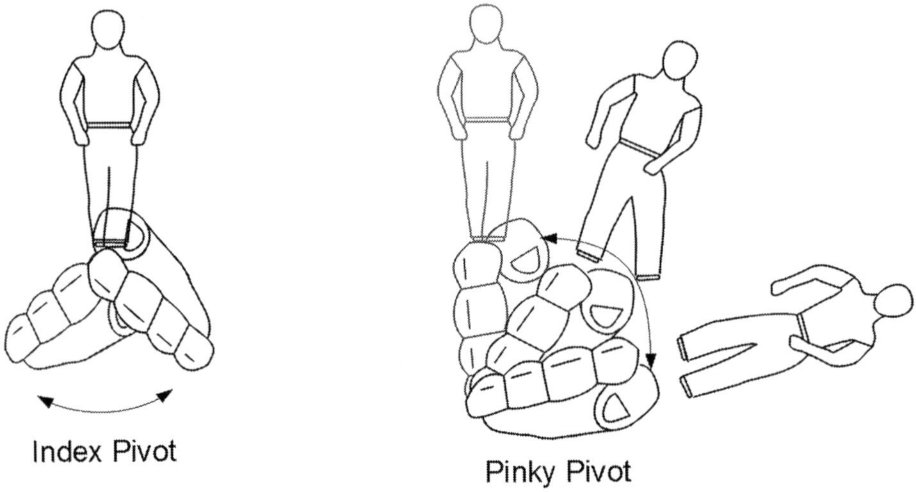

Index pivot has no effect on Uke; pinky pivot replicates the falling off the fence scenario

Do you see that the index pivot has very little effect on Uke? It takes a pinky pivot to collapse the fence (when Uke is leaning on the top of our arm).

To drill this particular scenario, stand as depicted below. Use your free hand to support the bottom of the grasped arm (see below).

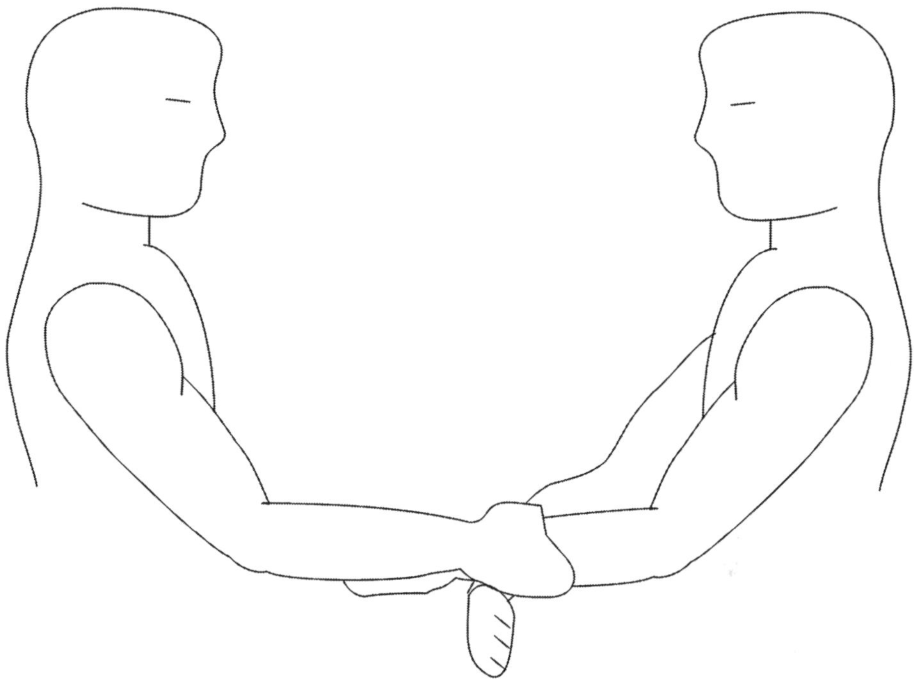

Using the free hand to support the grasped wrist and act as a guide for pinky pivot

Collapse the fence by leaving your left hand pinky in contact with your forearm and turn your hand so that your palm is facing the floor.

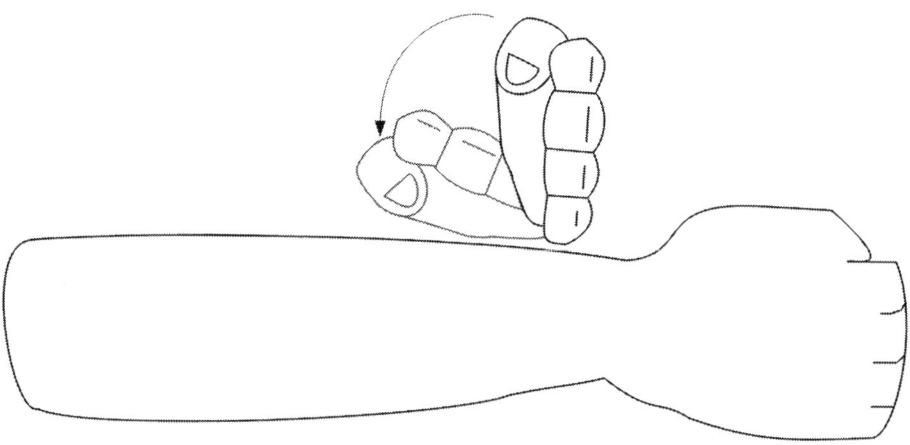

Uke's view of Tori rotating the wrist inward using pinky pivot

You will know you are doing it correctly when Uke lurches forward and downward as you turn your wrist.

Let us take a look at how falling off a fence applies to lever arms, again, in the context of yin connection.

Lever arms and Yin Connection

As the name implies, lever arms is how to turn your arms into an appropriate lever.

To achieve that goal we need our arm, a fulcrum, and just a bit of fulcrum placement know how.

Let us, again, make some connections to the falling off the lever by making comparisons to the key elements of the lever. Once we understand where the lever is, we improve the comparison by switching to falling off the fence.

Uke grabs our wrist

In a situation where Uke grabs our wrist, Uke represents the supported object (the square block), our arm is the arm of the lever (lever arm), and the conjunction point is the fulcrum. (Conjunction point is the contact area between Uke's hand and our wrist.)

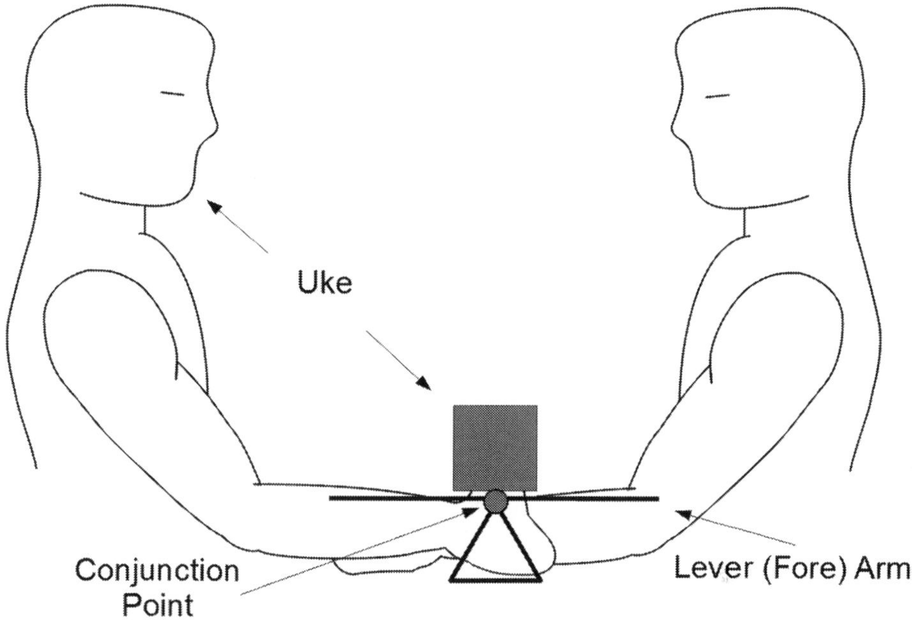

Relating the falling off the lever analogy to wrist grab

Uke grabbing our wrist is like the square coming in contact with the arm of the lever, but something is missing. The lever had gravity as an assistant. Gravity forced the square to rest its entire weight on the lever. We are not so lucky. Uke has his own legs to support him. At this point, Uke has no reason to lean on us. Uke has simply attached himself to us.

How do we mimic the effect gravity had on the square? You guessed it! We touch Uke's center! (You probably remember this from the daito hands example.)

The action of touching Uke's center creates connection (affixing two objects such that one object leans on another). Our arms act as the bridge, and Uke is leaning on us to avoid or redirect our attack.

Let us assume that you are touching Uke's center correctly. Uke should be pushing against your wrist in attempt to halt or redirect your hand. Uke will sense that pressing on the conjunction point is similar to pressing on a table.

Just as Uke settles on the table of our conjunction point, we tilt and the conjunction point becomes an inclined plane. Uke finds himself sliding off the table (much like trying to support himself on the corner of a table where a table leg is missing).

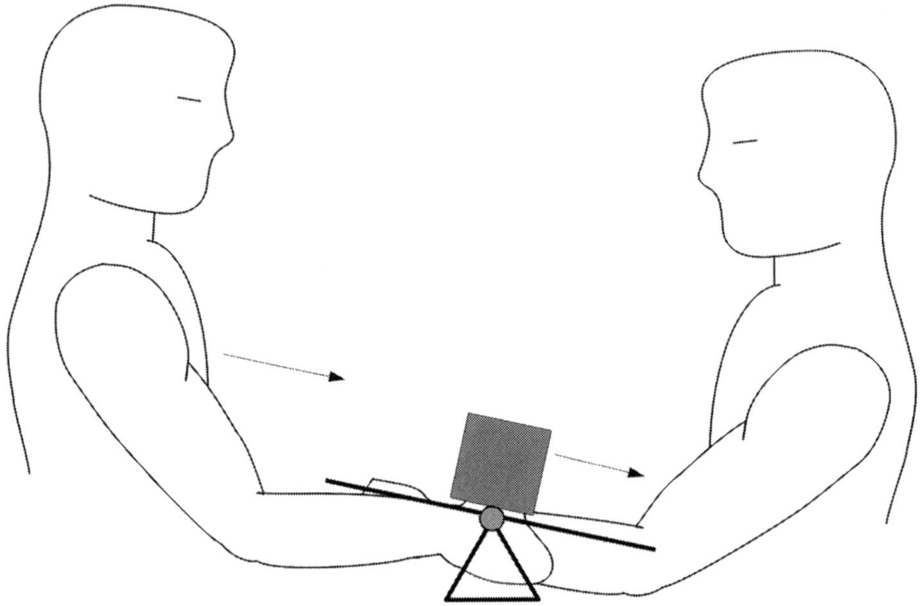

Uke falling off the lever arm (Aiki-Age #3)

The tilting action redirects (and does not contend with) Uke's force. It simply guides Uke's pressure around (over) the fulcrum.

Now, at any point, if we give Uke sufficient time, he will adjust and he will find a way to counter. The trick is learning how to keep a fluid motion. The typical goal is to change the tilt constantly and consistently. Fortunately, you will not need very much motion to direct Uke into a technique.

Improving the lever arm

The lever arm explanation thus far lacks some detail in how we best "leverage" the fulcrum.

Uke's sense of falling off the lever is based upon Uke's point of contact moving off of the support.

Earlier we described how adding width to an actual lever's arm improved the lever's ability to move objects off of the fulcrum's support. The same idea applies here.

Here is a real world example coupled with some insight to issues.

The beginner's mistake with lever arms is to bring the fulcrum (pivot point) directly to the conjunction point. Placing the fulcrum in this way is the equivalent of using a thin lever arm. It is just not efficient at moving Uke. Uke's contact point stays almost statically above the fulcrum. It works some of the time, but it is not the easiest way.

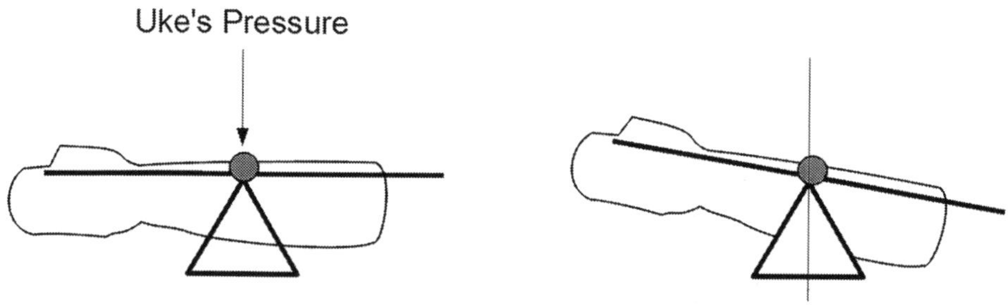

Placing the fulcrum at the point of contact; tilting here works inefficiently

Consider the effects of placing the fulcrum on the opposite side of the arm.

It is the same ten-degree tilt, but this time, Uke's contact point is moved considerably further off of the fulcrum's support. It is the same basic motion, but such a subtle change in focus can deliver considerably different results.

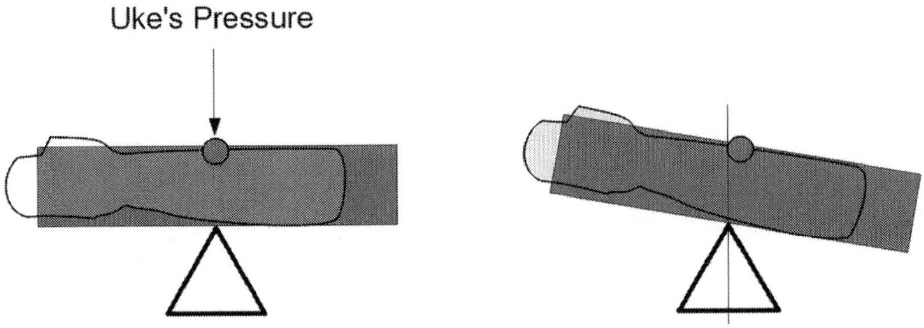

Placing the fulcrum at the opposite side of the arm

The challenge in making this correction is ignoring the contact point. The conjunction point is a point of contention and the point at which you receive direct input about Uke's actions. There is a lot of action happening at this spot. All of that noise makes the point of contact irresistible, but you can get past this issue with just a little practice and a bit of help. Here comes the cavalry.

First, try tilting Uke the hard way; with the pivot at the point of contact.

Have Uke grab your wrist as in the pictures above, touch his center, and then tilt your arm at the point of contact.

Having trouble knowing if you are doing it as prescribed? Use your free hand and touch a finger to your grasped arm at the point of contact, at the web of Uke's hand (flap of skin between thumb and forefinger). Pivot your arm around your finger. You should sense some amount of motion in Uke, but not too much as we have placed the fulcrum right up against the conjunction point.

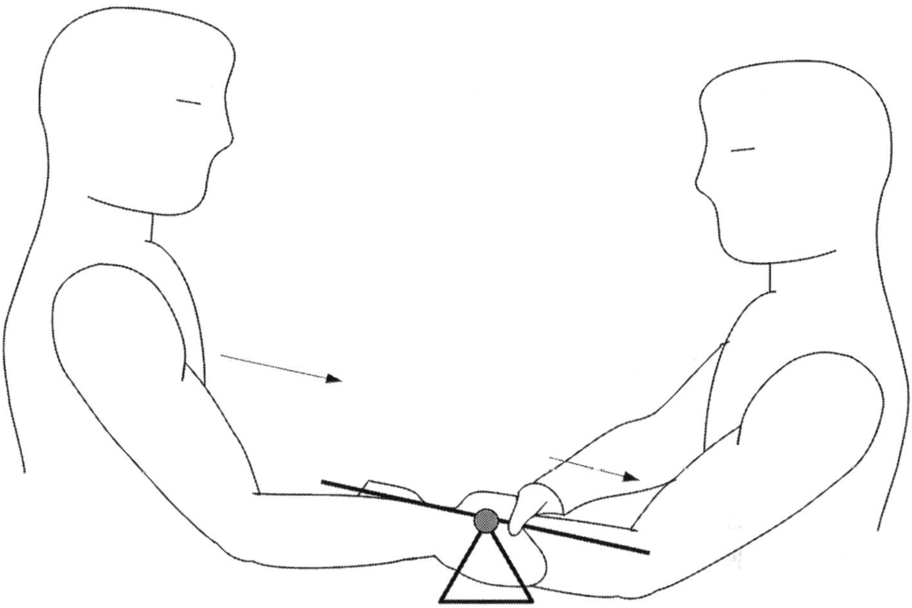

Using finger from free hand to set up pivot at (near) the point of contact

Now try again; this time with the fulcrum (pivot point) directly below the conjunction point, but on the bottom of your forearm. How, you ask?

The drill for lever arms is simple.

Line up facing Uke, have him grab your wrist, and touch Uke's center.

Now, place the wrist of your free arm below the contact point and pivot on your free hand wrist.

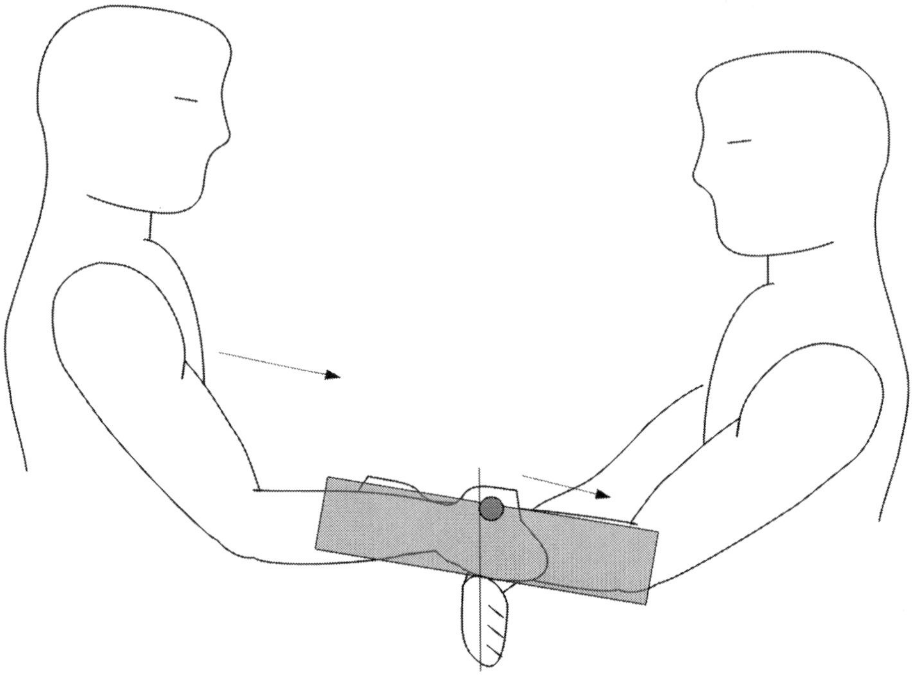

Using your free arm (right arm in this case) to support the conjunction point

Please take notice that tilting your left arm should involve the rest of your body. This means you will have to bend your knees. You may have noticed that Tori drops down in these pictures. I was doing my best to imply that the legs do most of the work.

You may have also noticed that this solo lever arms practice looks exactly like the drill for daito hands.

Combing the lever arms and daito hands drills

The similarities in the lever arms and daito hands drills allow us to improve our lever arms drill by adding falling off the fence.

Set up as before (Uke grabs, touch his center, place free hand wrist into position), but this time, perform a pinky pivot daito hand with your free hand. Allow your lever arm to ride the daito hand.

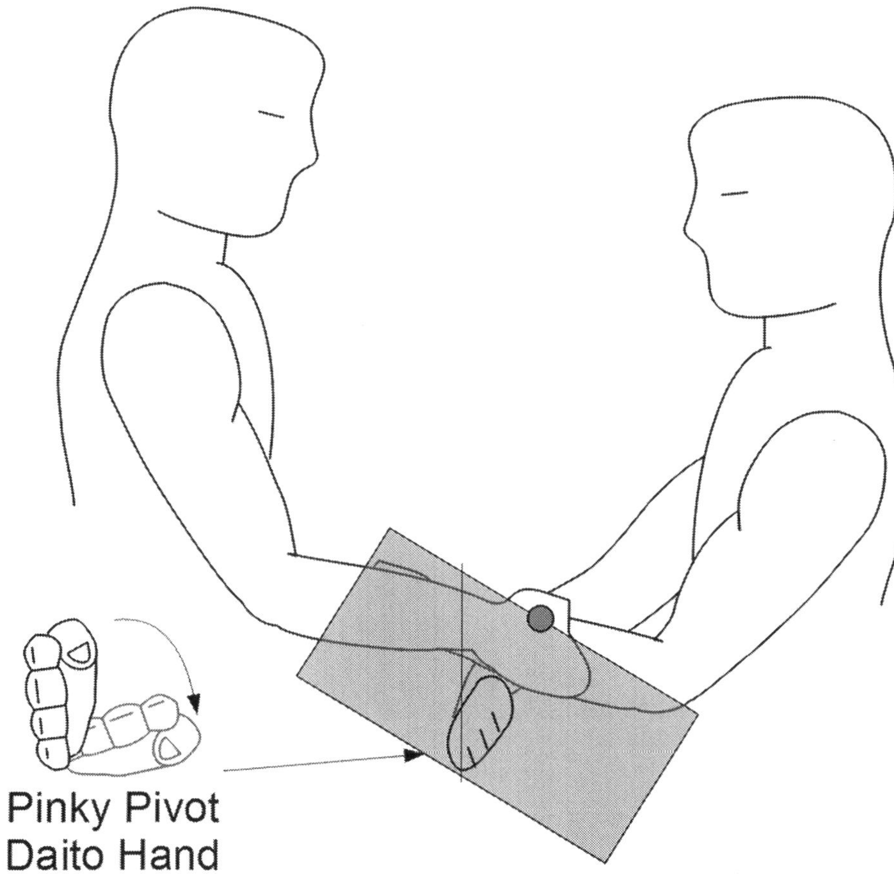

Using a right-hand pinky pivot daito hand to support and create left-arm lever arm

This action drops the fulcrum down even further from the point of contact and will have a more drastic effect on Uke.

This method of mixing the daito hand with the lever arm has been a most successful way to teach lever arms. Lever arm can be an awkward motion to develop. The daito hand support seems to help the student get past the noise and distraction at the conjunction point.

A bonus to this combination drill is that most students experiment with pure daito hands by removing the left arm and allowing Uke to grab the right wrist (daito hand). The conclusion drawn is that a daito hand twist works even when the forearm is positioned across the body (and not fingers pointed outward as in the first drill).

If you do get experimental with the daito hand across the body, be certain to try collapsing toward and away from Uke. You should be sensing that lever arms works in both directions.

You will know you have mastered this lesson when you feel Uke floating out of his position in a forceful manner.

Play by play review of creating connection with yin-side lever arm

So ends our exploration into yin connection, but before we move on to yang connection, let us do a bit of play-by-play of how yin connection is created when Uke grabs Tori's wrist.

We will use the context of Uke advancing toward Tori as Tori applies a lever arm and describe the action as if we were playing both roles.

From Uke's perspective:
I grab Tori's wrist and sense structure through the conjunction point. What I am sensing is that Tori's center is moving directly into mine and collision is imminent. I begin to repel or at least attempt to redirect Tori's structure. Just as I lean on/push against the conjunction point, the pressure I was reacting to changes as the lever arm tilts. I experience a sensation much like trying to push open a door as someone else pulls it open from the other side. My brain senses that something is awry and that I am not in a stable position. Subconsciously, I realize that I must readjust in order to maintain stability and balance or begin falling. I attempt to use my arm as a means of support, but of course, Tori continues offering structure but not stability. I never regain stability, to the point that Tori leads me into full technique.

From Tori's perspective:
We begin by touching Uke's center through our conjunction point. By owning our space, Uke senses that he is walking directly into the tip of the

arm of a turnstile. In other words, Uke has met the extension of our center, projected through our conjunction point. Said again in yet another way, we establish a bridge using direct horizontal pressure between our COB's. We touch Uke's center and then relax. In that relaxation, we allow our arm to tilt with the pivot at a point on our forearm opposite of the contact. Uke begins floating out of his position, and we continue directing Uke's momentum into a technique.

Directing Uke's fall is what we call techniques. Using a yin connection, we move, and that movement directs Uke's inertia (fall) into a motion we might call "Ikkyo," "Nikkyo," "Shihonage," or "Tenchinage," etc. Some of these techniques start with a wrist grab and some do not, but it will not be hard to figure out when a lever arm or daito hand is applied.

Keep Uke busy at falling off a fence. You will maintain the upper hand, and "your will be done."

Now onto yang connection.

Yang side of connection

The yang side of connection is just as easily understood if you keep in mind that it is not much more than the yin side placed upside down.

In fact, you have already been introduced to the best drill I know to learn the yang side of connection: elephant arms drill with palms down.

How about we back that statement up with a bit more detail and an additional drill or two?

If you have not already, I encourage you to reread "Precept 4: Sagittal Plane; First Belt Hoop" to reinforce your understanding of what it means to apply indirect vertical pressure on the COB. You are going to need a clear understanding of indirect vertical pressure.

Below is a repeat of an earlier Precept 4 illustration that depicts how indirect vertical pressure is created. This particular diagram shows Uke leaning on us. Simply reverse the roles and this becomes us leaning on Uke.

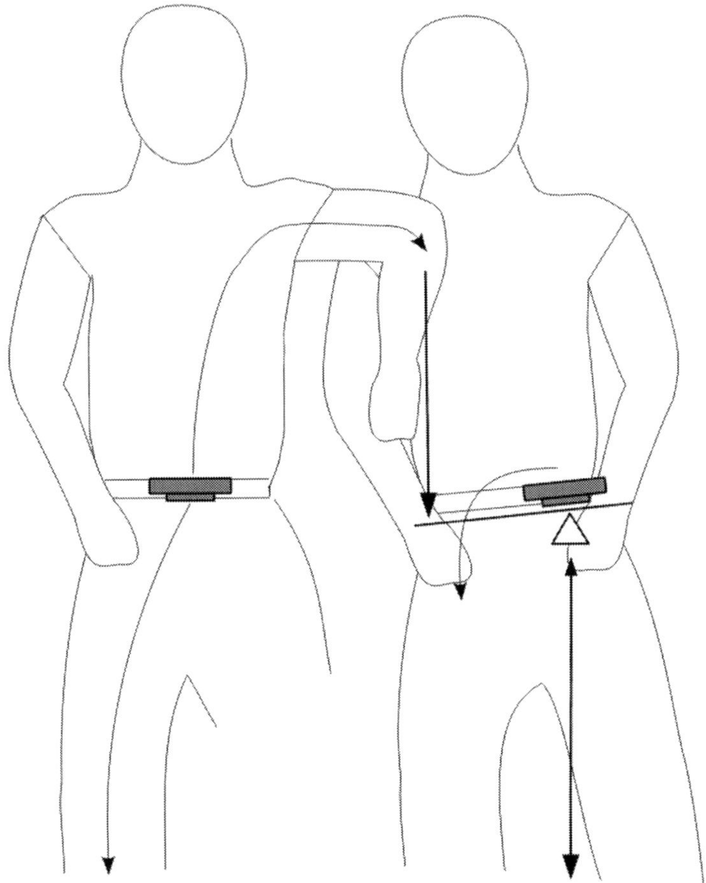

Post-left stance; Uke applying indirect vertical pressure to our COB

Let us begin.

I know I just said that yang connection is upside-down yin, but instead of simply turning the lever and block analogy upside-down, I want to open your mind to a new and much more accurate analogy: the concept of compressing and twisting Uke like a bow.

Why not continue using the lever and block scenario?

We could try to use the lever and block analogy to explain yang connection, but there is a major flaw if we allow Uke to become a block.

The flaw is that blocks are solid and do not bend. If the block is solid and adequately connected to the ground, the best we can do is try to crush the block under our weight. That would be the equivalent of jumping up into Uke's arms and hoping it will make him fall. It might work if we are bigger or nearly the same size as Uke, but this is will not work in all cases and it certainly is not Aiki.

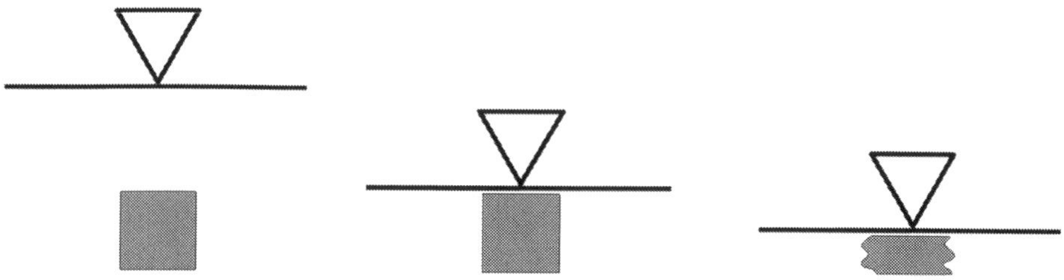

Lever crushes the block

Instead, we replace the block with a bow (traditional re-curve bow).

The reason we chose a bow is that, when burdened, Uke behaves like a bow.

How do we burden Uke? Heavy hands!

In fact, yang connection centers almost entirely on the application of heavy hands.

Heavy hands creates indirect vertical pressure on Uke's COB. The indirect vertical pressure coerces Uke to become rigid and then unstable. We can then topple Uke if we push in the correct way.

If you have read the basic terms section, you have a good idea of the heavy hand two-step.

- Step 1: Give Uke a reason to create structure by touching Uke's COB with indirect vertical pressure. In other words, lean on Uke.
- Step 2: Shift the pressure (your weight) to an unwieldy position for Uke to support. Recognize that shifting your weight to an unwieldy position is also indirect vertical pressure on Uke's COB, but in this step, the vertical pressure induces instability in reference to Uke's newly formed structure.

The somewhat overlooked part of that explanation is how to put our weight into our hands.

What we are going to do is give some direction to putting our weight into the hands as we trim down the heavy hand two-step into two words: compress and twist.

We explore compress by taking a look at compressing the bow and walking with a walker.

The twist converts falling off the fence into twisting the bow. The twist is not quite as simple to explain, so we have a couple of perspectives to help learn the twist.

We finish by putting these concepts together using a drill that looks similar to our yin drills.

Compressing the bow

Compressing the bow means we bring the two tips of the bow toward themselves. You can liken this action to how one would manually take the string off of a re-curve bow. We, as the lever, fall indirectly upon the bow, and the bow bends under our weight (in other words, the tips of the bow move closer together). The result is a relaxed string.

Bringing the tips of the bow toward each other is an application of indirect pressure on the bow's COB (shown below as a circle with cross-hairs.) Notice that the tips of the bow are not directly above the bow's COB.

This is why applying our weight to the tip of the bow effects an indirect pressure on the bow's COB.

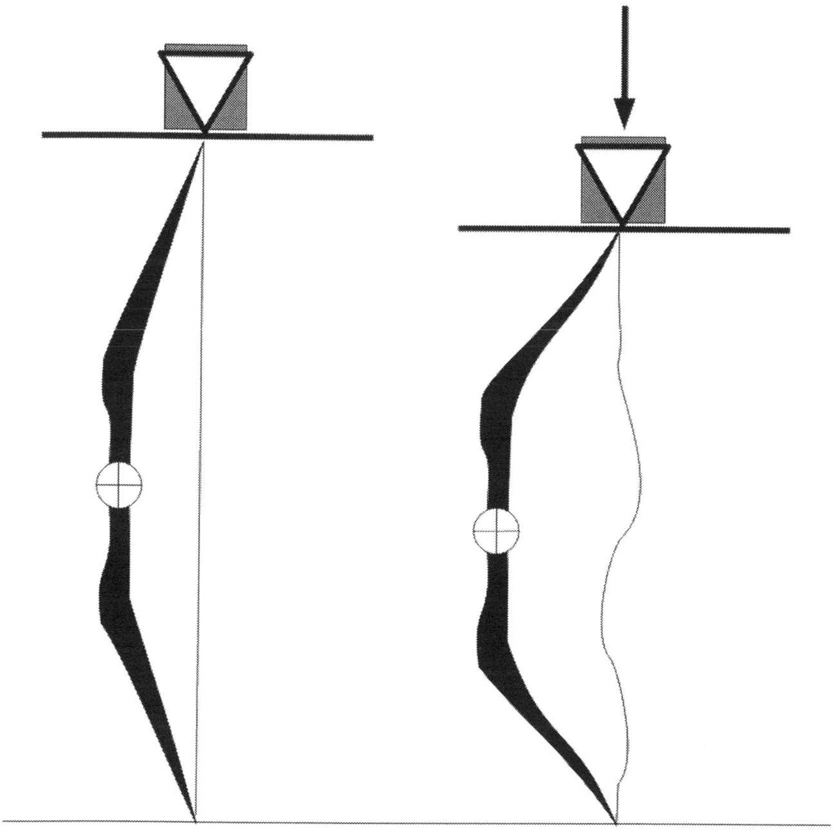

Applying our weight to compress the arms of the bow

Take notice of the position of the lever in comparison to the bow. The lever's fulcrum attaches to the bow tip.

The reason for the fulcrum being placed at the conjunction point is that the fulcrum is the only part of the lever that can apply weight. Trying to apply weight using other portions of the lever would simply spin the lever arm.

The less fancy way to say this is the lever must project direct force from its center (its fulcrum).

You should also notice that the bottom tip of the bow is pressed against the ground.

It is a simple concept, but it does not explain how to use my hands to effect the compression. Where do we go from here?

Heavy hands and walking with a walker

There are plenty of ways to attach ourselves to Uke, but the primary method is to use our hands.

Using a yang connection relies on placing our weight upon Uke.

So, this leads to the conclusion that we need to find a way to place a substantial portion of our weight into our hands without losing our stability or balance.

Putting our weight into our hands is nothing more than using our hands (and arms) to support our COB. You could substitute that description with "standing on our hands."

I am not implying that you need to learn to do a handstand to learn Aiki. What we do need to learn is how our hands can assist our legs as we walk. By assist our legs, I mean help our legs support our COB. The analogy that teaches this technique best is walking with a walker.

Many of us have had to use crutches to get around. Having experience with crutches will assist in learning this technique, but I would rather focus our attention toward how an elderly person typically makes use of a walker.

The reason for this is that younger persons have a bit more spring to their step. They have the tendency to use their healthy rear leg to launch themselves onto their crutches. They literally are jumping onto their crutches, and that is the equivalent of rear-wheel drive. (Bad!)

Elderly persons using a walker are more apt to relax into their step. They place the walker away from their body (Frame 1 below), use their *latissimus dorsi* muscles to lead their center over their toes, forward cam their hips to get one leg forward (Frame 2), effect a weight shift by continuing the lat pull, flexing their triceps (which drives the hands downward onto the walker) and straightening the forward leg to keep themselves supported (Frame 3). The rear leg supports no weight, so they relax the trailing leg and let it passively swing underneath (Frame 4).

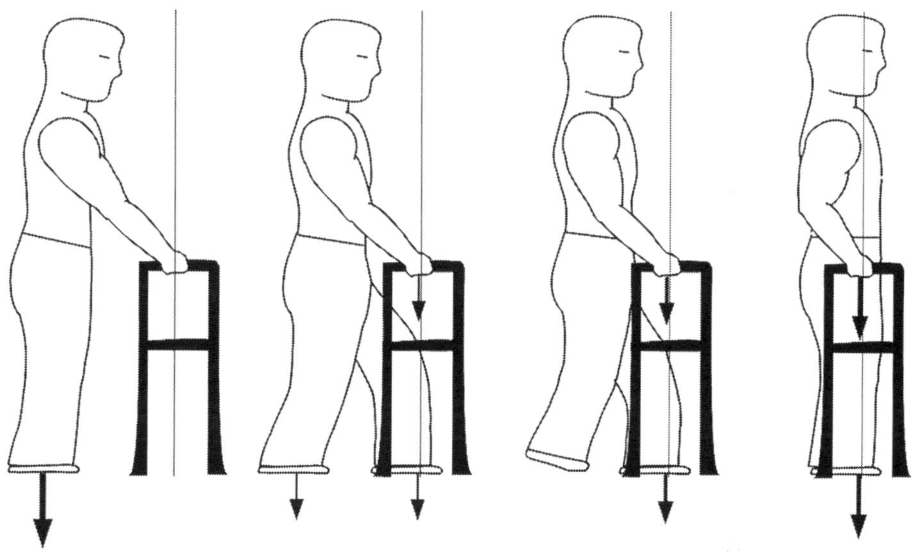

Using front-wheel drive as we walk with a walker

Focus on how the weight shifts. The "walking with a walker" action is a perfect example of applying the front-wheel drive principle with both the hands and legs.

The process of walking with a walker is how we enter into yang connection.

We begin by attaching ourselves to Uke. We push down on Uke's hand and begin stretching Uke's arm. This action creates the bridge (takes the slack out of his joints, stretches his arm like a rope bridge). We complete the yang connection by using a forward cam, shifting our weight, and sharing the burden of supporting our weight between both the hand(s) and leg. Uke is our walker.

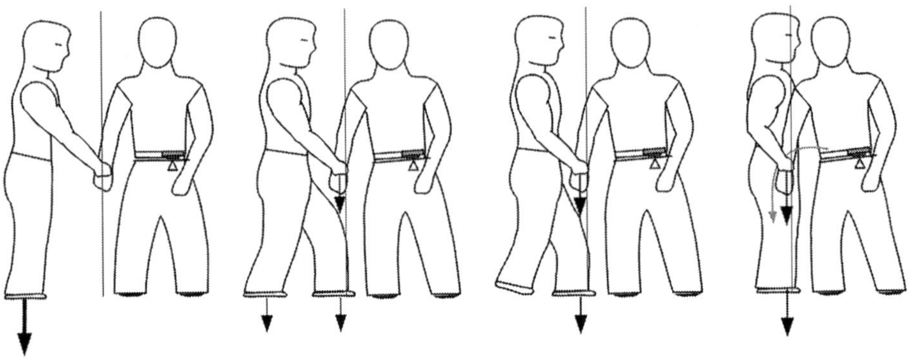

Using Uke as our walker

Twisting the bow

All right, so we now have Uke compressed.

We have our weight in our hands and Uke is somewhat burdened.

Something is still missing. The twist!

There is a slight wrinkle to using Uke like a walker. We want a walker to remain stable and capable of supporting us. We want the exact opposite of Uke.

How do we make Uke uncomfortable? We twist the top of the compressed bow!

"Which bow?" you ask.

If we have used Uke as a walker, Uke has reacted to our weight and is attempting to re-stabilize and restructure himself under this new load. Uke will eventually find stability under this condition. Burdened, but stable, Uke has formed a structure to keep himself from falling.

Uke's new structure resembles a bow. Here is the sneak peek at Uke's bow-like structure.

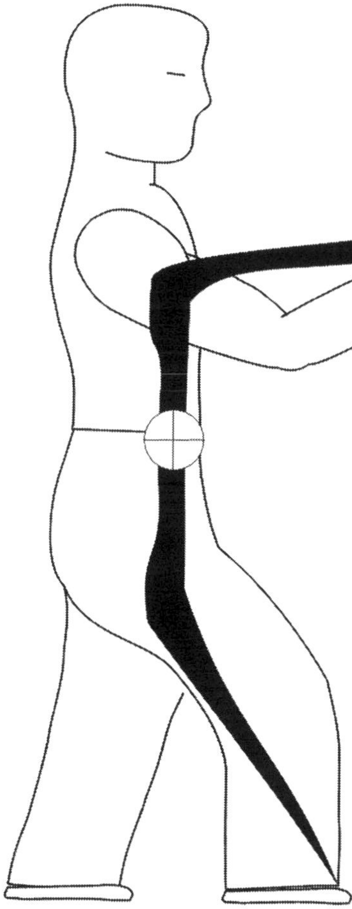

Uke and the bow

We have not yet thrown Uke because Uke is prepared to adjust to this one-dimensional, vertical pressure on his COB. We have loosened the string, but Uke is built to snap right back into shape.

If we hope to topple Uke, we must combine the initial downward pressure with a twist.

We create that twist, and add additional vertical spin on Uke's COB, by moving some of our weight off-center of his support.

The catch is that this twist has to be made in a particular direction.

Let us first investigate a common mistake: continuing along the line of the initial force. In other words, more of the same vertical pressure, no twist.

We start by attaching to the bow.

We then apply our downward pressure (using the walking with a walker method).

Lastly, we shift our weight slightly to one side of the fulcrum. Shifting our weight slightly to the side of the fulcrum is correct, but we mistakenly move along the bow's center axis. In effect, we simply bring the tips of the bow closer to each other.

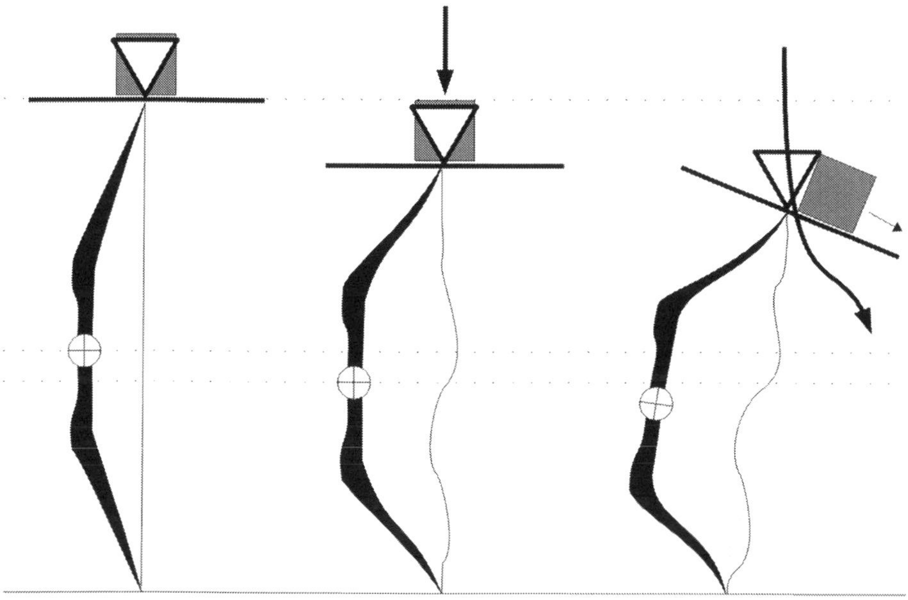

Compressing and then shifting weight onto the bow

Both the initial and secondary downward pressures create indirect vertical pressure on the COB, but the net effect on the bow is not complex. Our second dropping motion, (the weight shift), continued the bow's bend along the same direction as our initial weight drop (it drove the tips of the bow even closer to each other). All we did was compress the bow further in the same direction. We delivered a one-dimensional attack.

Uke can withstand most one-dimensional attacks on his balance.

Let us give Uke something extra to deal with. Let us change the direction of the second pressure and create a twist!

In order to do so, we have to approach the bow from a different perspective.

Let us again try dropping the weight via walking with a walker, but position the lever perpendicular to the supporting bow.

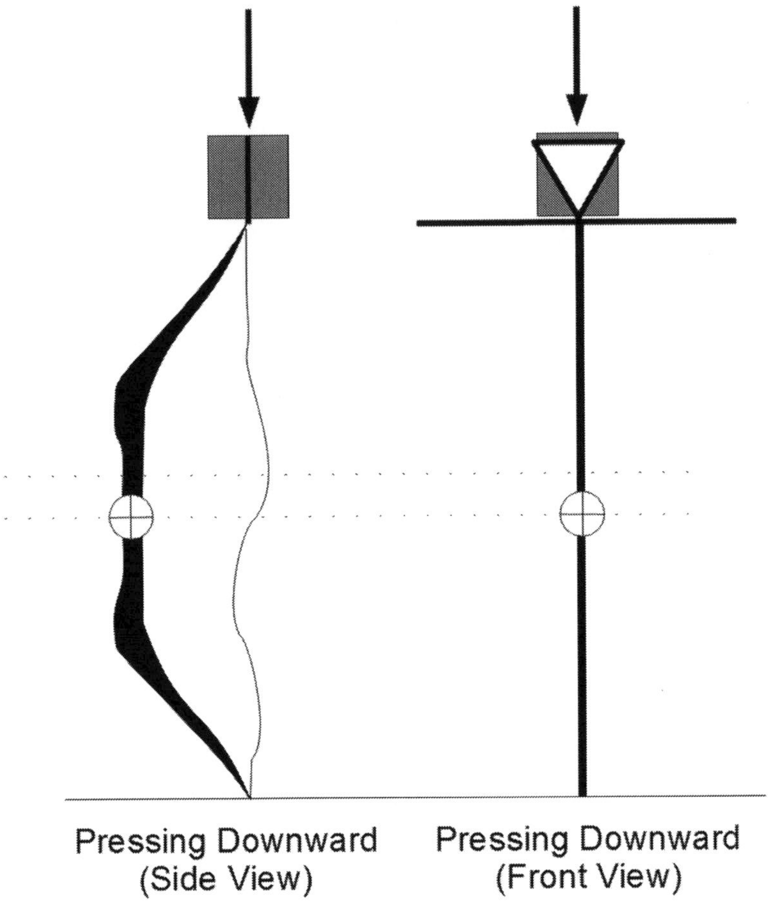

Placing the fulcrum perpendicular to the bow

With the initial weight drop in place, we shift our weight slightly off center of our fulcrum. This weight shift applies a second indirect vertical pressure on the bow's COB. The tip of the limb, already supporting the initial weight drop, is now being pulled off of its base. This is called twisting the bow.

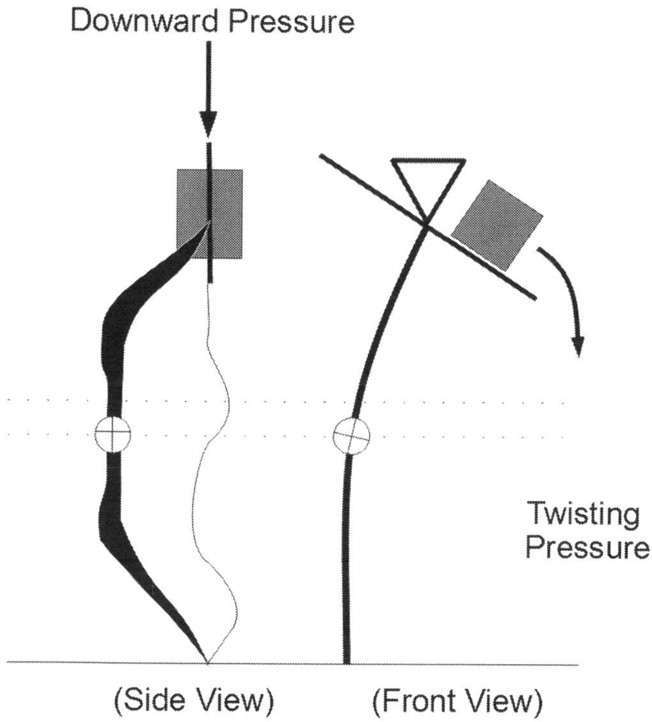

Combination of an initial downward compression and a second side-ward twisting pressure

The bow is strongest in resisting pressure that would bring the tips of the bow together. It is less resilient at supporting the sideways, twisting pressure.

The initial (walker) weight drop creates and burdens the structure. The second, sideways weight shift brings the structure out of alignment and seeks to break the bow.

Let us apply this same one-two process toward Uke.

Heavy hands: Bringing it together with drills

You can use the elephant arms drill with your palms down to learn heavy hands. The two important moves are there to discover. You find awareness of walking with a walker as you explore leaning on Uke's hands. Twisting the bow is no further away than tilting your hands.

For those that want things spelled out with a bit more detail:

Step one of this drill (compress) details how Uke becomes our walker (using top-down viewpoint diagrams and a quick review of the bow in Uke's stance). You can skip the optional Step One Advanced section called "Tilting the Bow" as it may confuse. I kept this explanation in here because tilting the bow benefits us by offering another way to float Uke's COB forward when he is trying to root himself on his back foot.

Step two is where we learn the complement of our earlier yin connection lever arms drill. We will attempt to explain using a variant of the falling off the fence motion, but we will additionally translate that motion into another analogy called tilting the table.

Step 1: Uke is our walker
We begin by lining up face-to-face, right-foot forward stance, touching right wrists with Uke.

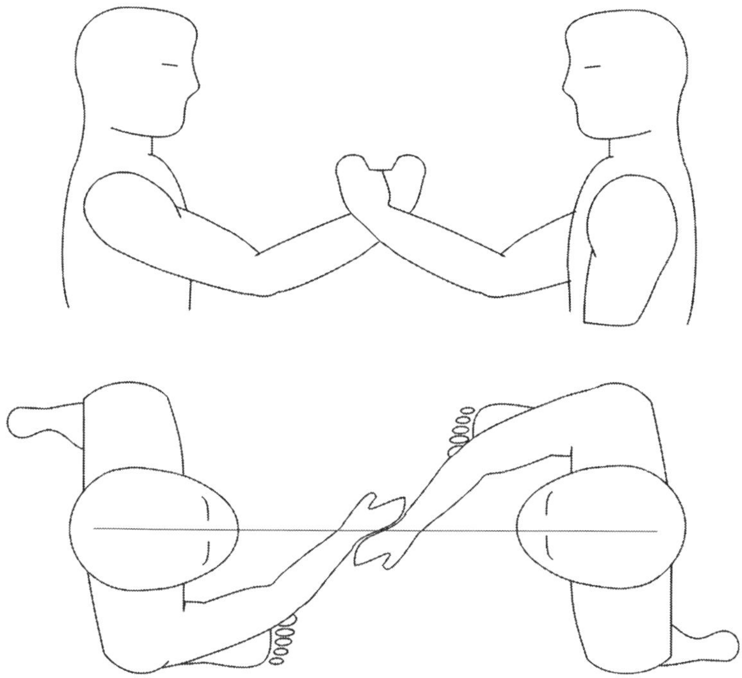

Starting position for learning walking with a walker drill

Step your left foot outward and grasp Uke's wrist. Stop for a moment in this wide leg stance (e.g., leave your right foot in place; your left knee should still be bent).

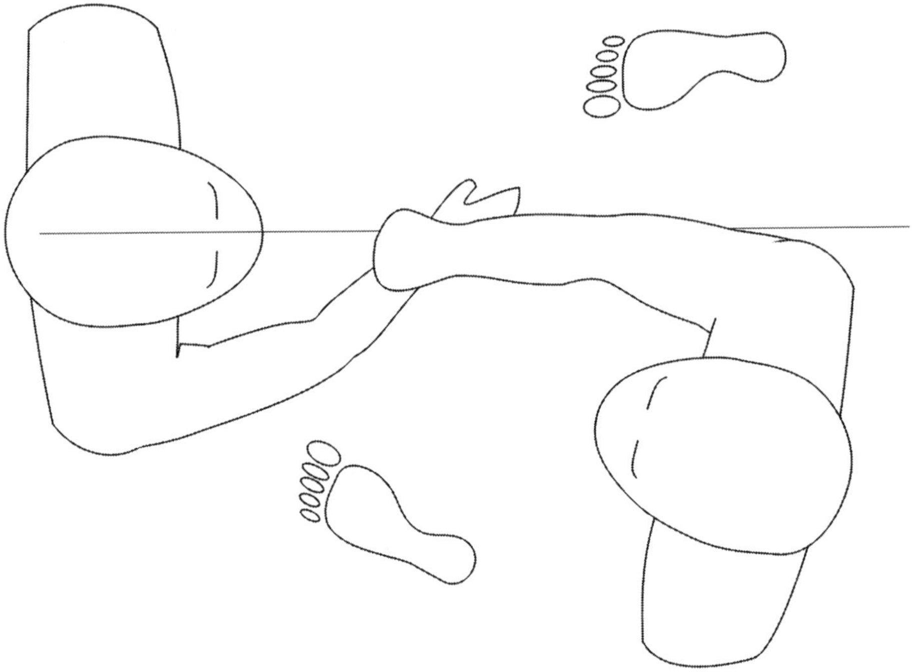

Stepping left and grasping Uke's wrist

Now practice completing the step (rising up) by pressing down with your right hand onto Uke's wrist as you extend your left leg. Allow your right leg to relax and you should find your right leg passively falling inward to complete the step (e.g., your heels will come together).

Optional: it may help develop your sense of front-wheel drive if you keep the entire bottom of the right foot dragging lightly on the floor as your legs close.

The focus of this practice is applying your weight onto Uke's wrist. Uke should feel as though he is supporting you from the moment you touch him. We never remove that pressure. Uke should still be feeling our weight even after we complete the step.

If Uke is not feeling your weight, it is likely because you are not using a centripetal arm. Be certain to draw your right hand downward and toward the bottom of your pants pocket on the same side as your COB (in this case left side). This should feel similar to the elephant arms drill. Failure to keep your hand in synch with your COB will cause a world of problems.

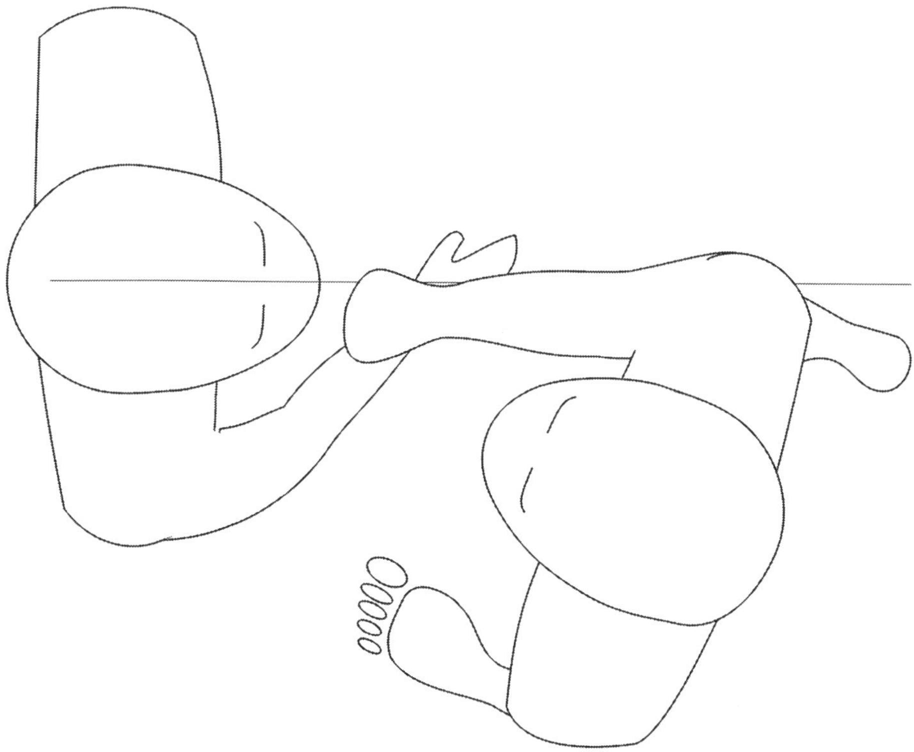

Completing the step and dropping Uke's arm as you apply your weight

If we have done this correctly, Uke's arm is stretched and we should sense that he is pulling backward/upward or at least pushing hard on the floor with the ball of his right foot to keep from toppling forward. Uke's lower back should have tensed a bit.

You should find that you were using Uke's reaction to assist you in rising upward.

The sensation you are experiencing is yang connection. It is not complex enough to cause Uke to topple, but it does give us a sense of what it means to vertically touch Uke's center by stretching his arm (extension connection). Practice sensing Uke's structure and take additional notice of where Uke has placed his COB in response to your attack.

Let us take another look at Uke's structure and the idea of Uke as a bow.

Uke's body becomes the bow in response to our first weight drop. We have grabbed his wrist and are driving that hand (and by proxy, his shoulders) downward. Uke must respond to that weight drop or find that his face is moving rapidly toward the floor. Uke creates a structure that counters this downward motion and puts his COB at rest (static position).

For all intents and purposes, Uke has created a bow.

The tips of the bow become his extended hand and the ball of his forward foot. The COB of the bow is Uke's COB.

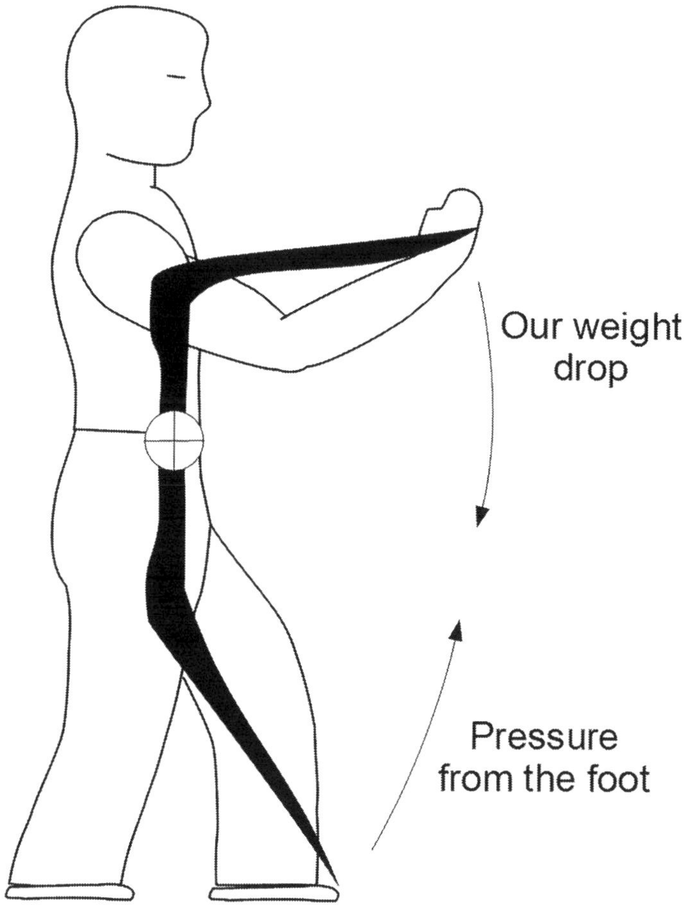

Uke and the bow

The downward, clockwise pressure on his wrist (from our weight drop) is counterbalanced with an upward, counterclockwise pressure from the ball of his foot. There are muscles all along the path in between those points that Uke had to tense in order for that to happen. (One easily noticeable point of tension is Uke's lower back.)

Step 1 Advanced: Tilting the bow for more effect (optional)
Bonus time! Let us take an aside to investigate how to add even more discomfort to Uke without using much additional force.

This lesson will pay dividends when you find an Uke that likes to sit on his back leg.

There is an interesting behavior hidden in the shape of a bow that helps us apply additional stress (vertical pressure) to Uke's COB. This additional pressure is in the same path as the initial drop (and therefore one-dimensional), but it is useful to know it is there.

The hidden trick to increase the initial downward vertical force applied to Uke's COB is to tilt the bow.

What do I mean by tilting the bow?

Let us reveal the advantages of tilting the bow by adding, changing, and then removing extensions to the ends of the bow. The point is to see how much of a burden is placed on the bow and then look for the same effect in Uke.

In the diagram below, we have extended the arms of the bow and moved the weight to the edge of the upper limb.

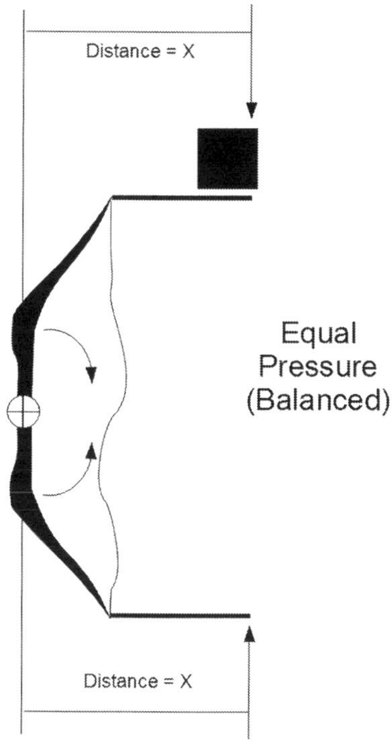

Equal vertical pressure(s) on the bow

The pressure from the top is negated by the pressure coming from the floor.

The bow is under pressure, but stable.

What happens when we shorten the bottom extension (footer)?

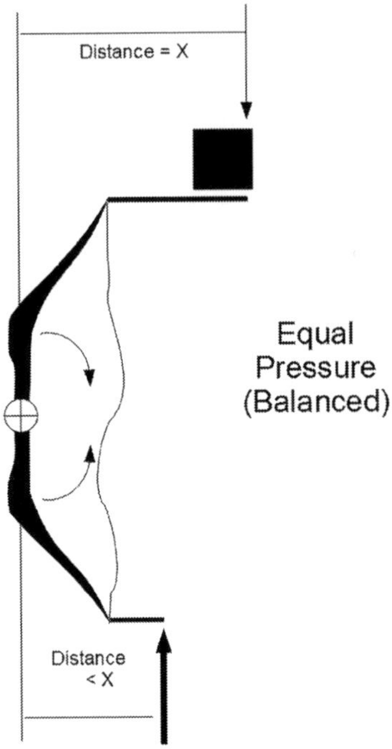

Greater force required on the bottom (footer) of the bow to equalize pressure on COB

It takes significantly more pressure coming up from the floor onto the bottom extension to keep the COB in a balanced state. (You should almost be able to sense the bow in this picture wanting to topple.)

The magic happening here is that the weight on top is applied at a greater distance from the COB (fulcrum) than is the upward pressure from the floor. You can resolve that although the torques are again balanced, the amount of force (or you could think of it as pressure) on the COB is increased, simply by moving the weight further off of the support.

Let us remove the extensions and take another look.

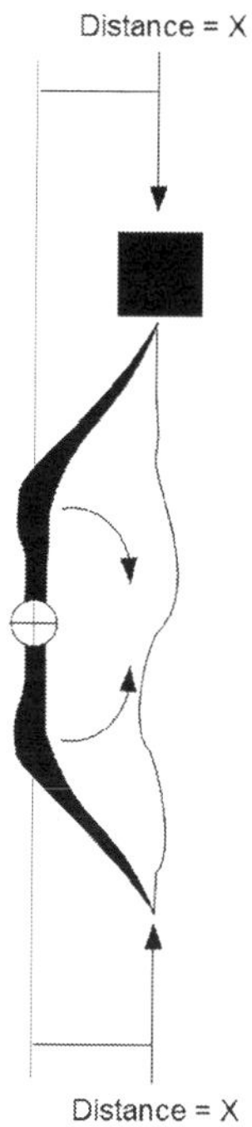

Standing bow with weight balanced on top

Again we find a perfectly balanced condition. The weight compressing the top arm of the bow is balanced by the pressure from the bottom.

Pay close attention to the distance from the COB to the tips of the bow.

Let us tilt the bow and see what happens.

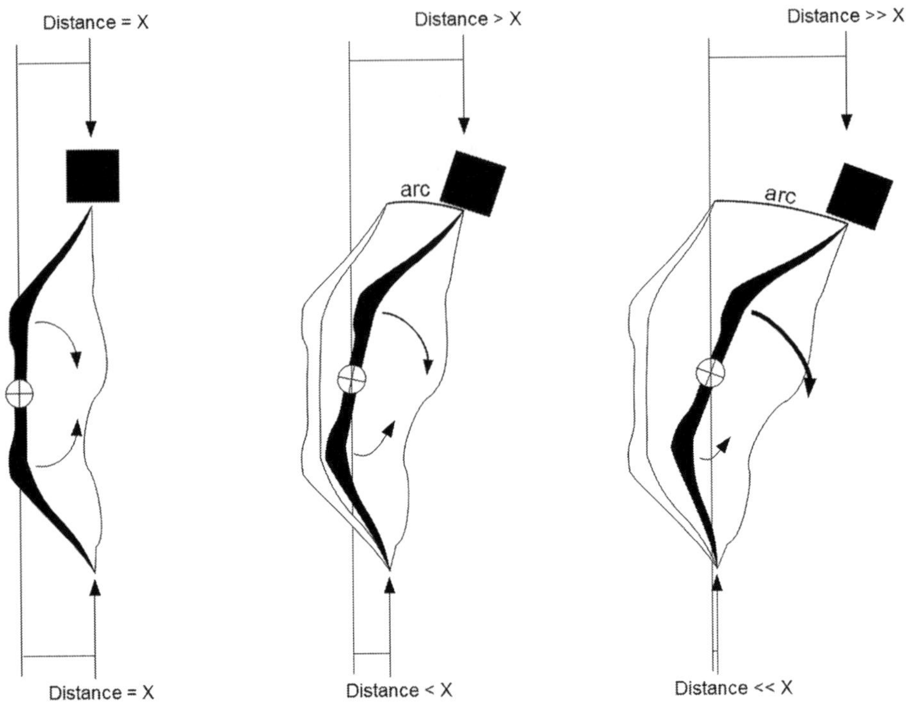

Tilting the bow to 12 and 21 degrees; increasing the vertical pressure on the COB

Tilting the bow results in a rapid decrease in the distance between the COB and the bottom support. (Look for the change in the bottom distance.) Tilting also increases the distance between the COB and the upper support.

The decrease in distance between the bottom tip of the bow and the COB makes it difficult to apply the same amount of upward (counterclockwise) pressure as is being delivered via the weight on top of the bow. This effect worsens as the bow continues to tilt and the weight moves further away from the support. (Right-most picture above.) The amount of torque (downward vertical pressure; clockwise) on the COB increases until the bow is driven off-balance and begins falling.

Again, take notice that we did not alter the "form" or "shape" of the bow to produce this effect. All we needed to do was move along the natural arc created as the bow toppled. The bow remains intact, but is burdened by its own weight (and worsened by any additional weight we might apply to that structure—hint, hint).

Additionally, take notice that the bow and the object it is supporting become a unified structure. Their weight is being supported by the earth. The structure is basically weightless along the arc. There is no push or pull on the arc, only falling. (No push or pull, only falling. So important I had to say it twice.)

The bow is allowed to be itself. The structure is kept intact as we move the bow (structure) along a path it was easily capable of traveling.

Tilting Uke
We can tilt Uke in the same way we did the bow to produce the same result.

We learned about how the initial weight drop onto Uke's arm causes Uke to create a bow-like structure. (Uke senses that his head will hit the floor if he does not adjust to the newly added weight.)

At this point, Uke is shaped like a bow from hand to the ball of the right foot.

Keep the pressure on Uke (constant pressure in your right hand and left foot) as you shift to a post-left position.

Lock your right arm in place, and rotate clock-wise around your COB. Use this hip-driven motion to draw Uke outward as you allow your hand to drop downward and along the arc. You should be able to see Uke moving along the arc formed by his shoulders.

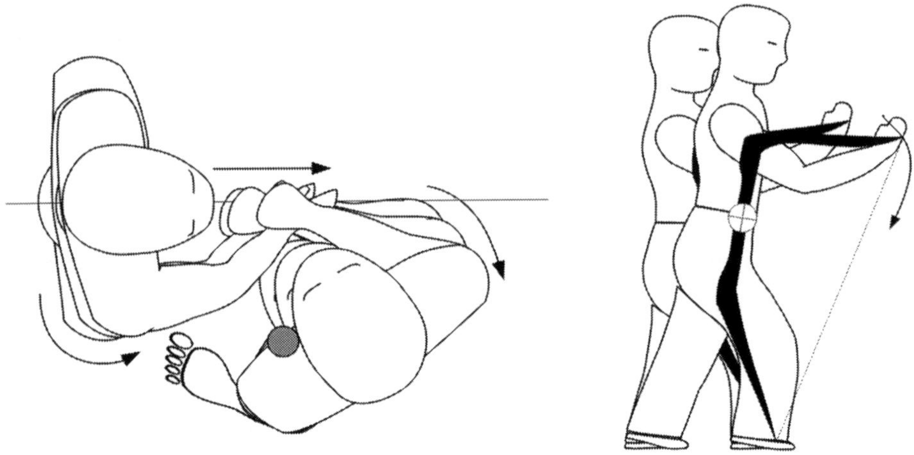

Using left-post clock wise turn to tip Uke; Uke as a bow tipping

I find that I have to resist the temptation to pull horizontally outward on Uke's arm.

Your hips must be the motor for drawing Uke forward as you exercise a lat pull-down.

The telltale sign that you are having the same issue I typically have is that your right shoulder becomes tense. The tension should be in your *latissimus dorsi*. It may make more sense to you if you concentrate on bringing your right shoulder blade closer to your spine (as if you were going to puff out your chest).

Your hand is moving along the arc, but the mental picture you should be using is to allow your right hand to follow the string (imaginary string of the bow). In other words, drop your hand in such a way that it feels as though you are following the bow string to the other bow-tip. Stay slightly to the outside of the bow string. (See arrow in the right-most picture above.)

Use tilting the bow when you find Uke has dropped his weight to the far side (Uke has posted left and has little weight in his right foot.) Posted right or left, the drill still applies.

You may sense a slight rise in Uke as you uproot him from this back-weighted position.

I suggest practicing with Uke in post right, left, and double-weighted positions.

Posted left is, for me, the most difficult version (and the most rewarding!).

Step 2: The twist
I am going to explain this step in two ways. The first is for those that want to keep with the daito hands type drill to parallel falling off the fence. The second explanation, tilt the table, is how we teach this to white belts and seems to be the easier way to get the point across.

Daito hand version
In step two, we again get into a left-foot forward, wide stance as we grab Uke's wrist.

Wait here for a second as we are, again, going use front-wheel drive to rise up and burden Uke. The difference this time is we are going to add a twist.

Adding the twist is practiced via a modification to the falling off the fence/daito hands/lever arms drill we used earlier.

From the forward step, grabbing Uke's wrist position, place the blade of your left hand on top of your right hand. (Looks a bit like an x-block. Hmm. Coincidence?)

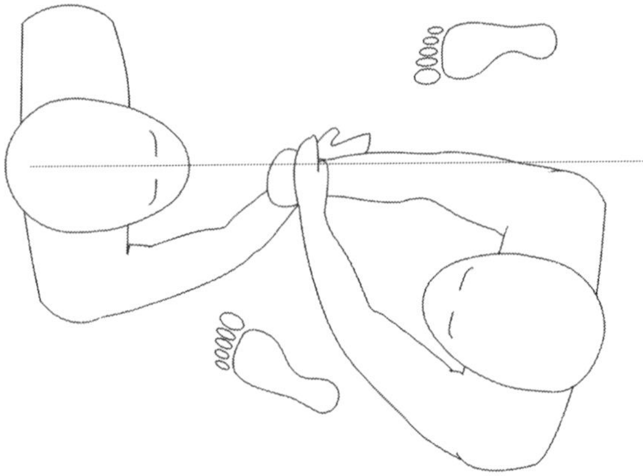

Stepping left; grabbing Uke's wrist; left hand-blade on top

The blade hand will act as the daito hand, similar to how we used it in the yin connection drills.

In lieu of falling off the fence, this time the daito hand is there to add the twist to the bow.

Complete your front-wheel drive step as you simultaneously drop your left hand through your right hand.

From the perspective of standing in front of Uke and looking directly down the line at a cross-section of Uke's wrist, the action looks as below.

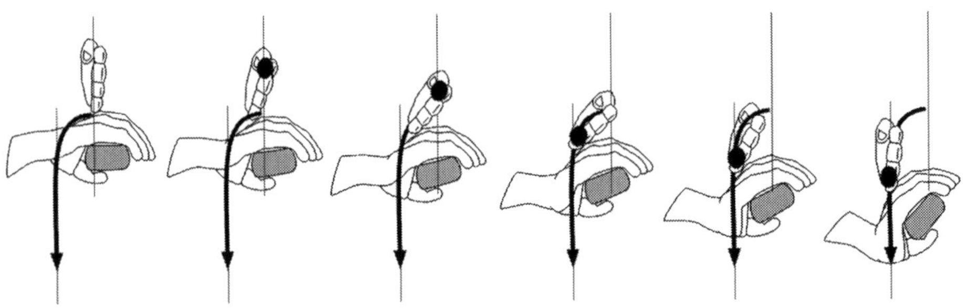

Using the upper hand to guide the grasping hand in yang connection

Notice the switch from index pivot to pinky pivot in the blade hand.

The index pivot is used to knock Uke's wrist out of alignment and the pinky pivot is used to drop our weight just to the side of Uke's arm.

Dropping to the side of Uke's arm is how we become unwieldy for Uke to support.

Here is a closer look at how the hand blade drops through this motion: index and then pinky pivot.

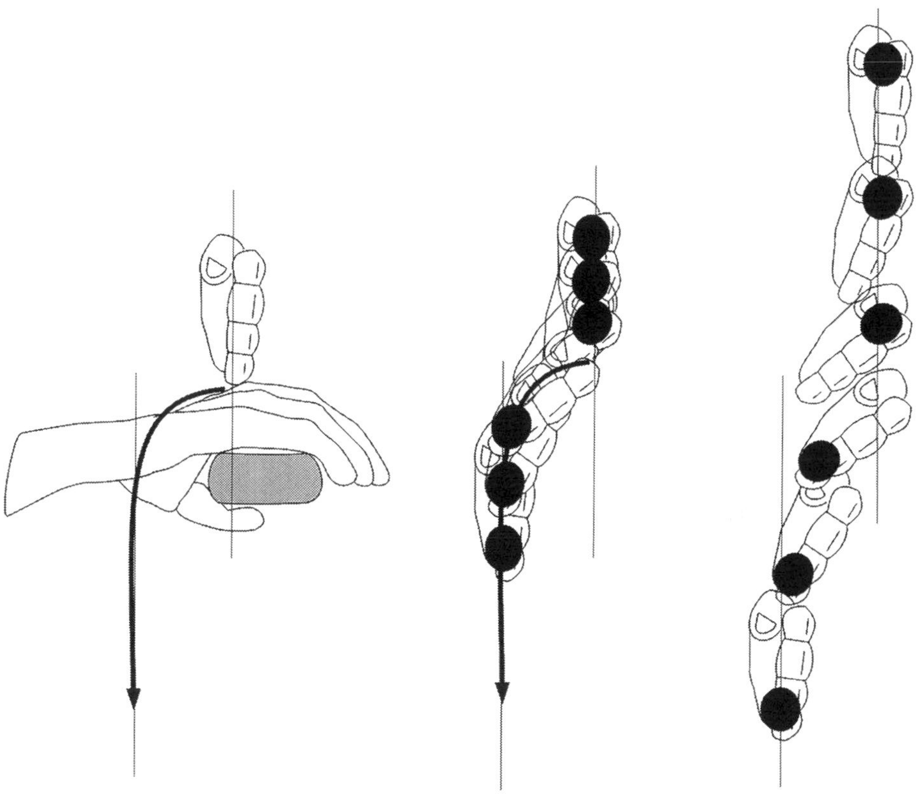

Path of the blade hand in yang connection drill

The walker (initial) weight drop will create the bow (optionally, the hip turn tilts the bow to create additional tension) and downward falling off the fence (second weight drop) twists the bow.

You will have to keep your right wrist supple in order to apply the second weight drop correctly.

Tilt the Table Version
Here is a less intense way to visualize twisting the bow.

Have Uke stand right foot and right hand forward, with his palm upward. Uke's right forearm should be parallel to the floor, soft-side upward.

Stand to the side of Uke in a comfortable stance (I prefer one leg a bit more forward than the other) and place both hands on Uke's forearm. You may want to have Uke post right as you first try this.

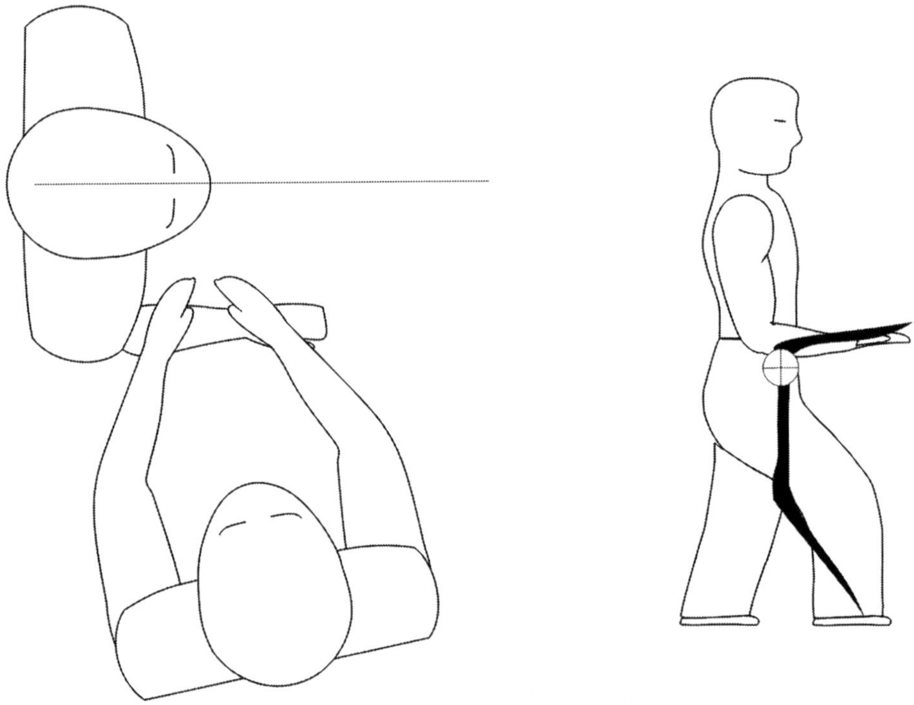

Lining up to learn how to tip the table

Use the walker analogy to press down slightly onto Uke's forearm; this action should compress and tilt the bow just enough to get Uke into a structure. (For example, touch his center by extension. In this case, stretch his shoulder downward. Uke keeps his face off the ground by pushing against the floor with ball of the right foot and tensing the lower back.)

Now visualize Uke's forearm as if it were a table. Imagine an object sitting on that table somewhere between your hands. (I typically imagine a glass salt shaker.)

Tilt that table in such a way that the imaginary object will slide off of Uke's arm and land on your toes.

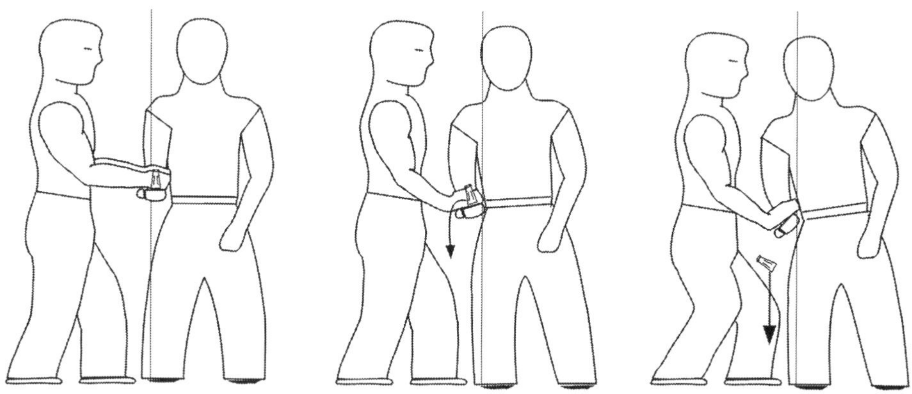

Side positioned yang style connection drill

It is very important that you have the object land on, or just in front of your toes.

Try having it land behind your forward foot and see what happens. Doesn't have the same effect, does it?

If someone were to stand in front of Uke and consider Uke's forearm bones as the table, the imaginary event would look a lot like this.

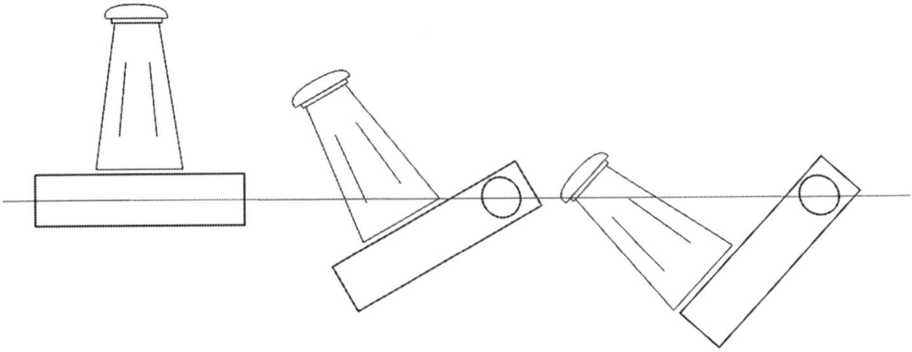

Imagining a salt shaker sliding off of a table

If you did not get it correct, be certain you are not putting Uke's elbow back into his hip. We want to make certain Uke's arm is not directly supported by his right leg. Uke's elbow should be falling along his side.

Switch to the other side
Let us try that same tilting the table drill from the other side of the arm.

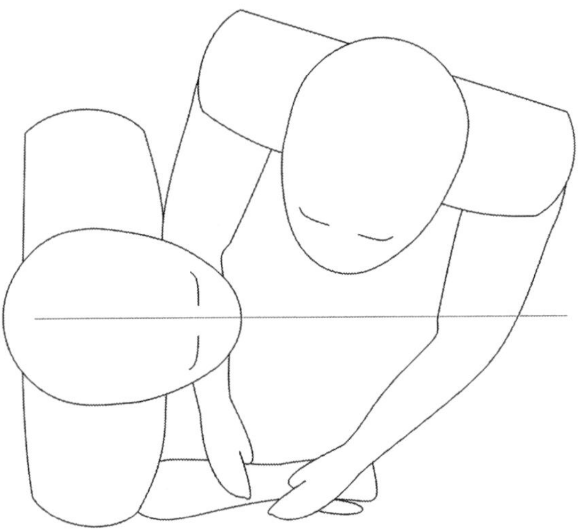

Lining up on inside of Uke's stance for yang connection drill

This was a seriously difficult modification for us to tackle at first. It was frustrating to vividly see the salt shaker and have repeatable success at dropping it upon our toes from that outside position, but when we moved to the inside position, we lost all ability to repeat the task.

The extremely common mistake to make in this position is, again, to push Uke's elbow into his hip.

Putting Uke's elbow in his hip allows Uke to move all the weight (ours and his) over his right leg and support us. This is highly undesirable.

To compensate, we created another analogy that I hope will save you time: riding the sled down the side of the leg (interchangeably, sliding down the calf).

When performing the drill this way, convert the table we made of Uke's forearm into a sled. Tilt the far side of the sled (Uke's forearm) and allow the sled to ride the side of Uke's leg. Follow the sled down to the floor. Uke will fall before you get very far.

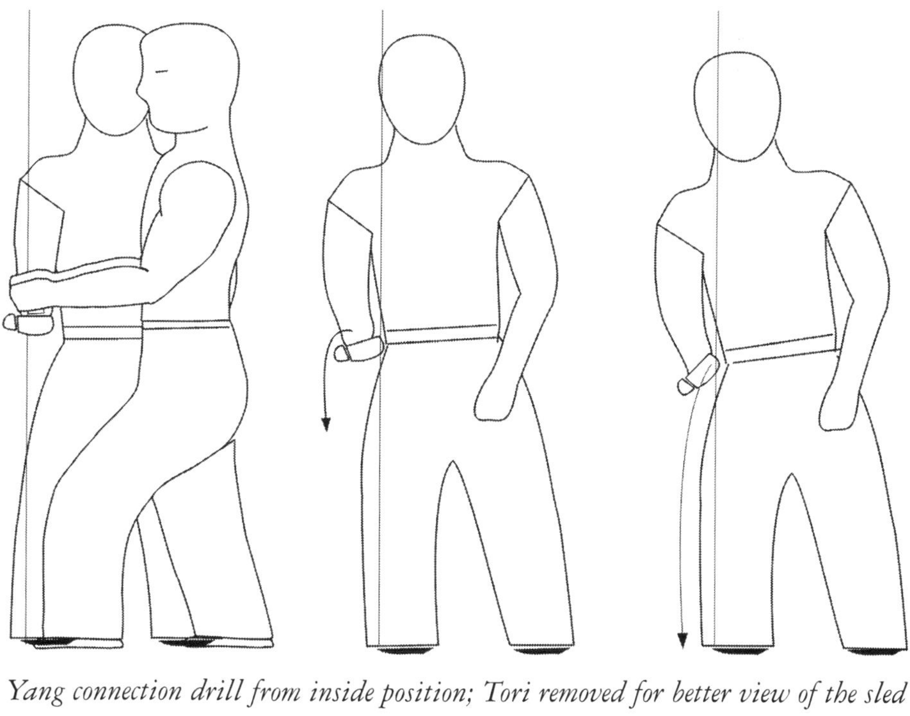

Yang connection drill from inside position; Tori removed for better view of the sled

So ends our Step 2, twist explanations.

Heavy hands summary

One brief, last comment to close our discussion on heavy hands practice.

Heavy hands is a singular, three-dimensional motion. It can be described through the two key elements of walking with a walker and twist the bow, but keep in mind that we bring these two together and use them at the same time. Work to make the two steps one fluid motion.

What else did we learn? Attacking Uke's base!

I could not pass on describing a tangent progression that may have skipped your notice.

In the yang connection drill, we describe dropping that salt shaker onto our toes. I hope you took the time to drop that shaker on your heel or even further back (like maybe to your back foot). You should have found that the effect on Uke was less desirable the further you moved away from Uke.

Why does it work so well when we drop the salt shaker on our toe? We are attacking the knee joint!

Ask a personal trainer how to do a deep knee bend and what advice should you expect to hear? The knee must track over the toe. In other words your knee must bend in the direction it was designed to work. (Or gain the nick-name "gimpy." After your recovery, of course.)

The manner with which we put weight on Uke's arm during these latter yang connection drills is putting stress on Uke's knee and is an attack to his basic structure. Uke's knee joint does not like it, and he will move his hip to try and get that knee tracking over the toe again.

This attack to the knee completes a set of three attacks to the structure of Uke's base.

Working from the floor upward we have attacked the:

- Feet: no-line and the 20, which is an attack toward Uke's feet. We are working on lines where Uke's feet cannot provide support.

- Knee: just inside or just on the outside of Uke's knee is manifested by directing ours and Uke's weight to a point on the floor just to the side(s) of Uke's feet. It most effective when applied in conjunction with twisting the bow (which is why we did not cover this concept until now).

- Hip: sliding Uke means we are spinning his COB as we move him along the weak lines of his stance. This opens or closes Uke's kua and locks his hip joints.

Attack the feet, knee, or hip. You may apply one or all three in any given technique.

Yang connection summary

Yang connection is based on us leaning upon Uke for a portion of our support.

The advantage in leaning on Uke (versus Uke leaning on us) is that most of the motions result in extending Uke's limbs. At some point, his arms will fully extend. Uke's fully extended arms remove the need for a joint lock or stiffened joints. If we skip the arms and place our weight on Uke's body, well, then we have a direct connection to Uke's spine and COB.

The disadvantage is that we have to be careful to never use direct vertical pressure on Uke's center. In other words, we cannot place our weight directly on Uke's COB. The control of Uke's balance will disappear if Uke can easily support us. Uke will take over because he has us in a yin connection.

Take your time and burn in your practice of daito hands and lever arms. You are going to want to have that foundation as we move to the last precept.

Precept 6: Aiki-Age and Aiki-Sage

[Review the latter portion of the basic terms section before moving on with this section. We are going to assume familiarity with the basic terms material as we introduce new analogies.]

The sagittal plane section included explanations of the belts and focused on how we rotate the COB horizontally.

Aiki-Age and Aiki-Sage are the complement to the sagittal plane lessons, as "Age" and "Sage" are how we place vertical pressure on Uke's COB.

Put simply, Aiki-Age spins the COB downward and Aiki-Sage spins it upward (and over).

Developing an understanding of Aiki-Age and Aiki-Sage requires an expanded view of the COB. Let us synch on a few concepts before we directly address Age/Sage and describe some drills.

The COB as a dynamic orb

You should recognize the COB as a dynamic orb.

The COB is a three-dimensional fulcrum, better known as a ball. Ball = orb. The dynamic part is the fact that the COB moves and, according to our purpose, can be differing sizes.

By now you should be comfortable with the concept of the COB being round and that it moves. The deeper awareness is understanding how the COB shrinks or grows and gaining familiarity with what happens when we manipulate the COB.

As far as the size of the COB, at its smallest, the COB is no larger than a speck of dust. We can grow its size to infinity by adding layers of concentric orbs around it. (Much like building our own pearl.) The varying widths of the orb can be likened to the stratified layers of the Earth. (Although the

COB can be varying sizes, the practical range of diameter for the COB is between eight inches and six feet.)

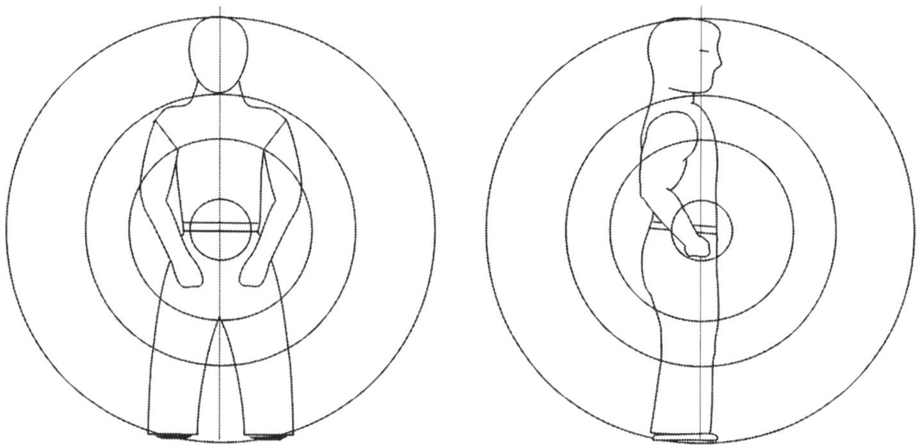

Uke and the orbs; Uke in double-weighted stance

Viewing Uke in a double-weighted horse stance, we can see the COB aligned with the center of the body (just below the navel).

The diameter of the largest orb depicted (outer most edge) is approximately equal to the height of Uke. This coincides with the width of the outstretched arms and should put you in mind of Da Vinci's picture of the symmetry of the human body.

Take note of the smaller, inner orbs. These are often disregarded or simply not recognized.

If we move one layer of the orb, what happens to the rest of the layers? In short: the COB's "many orbs in one" move in unison. Let us take a closer look at what that means.

The orbs are glued together. In other words, they are all layers of the same orb and always move in the same direction at the same time. I do mean any direction. Whether they are rotating around the center (e.g., spinning) or moving along the X, Y, and Z planes (e.g., bouncing the ball), all the concentric orbs move together. For example, all of the orbs will complete a horizontal revolution at the same time.

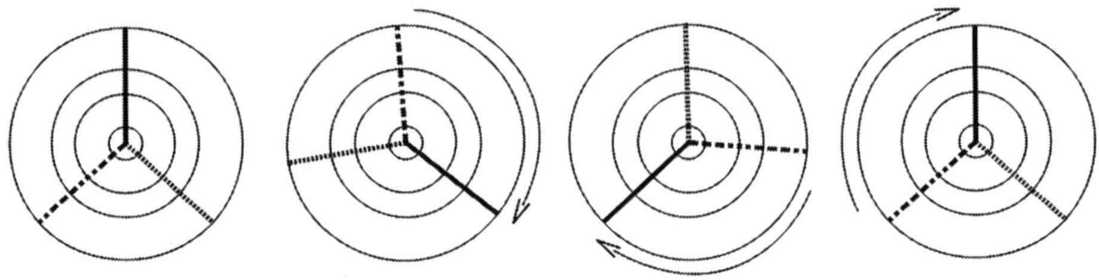

All orbs move with each other

To help put this glued together behavior in perspective, imagine yourself spinning around as you held your arms outward. Your arms were as far from the center as they could be and traced a wide circle. Your nose was very near the center and traced a smaller circle. No matter how many times or how quickly you rotate, your nose and your arms will always maintain the same number of revolutions. This is the same for the orbs. No matter how small or large, they all maintain the same number of revolutions.

Even though the orbs move together, there are differences. Notably, the outer orbs have less pronounced arc, cover more distance in the same amount of time, and thus, have greater velocity than the inner orbs. These aspects have an extremely influential effect on how an Aiki technique works (or does not work).

We can experiment with one size orb or another as a method to break through plateaus in our practice. In that, we may find it easier to play with a more inner orb to get a feel of how a technique should be performed and then switch back to using an outer orb (or vice versa).

What is the point?

Tori's greatest influence on Uke's COB happens when Tori is traveling along the surface of the orbs (three-dimensional parallelism).

Any contact with Uke is made at a particular distance from his COB. Under certain conditions, the most effective way to spin Uke's center is to push that contact point on a path that maintains that distance from the center of the COB. Much like tracing an arc along the surface of a ball.

In most cases, Uke's body is not designed to resist spin. With just a little bit of friction, Tori can spin Uke's orb just as though he were spinning a foam ball floating on the water. As you will come to understand in the last section of this book, spinning Uke's center is the basis of Aiki.

Of course, not just any spin will do. We have to spin Uke's center in the appropriate direction if we hope to topple him. Typically, we cannot topple Uke with just horizontal spin (the belts), we need to spin Uke's COB vertically (Aiki-Age, Aiki-Sage) if we ever hope to knock him down.

It is a good idea to look for the arcs in an Aiki technique. The somewhat tricky part is to find the arc within the rather awkward shape of the body, especially as Uke shifts his weight (e.g., steps.)

All that weight shifting makes for some complicated arcs. Most Aiki techniques require pushing the contact point as if tracing parabolas or ellipses, but the effect on Uke's COB is an arc.

Let us take a moment to analyze where the arcs go as Uke moves.

Which way did Uke go?

Uke shifts his weight, and the COB moves within the body.

Every time the COB moves, it takes all of the orbs with it. (The orbs are, after all, extensions of the COB.)

This creates some interesting complexity for those that only see the COB in the center (always just under the navel).

Look at what happens to the relationship between the orbs and Uke's body when Uke puts all his weight on one side (i.e., Uke posts right or left).

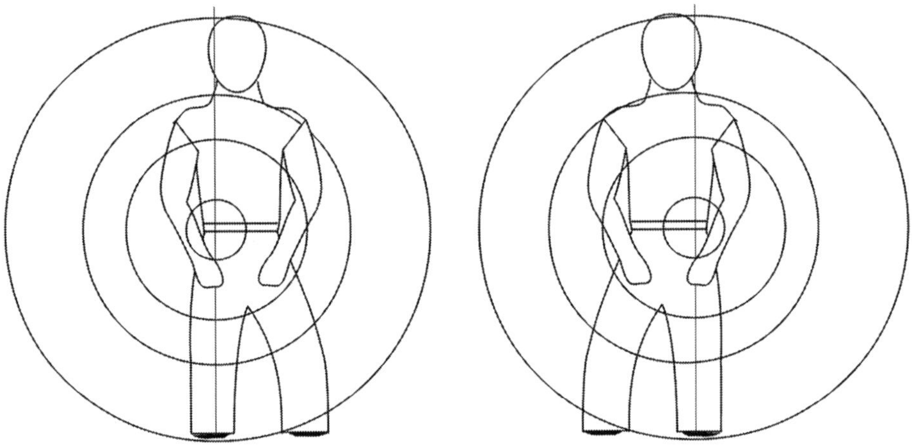

The orbs move as Uke shifts his weight right and left

The orbs have shifted and so too have the arcs created by the surface of the orb. (I only showed four orbs above. We could have drawn an infinite number of orbs. I like these four in particular as they have a great deal of utility.)

What exactly do I mean by arcs?

The arcs are paths along the surface of the orb (whichever sized orb you are working with). The arcs remain at a constant distance from the center of balance. The arcs represent the three-dimensional parallelism we seek to use when making Uke's COB spin.

If the COB moves in the X, Y, or Z dimensions (or more importantly, *as* the COB moves in these dimensions), we have to recognize the shift and adjust our arcs accordingly.

The arcs present when Uke is double-weighted have less than optimal effect when Uke posts to either side. Similarly, the double-weighted arcs become dead spots when Uke posts to either side.

This is especially true at the height of the chin.

The path from chin to the back of the head works well to spin Uke when Uke is in a double-weighted stance, but becomes significantly reduced in its effectiveness when Uke posts to either side.

Here is why.

Following a path from Uke's chin toward the back of his head, while Uke is posted either right or left, no longer takes us longitudinally through the very topmost point of the orb. We will effect some vertical pressure on Uke's COB, but we will also begin spinning Uke horizontally. This horizontal spin can assist Uke in warding off our attack.

Uke knows this instinctively. You will find that anyone, and I mean anyone, trained or untrained, with even the basest of desire to remain standing and basic athletic awareness, will naturally shift their weight to either side and attempt to spin out of Shomenate #1. This is why most of your techniques do not work on your spouse when you try it on them at home.

All arcs have their uses, but some arcs are more appropriate than others.

We feel heavy to Uke when we influence Uke's center vertically. We do this the best if we move longitudinally along Uke's orbs (move along the arcs but directly toward the very top or bottom).

The longitudinal arcs apply the greatest amount of vertical pressure on Uke's COB because they travel directly toward the poles. By the poles I mean the bottom and top most points on the orb (highest and lowest, e.g. the North and South poles of the Earth). Traveling along the longitudinal lines of the COB removes horizontal rotation and focuses all our efforts toward rotating Uke's COB vertically, in other words, moving toward the poles creates pure indirect vertical pressure on the COB. (Important! Remember that statement.)

Here is one quick tangent that ties the COB back to an earlier lesson. We describe the line that runs directly between the north and south poles as the vertical axis.

The vertical axis always runs through the hand grip area of the bow. The tips of the bow are not the NP and SP (pronounced: En-Pea, and Ess-Pea, i.e., north and south pole). I mention this point to highlight where the vertical axis and bow intersect so that you might apply either as needed. All of the precepts are intertwined, but are not the same concepts. It helps to know when and how you can cross over between the concepts.

So what are we faced with? Always look on the bright side.

The title of this section says it all. Exactly what are we facing when we attempt to throw Uke?

We like to say that we are always looking at the bright side or light side of the moon when we address our relationship to Uke's COB.

It does not matter which direction Uke is facing, the half of the COB closest to us is considered the bright side.

In a sense, we are the Sun.

Most of our techniques will attach to Uke on the bright side of the COB, but there are cases where we make contact on the edges just out of sight, on the dark side of his COB (ala Ushiroate #5).

The bright side and dark side analogy is extremely useful when you begin to think in terms of how we rotate Uke's COB.

We describe that edge between bright and dark sides of the COB as the corona.

Now let us get to the heart of why we wrote this chapter: Aiki-Age and Aiki-Sage.

Aiki-Age

Aiki-Age is the direction we spin Uke's COB and not a particular technique. Aiki-Age is how we spin the bright side of Uke's COB longitudinally downward, toward the SP. (Conversely, the dark side is moving upward toward the NP.)

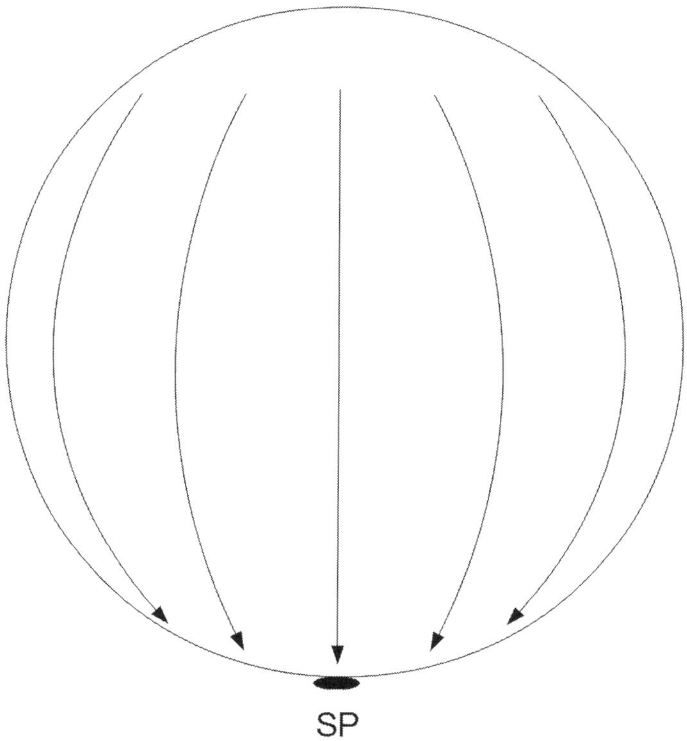

Aiki-Age spins the bright side of the COB vertically downward toward the SP

Aiki-Age is a connection builder. Aiki-Age is one of the two potential conditions created when one person is leaning on the other. (The other condition is Aiki-Sage.)

The basic terms section revealed four lever-arm methods to create Aiki-Age (rolling Uke's moon downward toward the SP), but Aiki-Age can just as easily be created using daito hands.

Both Aiki-Age and Aiki-Sage always use the same formula. We touch Uke's center (compression or extension) to form a bridge. Once the bridge is formed we selectively position our fulcrum and then tilt the lever. This tilting action does one of two things. The tilting rolls Uke onto the semi-support of our fulcrum (yin connection) or Uke finds that he is trying his best to adjust to us leaning on his COB in an unwieldy way (yang connection).

This one person supporting the other condition is the final ingredient that converts a bridge into connection.

Once we have connection, all we need do is to move our support and Uke follows. Alternatively, once we have connection, we can let Uke's COB spin around itself. Sounds easy, but it takes practice.

If you had any difficulty in attempting the Aiki-Age drills described in the basic terms section, it likely came down to the ability to use a centripetal arm.

So what is a centripetal arm?

The centripetal arm describes our motion as Tori. It is how we move our arm so that it feels heaviest to Uke. It combines moving along the arcs with putting our weight into our hands. Let us investigate.

Centripetal arm: Paint the wall to paint the ball

The abbreviated version of how to apply a centripetal arm is to paint the wall. (We could have painted a fence here, but we already used a fence in another analogy.)

Now that you think you know what I mean, let us dive deeper.

Let us focus on the downward stroke; the one we depicted in our yang connection explanation (Precept 5 discussion). The right hand (lower hand) is the one painting.

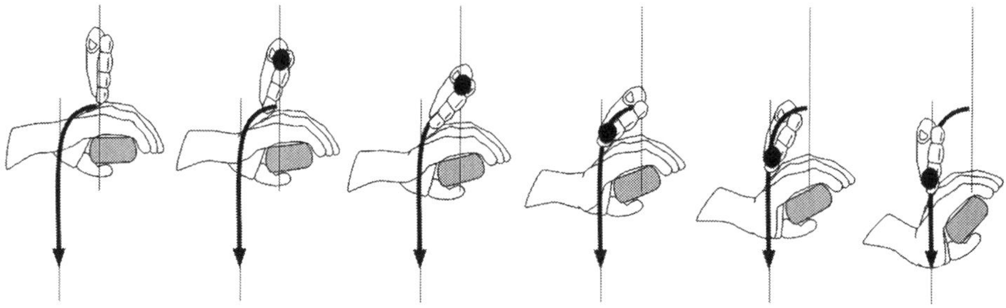

Yang connection drill; paint the wall

Let us ask ourselves a few questions.

When painting a wall, does our wrist ever touch the wall? Do we grip the brush with extreme intensity? Do we maintain a constant and even pressure between the bristles and the wall throughout the motion?

The answers are obvious, but speak to a deep sense of body awareness.

No, we do not actually touch the wall with the wrist. The wrist leads the hand in a path parallel to the wall. (Take notice of that statement, the wrist leads the hand!)

We grip the brush, but not so hard that we see white knuckles, or so loosely that the friction between the brush and the wall rips the brush from our hand. The hand is relaxed but structured. Liken it to an un-bendable arm expressed via our hand.

Finally, yes, we maintain a constant and even pressure between the bristles and the wall or our paint will look awful.

This paint the wall analogy would be perfect description for a centripetal arm except for one important understanding, the wall is flat and vertical, and Uke's COB is an orb.

We improve the analogy by changing the object we are painting to an orb, and we get paint the ball.

Paint the ball (run your hands along the surface of Uke's COB) while using the body awareness we just described.

What? The orb has two sides?
An orb may be round but it has two sides that we can paint: the inside and the outside.

It will help to think of the COB orb as though it was one of those rigid plastic balls that you put a hamster into for exercise. We are not using this example for the purposes of setting the COB's size; we grow or shrink the ball as necessary. The point here is that you could conceivably paint either the inside or outside of that ball.

The importance of the two sides of the orb becomes apparent when we apply an extension or compression touch upon Uke's center.

Touching Uke's center with a compression is much like putting pressure on the outside of a ball. In fact, we use a large inflatable workout ball to teach painting the ball with compression. We hold an exercise ball with two hands and allow the student to focus on spinning the ball, not moving it.

Paint the outside of the ball when using compression. (There are exceptions, but compression is typically when we are moving toward Uke's center, e.g., using direct horizontal touch on Uke's center to stiffen Uke's arm joints, or putting your hand to Uke's chin to knock him over as in Shomenate).

Paint the inside of the orb when using extension. (Again, exceptions exist, but extension is typically when we are moving away from Uke's center, e.g., dog on a chain—taking the slack out of Uke's joints by stretching his limb.)

When we touch Uke's center using extension, it is much like our hand is trapped on the inner surface of the orb. It is the bridge that keeps us at a constant orbit around Uke's COB. I do not do this as a practice myself, but you could get the feel for this by tying a string to a steady spot (e.g., a door knob), grabbing the loose end of the string, and moving your hand in the arc(s) permitted by that string. The goal is to keep the string taut, but not pull too hard on the string. The challenge is to imagine that the inside surface of the COB is forcing your hand into an arc. We are wiping our hands along the inside of Uke's orb (painting the inside of the ball). I expect you will find this practice feels somewhat similar to ryote-mochi techniques.

Centripetal arm: Using the rings

Painting the ball helps us trace arcs.

Using the rings analogy helps us focus our weight into our hands.

The analogy is simple. Imagine that you have a large, heavy metal ring around your forearm that can slide from elbow to wrist as you tilt your arm. We use the ring to focus our attention and our weight. The ring allows us to engage our mind as we act.

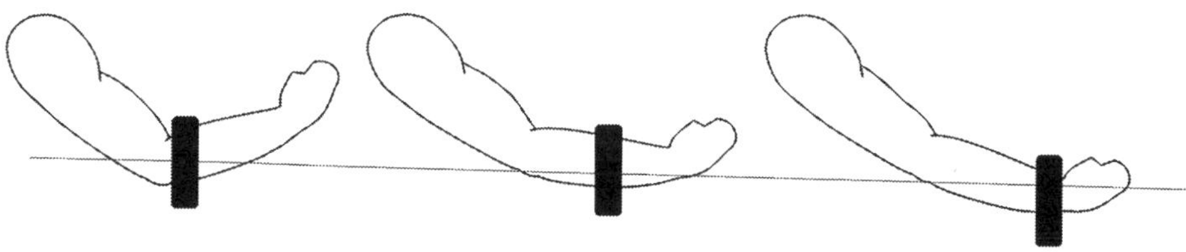

Imaginary ring on the forearm

Let us combine the ideas into a single drill.

Aiki-Age drill

Extend your arm approximately halfway and grasp Uke's lapel at collar bone height. Begin by imagining the ring forcing the top of your forearm nearest your elbow downward as you begin moving your hand along the orb. (The orb in this case is the one that passes through the point at which you have grabbed. Supposing that your Uke is about six foot tall, his collar bone should be about two feet away from very center of his COB. Draw Uke along that four foot diameter orb.) Draw Uke onto his toes before you start tracing the arc. (Next chapter explains why.) Tilt your arm in such a way that the imaginary ring slides toward your wrist as you continue the motion along Uke's orb. You will find that you have to step backward or even make a turning step to allow Uke to drop to the floor. Uke should have very little ability to resist your action.

This particular drill is designed to touch Uke's center using extension, so be certain to paint the inside of the orb as you make certain that your hand is moving longitudinally toward the SP (or likely find that this drill is not going to be as effective).

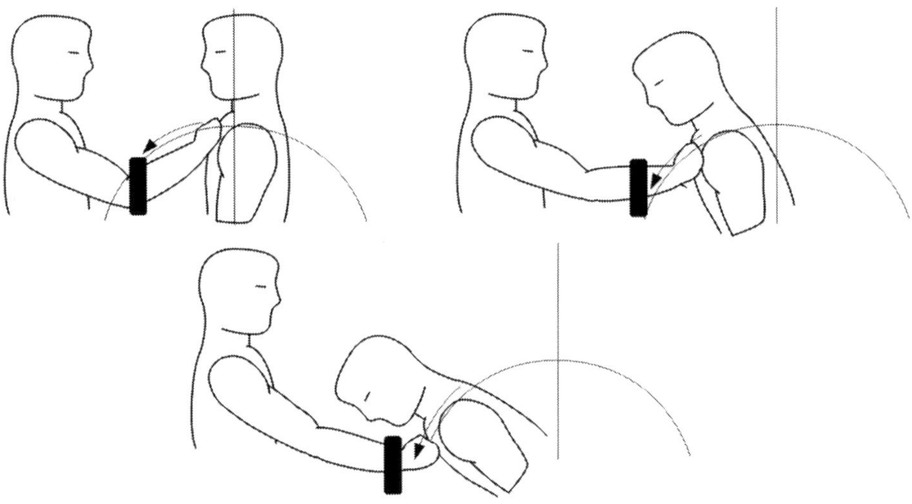

Using the rings, Aiki-Age drill starting, middle, and end point

The ring should always be imagined as being in contact with the forearm. For now, never allow it to rest on the bicep or thumb.

This analogy points out a key understanding: the position of the hand is not important. The imaginary ring should be applying pressure along the forearm. The tilting of the forearm (and motion of the ring) creates the Age and Sage motions. The relationship of your hand and wrist is only relevant to how you attach to Uke.

For example, one could use the centripetal arm to create a rising motion (and effect a Sage) while keeping the fingers and wrist bent downward toward the floor. The same can be said of applying a falling motion (or Age) on Uke with the fingers pointed upward.

Combine the rings with paint the ball and see how well you grasp Aiki-Age.

Aiki-Sage

Aiki-Sage is the complementary motion to Aiki-Age. Aiki-Sage makes the trip to the NP.

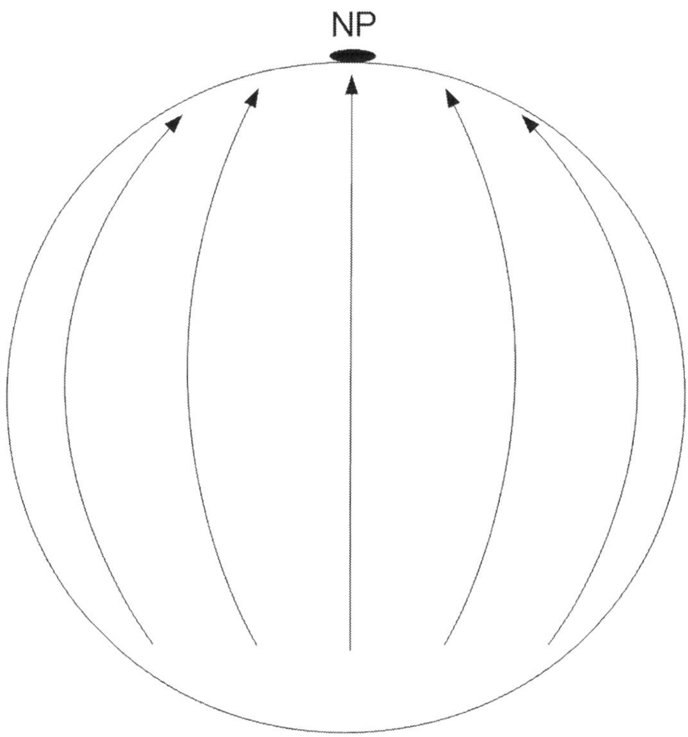

Aiki-Sage spins the bright side of the COB vertically upward toward the NP

The rules of using a centripetal arm and moving along the longitudinal lines toward the pole still apply. The sensation of painting the ball is there as well.

The same basic equation is used to create connection in Aiki-Sage: touch Uke's center to form a bridge, position the fulcrum, tilt the lever, and roll Uke into the semi-support of our fulcrum (yin or yang connection).

I like to abbreviate that equation when describing Aiki-Sage as up and over.

Simple to remember, but there is a catch.

There are two tricks to Aiki-Sage.

The first trick is to remember that you (almost) never start at the NP. It may seem silly to point this out, but the NP represents only one small point on the orb. There are times when we start at the NP, but it is not the common practice. I find that most techniques we practice begin touching Uke's COB approximately 85% of the way up the orb.

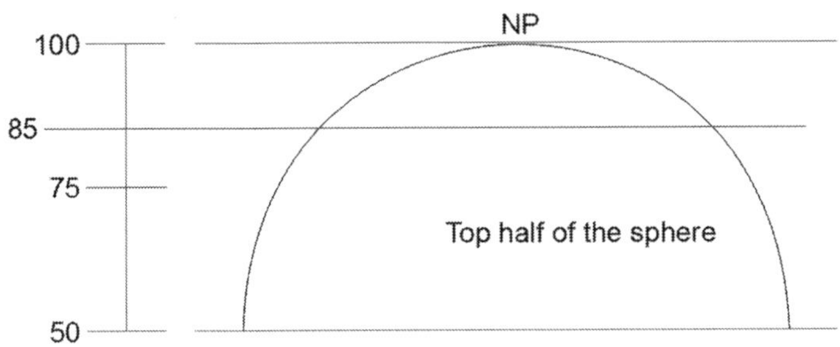

Illustration of where 85% of the way up the orb is located

Since we do not typically start on the NP, we must paint the ball and trace our way upward to the NP. This is the up portion of the equation.

Any path moves away from (off) the surface of the orb, or one that goes through the COB (into the orb) ceases to be on the arc. This will result is losing the nothing but spin effect.

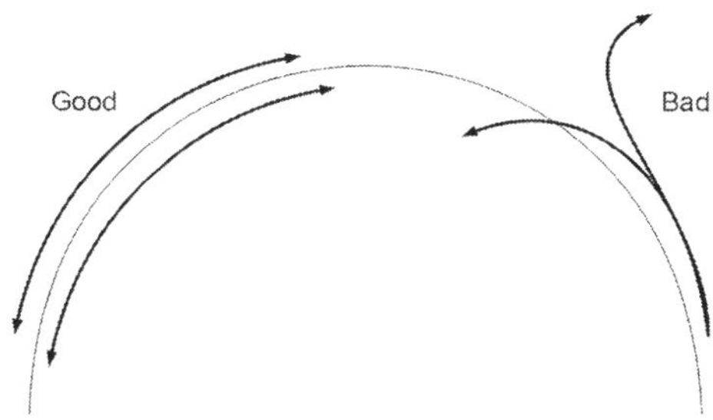

On left, moving along surface of the orb; on right, going through or off surface

The second trick is to know when you have reached the NP. Once you make it to the NP, you must stop moving upward and begin heading over (downward toward the SP on the dark side of the COB).

Another quick tangent. Extension or compression at the NP is purely vertical (completely with or against gravity). Compression or extension touch (i.e., lifting or dropping) at the NP is a direct vertical touch on Uke's COB. We are not spinning Uke with direct vertical touch, we are either pushing the COB down or lifting it up. We are moving on a path from the NP directly toward the SP. That path is called the axis, and it is the line around which the body spins horizontally.

Let us explore Aiki-Sage by performing a drill from two different heights.

Aiki-Sage low

Stand facing Uke at about an extended arm's length away (~3 ft.) with your elbows dropped to your sides, hands outward, and have Uke grab both of your wrists. (This looks similar to the oval drill.)

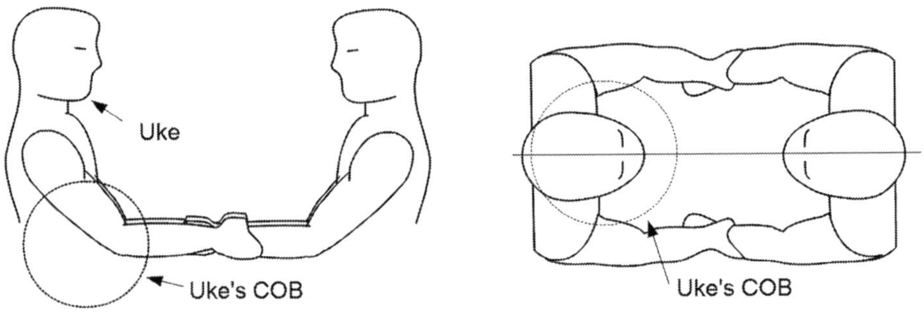

Lining up to attempt Aiki-Sage drill; Uke's COB in middle position

Follow the recipe.

Step 1: Touch Uke's center with both hands.

I suggest you use a forward cam motion (bend at the knees!) to drive your hands forward, keeping your elbows at your side. Look to see where Uke's center is and drive both hands to the sides of center, but along the bottom side of Uke's arm.

Uke should be defending himself by stiffening his arms to begin impeding (and/or redirecting) your approach.

Hmm? Uke does not have stiffened arms?

The most common problem at this first stage of the drill is reliably making Uke defend himself. In some cases, Uke is too comfortable with allowing someone to enter into their personal space. If you feel Uke is passive, have them imagine that Tori is holding a weapon. We are not asking Uke to be overactive, simply cautious that someone is driving their hands toward their torso.

It is easy to blame Uke, but the most common, and most likely, reason that you are having difficulty is that you, not Uke, are causing Uke to bend his elbows.

Do not despair. This drill is a rather advanced one, since we are not using an outright joint lock to control Uke's arm.

If you are struggling with getting the desired reaction from Uke, try experimenting with driving your hands toward differing heights along Uke's body. Try pointing at Uke's ears and see what happens. It should not work this way. It is too high. Try driving toward Uke's thighs. Too low. I think you will find the sweet spot if you drive just below the shoulder's ball joint. Another visualization we use is sliding our hands along the bottom of Uke's arm instead of driving directly into it, as if you were going to run your forearm along the bottom of Uke's, reaching for the armpit.

Keep working at it until Uke is locking out his elbows (or at least keeping an awkward, un-bendable arm). Try until you feel Uke's ring and pinky fingers providing the majority of the pressure to your forearm.

Step 2: Begin the up and over

At the point you feel his center, you have reached the outside of the orb at the 85% mark and can begin painting upward along Uke's COB. (You should notice that Uke is ever so slightly on his heels.)

The goal is to spin Uke's COB, not move it. We want to control Uke's COB with purely indirect pressures. The trick is to not drive Uke backward so far past his heels that we simply uproot him and make him step backward. This uproot is an excellent skill to develop, but it is not the goal of this drill. Guide Uke to the point that he is on his heels, but go no farther.

The orb is rather small at this height, and the arc we trying to travel along is abrupt. Depending on the height and arm-length of the persons involved, the arc should be somewhere between an oversized basketball or a medium beach ball. The up and down motion is noticeable.

Once you reach the NP, you could knock Uke down by bending your knees and driving your wrists directly down into the center of Uke's COB. (Driving downward through the center of the COB will serve to knock Uke over if Uke is amply unstable, but this is not the point we are trying to make just yet.)

Begin paying attention to the pressure Uke exerts on your wrists. As you crest the NP, you will feel the pressure from Uke's hands change considerably. It is difficult to describe exactly. You do not lose contact, but the pressure you were feeling at the underside of your wrist gets lighter. You might notice the friction between Uke's hands, and your wrists starts to dissolve as Uke falls away.

Follow the arc downward along the dark side of the COB, toward his SP. You will not get far as Uke will be falling at this point. Shed Uke as you ride over the orb.

Aiki-Sage higher

Let us take a turn at Aiki-Sage higher up on Uke by performing a drill that, in general, looks like we are simply reversing the path we took on the Aiki-Age drill (using the rings).

Place your hands on Uke's shoulders.

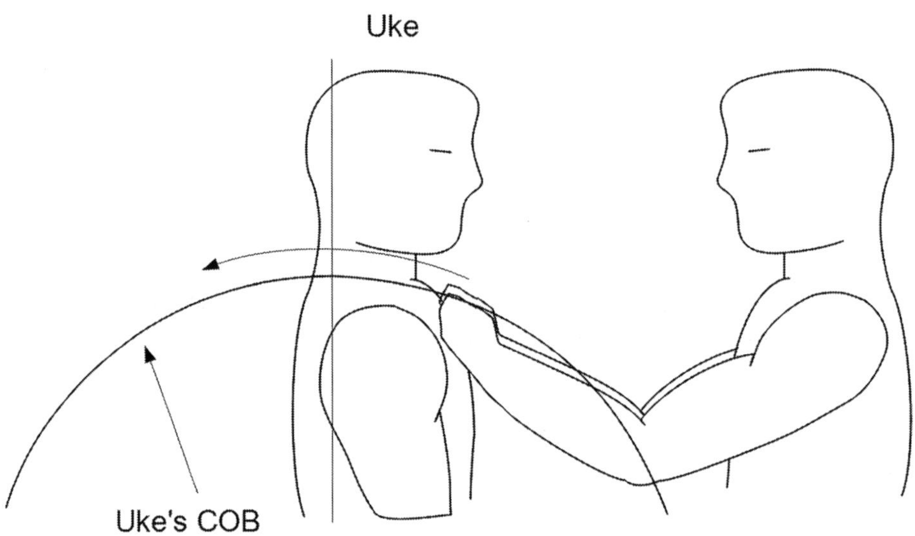

Lining up for Aiki-Sage higher; Uke's COB is pushed back against his heels

The good news is we are avoiding Uke's arm joints, but we have to take care to not apply pressure on Uke's collar bone(s). You are doing this drill incorrectly if you are hurting Uke.

The bad news here is that the actions we take here are going to be very subtle and very slight. The arc we need to follow is not as pronounced as before. Chances are that you will need to back off on the pressure and move slowly in order to develop awareness.

I suggest Uke stands in a double-weighted stance. It is typically easiest if you push along Uke's no-line. Find the no-line and drive both hands parallel to it.

We want Uke's sagittal plane in the center so that the trip to the NP will be much more predictable. By moving both hands at equal distances to the sides of the sagittal plane, we gain the benefit of using equal horizontal pressure with both hands.

We are going to begin by touching Uke's center.

If Uke is not on his heels, you will find that the trip to putting him there is a short one. With very little distance, you will be at the point where you can drive Uke off his heels. You have gone too far if Uke is stepping backward.

Begin the up and over.

Remember that the arc at this stage is much more slight than it was when we were working lower and closer to the center.

We are again using a compression, so trace along the outside of the orb, but keep pressure toward the center of the COB at all times.

Uke should fall out from underneath your arms.

Keep practicing to use less and less force to knock Uke down.

Connection builders summary

Lever arms and daito hands are how we influence Uke's center into an Aiki-Age or Aiki-Sage motion.

By touching Uke's center and allowing one person to lean on the other, we begin controlling balance and stability.

In practicing the final two precepts, what you will begin to find is that you borrow from the earlier precepts as way to fine tune the technique you are working on.

I am beginning to see glimpses of the first five precepts blending into Age/Sage.

These first five do not disappear, instead, all six precepts are beginning to look like the same action.

It is almost as if you need to see all six sides to understand that, together, they make up a six-sided die.

No one side is more important than the other. You cannot see all sides at once. If any one side was flawed or if there was no distinction between the sides, the die would cease to have purpose.

Once you know it is a die, you can give it a higher purpose. You can begin to play different games with it. You can focus on one side or the other to load that die and make it more predictable.

Find all six precepts within your techniques. It may begin by isolating each precept, but the magic begins as you study how they relate to each other within the technique.

Eventually, put the die back together and start playing again.

These precepts are not themselves a kata. The precepts are part of Aiki kata. They have always been there, just not highlighted or simply unrecognized.

The difference you create will be in your awareness. You will most clearly recognize what went correctly and what went awry (if anything). You will find your Aikido will be much more predictable, even as you venture outside of the kata.

If your experience is anything like mine, you will find out how little you understand.

The small bits written in this book are only the basest of description. There are so many other ideas yet to share, even about these precepts, but that will have to be done after I get a chance to absorb them for myself.

One last section before we part: "How to roll the dice." In other words, the secret to Aiki.

The Secret to Aiki

Many of you came to this section first. No mistake in that. I would have too if I had not had to write the rest of the book first.

I sincerely wish that someone had told me the secret to Aiki at the beginning of my training. Oh, the wasted years!

Those of you that skipped to this section should keep in mind that this is only one half of the story. The precepts tell the other half.

Enough suspense, but I warn that the following explanation(s) will not be as meaningful without an understanding of the precepts. I am not going to hold back using language established earlier in the book.

The abbreviated version of the secret is: pin and spin. Pin Uke's COB (center of balance) against the edges of his stance, and spin the COB.

Pin and spin is the root principle of Aiki. It is the basic math of Aiki.

We have a couple of names for this concept. When it first came to me I called it grinding the pearl against the glass. Others like to call it ball to the wall (this description only covers the first half of the equation, the pin). I now refer to it as pin and spin.

All are accurate, because they mean something specific to those who created them. I invite you to come up with your own description.

You would probably be better equipped to create your own description if I explain some more, huh? (Well, if you have read the rest of the book, I think you already have it figured out, but for those that do not know what the COB is and how it moves, keep reading. But good luck!)

On the mat, Aiki is demonstrated by controlling Uke's (and our own) balance and stability.

Balance and stability are related but are very different animals. Think of balance as the measure of support and stability as a measure of wobbliness.

Destabilizing Uke softens his structure and permits us to remove his support.

Let us look at the two siblings: balance and stability. We will make certain we understand their definitions, and then show how pin and spin affect balance and stability.

Balance

Balance is binary in the sense that either you have balance or you do not. There is no in-between.

Judging the condition of balance is simple: Are you falling? If you are falling, you have no balance; the structure that stood between your COB and the floor is gone. That structure is called your support. Balance cannot exist without a support to balance upon. If you are not falling, something is holding you up and you are balancing on that support.

Falling is gravity taking over and trying to re-introduce your COB to the floor. Relatively speaking, gravity is directing you downward and it is irresistible. (There is the temporary condition where we overcome gravity's pull by jumping upward, but unless you have the uncanny ability to reach escape velocity by leaping, you are going to start moving toward the earth again. What goes up...)

Do not confuse contact with the floor as having a support. If your legs buckle (completely relax), you may have contact (touch) with the floor, but your legs (that once acted as a structure) are now compromised.

While falling, unless equipped with a personal propulsion device (e.g., mini-jet engines or rocket pack!), we have nothing to push against to direct our motion. Gravity, inertia, or our opponent is in complete control.

It really is simple. If nothing is holding you up, you are falling. Balance is the condition when something is holding your COB at a particular distance from the ground. We have our balance when we possess active control over that support throughout our motion.

Quick note, I do not define balance as being rooted. I find that rooting or rootedness is a combination of balance and stability. Let us look at stability and maybe you will better understand what I mean.

Stability

Stability is wobbliness or strength of support. How much effort will it take to topple something? (Take note that I said topple and not crush! We topple Uke, we do not deform him.)

Stability is a gray area. Stability has perspective. Stability is constantly changing and has multiple states at the same time. You may be stable from the perspective of one vector of force and completely lacking stability from another. (And all degrees in-between! The Precept 1: no-line lessons should illuminate this point.)

We have learned that there is always a weak line in a stance, but that does not mean the stance is unstable. In fact, unless we are using the precepts, moving Uke along the weak lines in his stance is most likely to cause Uke to step, not fall. Uke's step will typically offer him stability against the action that led him to step.

Destabilizing Uke softens his structure and makes him easy to throw. Some might think that I am describing the word Kuzushi. I agree, but where I beg to differ is when Kuzushi is translated as "balance-break." That translation held me back for many years. Kuzushi is when Uke is unstable, not unbalanced. Breaking Uke's balance is what happens when we break/remove his support and make him fall. This is not a subtle difference. Precision in words is extremely important.

So how do we destabilize Uke?

Think about stability in everyday objects. Which is more stable: an object with a wide base, or one with a narrow base?

Ask yourself, "In which direction will the ice cream sugar cone stand best: on the wide side or on its point?"

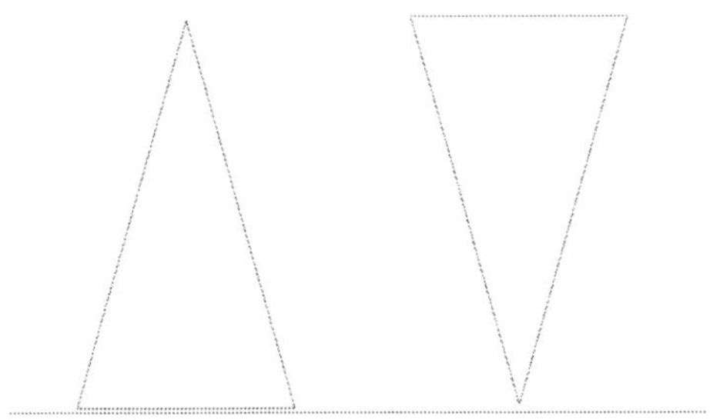

Ice cream sugar cone in two standing positions; which is most stable?

A wider base (the cone upside down on its wide mouth; on left) will be the most stable. Why?

Stability is primarily a measure of how far the COB is from the edge of the base (support) and secondarily upon how much of the mass is over (above) the base area.

If we use a top down view of the cone from the picture above, we can see two very different bases:

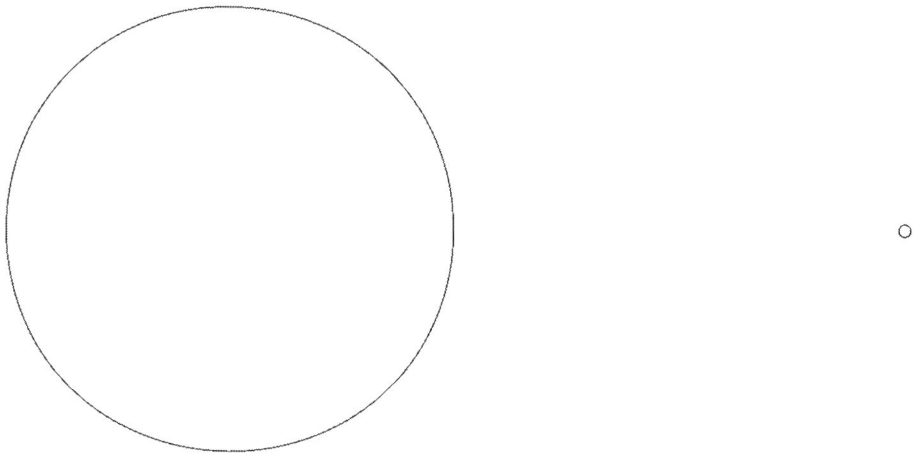

Top down view of the parts of the cones in contact with the floor; their bases

Which one of these would you rather try to stand on? We know the COB is smaller than a speck of dust, but even a speck of dust would have trouble standing on the base to the right.

Consider how much of the cone itself is sitting above these bases. The cone on the left (wide base) has 100% of its body above the base. The cone on the right has nearly all of its body hanging off the base. The cone on the left is completely balanced. The cone on the right is experiencing what you might call a precariously balanced condition. The cone on its point has to have a perfect spread of its mass or one side will pull down on the others.

So what?

Both objects are balanced. They are not falling, but one is more likely to topple than the other.

What will be the effect if we add weight to any part of the cone to the left (wide base)? Not much in the way of falling, huh? We can add enough weight to over-burden and eventually crush the cone. But it is going to be very difficult or near impossible to topple or knock this cone down by adding weight.

How much influence is needed to topple the cone on its point? Hardly any. The cone on the right lacks stability. In fact, the wind could blow and knock this object down. We could easily topple the cone by adding weight at almost any point on the cone.

Instability = wobbliness = Kuzushi. They measure how well you are supported.

Getting to the pin

I can almost hear you object, "Uke is not a cone!"

I agree, but he does have a base and we can use the same principles to destabilize him. Once Uke is destabilized, he becomes easy to topple (throw).

We have two options to destabilize Uke. Both options perform the same action: they bring Uke's COB to the edge of his base.

The first option is to leave Uke's base intact and then shift his COB to the edge of his base (move Uke's COB). I call that one "pearl against the glass" (others prefer "ball to the wall"). The second option is to reduce Uke's base. This option means we shrink Uke's base. The COB gets closer to the edge because the walls of the base close in on it. Sounds fancy, but it typically means that we make Uke stand on one foot. (It could also mean we get him to bring his feet closer together, or close his stance.)

Here is a quick repeat of Uke's base shapes. See the basic terms section for the additional explanation.

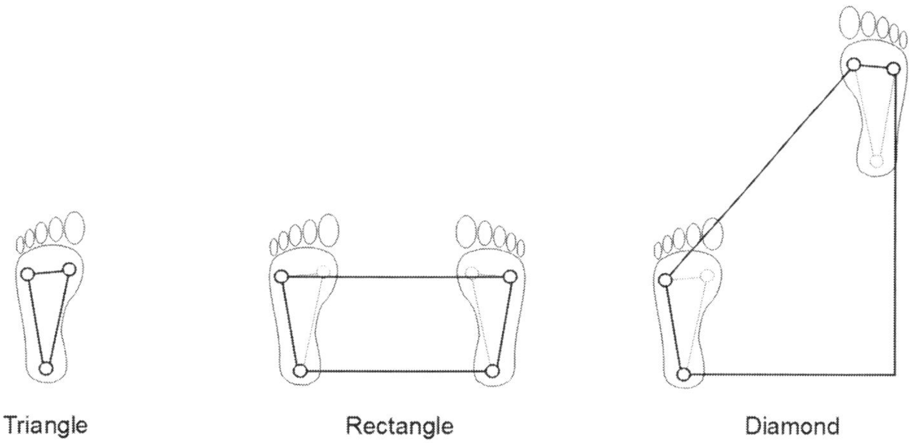

Uke's (and our) base shapes: the triangle in our feet, double-weighted rectangle, and diamond

Pearl against the glass

Each edge of the base shapes acts like a pane of glass. That glass extends upward from the floor to the ceiling. It is almost as if Uke is walking in a glass case.

The edges of the base shapes, the glass walls, are the lines of instability. You grow unstable as your COB gets near these walls.

Do not believe me? Try it!

Stand on one foot and shift your COB to the edges of your foot. You will feel stable with your COB stuck in the arch of your foot, but get that "edge of the cliff" feeling as you let the COB get close to your toes (the flat front glass wall of the foot) or that "about to fall backward" feeling as the COB nears your heels (near the point of the triangle).

Move your COB to the edge of any stance you desire. You should always feel balanced (supported), but definitely not as strong as you were while your COB was in the middle of the stance.

Shifting weight is the common way persons describe shifting the COB. We can shift Uke's weight just as easily as we shift our own, if we leverage the precepts! (This is why connection is so important. Connection allows us this control over Uke's COB.)

Uke will remain standing as long as his COB remains stationary (not spinning) within the field of the base shape. Bring Uke's COB to the glass wall, but do not breach the wall. (Do not break the glass!) If the COB breaches the wall, Uke will step and we have to start over.

Is bringing the ball to the wall a bit confusing? It may help to imagine a plumb-bob dangling from the bottom of Uke's COB. As Uke's COB moves, so too does the plumb-bob. The diagram below shows Uke in the starting positions. Shift his body so the COB drifts to the walls.

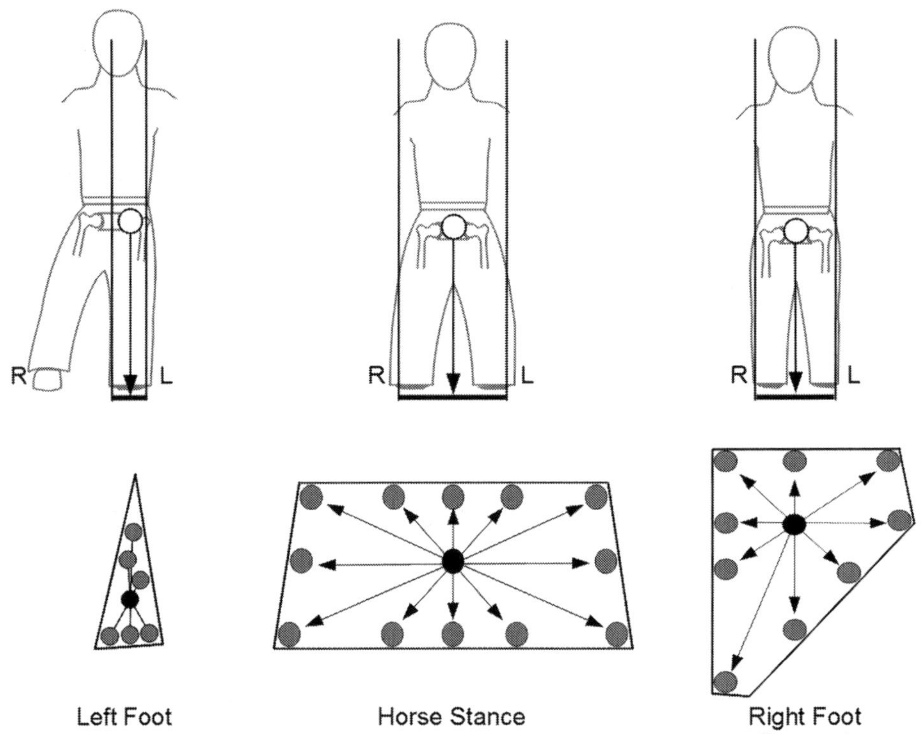

The base shapes; moving the COB around inside the base shapes; imagining the plumb-bob

Having Uke's COB against the edges of the stance is what it means to pin Uke against his stance.

We are in perfect position to spin Uke's COB, but let us first take a look at reducing Uke's base.

Reducing the base

For most applications, reducing the base means we make Uke balance himself on one foot.

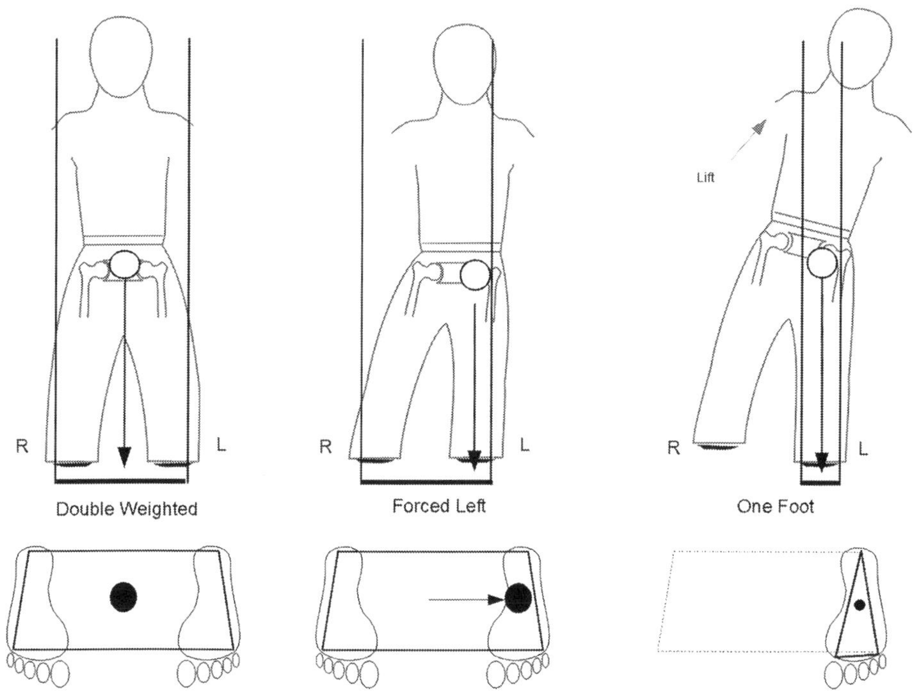

Shifting Uke's weight to one side; with a little lift, putting Uke on one foot; reducing Uke's base

It is not that difficult to put Uke on one foot, but it comes with a drawback. It is extremely easy to push Uke too far and breach the wall while Uke is on one foot. There is only a little wiggle room between breaching the wall and keeping Uke's COB in his arch or on the edges of his base (triangle). If we drive Uke's COB through the glass wall, he steps and we start again.

Uke is pinned, let us spin

Are you ready to topple Uke?

Uke is very pliable when he is unstable. (Everyone is, even the big people!)

Uke will remain unstable as long as his COB remains pinned against the wall, but unstable is not unbalanced. So how do we unbalance him? Where do we go now that we do not want to move Uke (and breach the wall)? Easy! We spin him!

The spin is an indirect touch to the COB. On the horizontal plane, we indirectly touch the COB and cause Uke's COB to rotate clockwise or counter-clockwise. (Top-down perspective, use the belts!) On the vertical plane, say hello to Aiki-Age and Aiki-Sage. Combine the techniques if you so desire. Get super fancy and start playing with Mobius strips.

The spin works because, while Uke is unstable, his structure is doing all it can to provide support. The spin creates torque within the support structure and that torque destroys the support. No support, no balance; a true balance-break is created, and Uke falls.

The spin should grind the COB against the wall of Uke's base. This is where grinding the pearl against the glass came from.

Spinning Uke's center is a bit trickier than it sounds. You must take care to keep Uke's center against the wall until he is falling. If your spin forces Uke's center to breach the wall, he will likely step and we will have to start over again. If the spin moves Uke's center away from the wall and back into the field of his base, Uke is most likely to regain his stability and control over the position of his COB.

You can grind the pearl against the glass without spinning it, much like someone would rub a ball of soap on a glass. In other words, you can make Uke's COB drop upward, downward, or even make the COB run parallel to the floor, along the inside of the walls. These actions are not as likely to cause Uke to fall, but are an excellent way to set Uke up for a specific throw (e.g., if you wanted to control the throw in such a way as to assist in stopping multiple attackers). I think you will find it easier to throw Uke when the COB is positioned in one of the corners of his stance.

Spinning or rubbing the COB against the walls of instability relies on the center of the COB staying at a consistent distance from the wall.

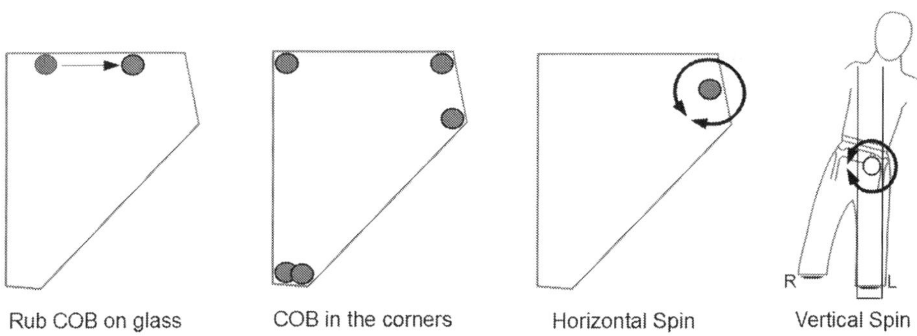

Rubbing COB on glass (no spin); COB in the corners of the stance; horizontal spin on COB when against the glass, and vertical spin on COB when against the glass (reduced-base, aka triangle of the foot base)

A quick thought about spinning vertically (advanced nuance to compression and extension in Aiki-Age and Aiki-Sage): Extension connection must be directed outside the base, and compression connection must be directed into the base.

Extension always leads to the spaces outside the base. Bring the COB to the wall and, while applying Aiki-Age or Aiki-Sage, be certain to keep your focus directed anywhere but inside the base of Uke's stance. You should also exclude moving Uke parallel to the floor, as this becomes a horizontal motion and ceases to be Age/Sage. You will find that there is a border of about six to twelve inches around the base that will create the optimal results. You can liken this to a pulley system, where our tug on the rope spins the pulley. The desired effect on Uke is diminished greatly if we direct our force inward, toward the field of the base.

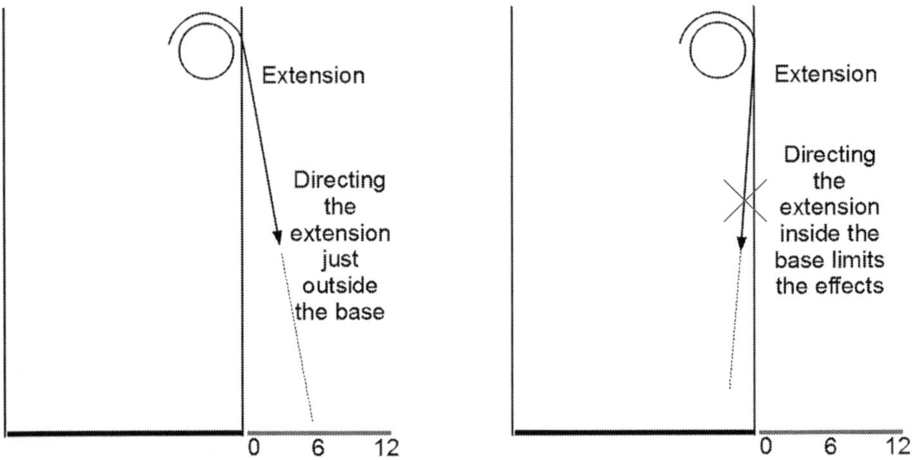

Extension applied just outside the base is much preferred to directing inside the base

Compression is the opposite. Always direct your compression into the base. Bring the COB against the wall and then rotate inward. It can be tricky, but be certain you keep the focus inside Uke's base. Many times I find that compression is difficult when Uke has a small, reduced base. It is easy to go too far and out the other side of the base.

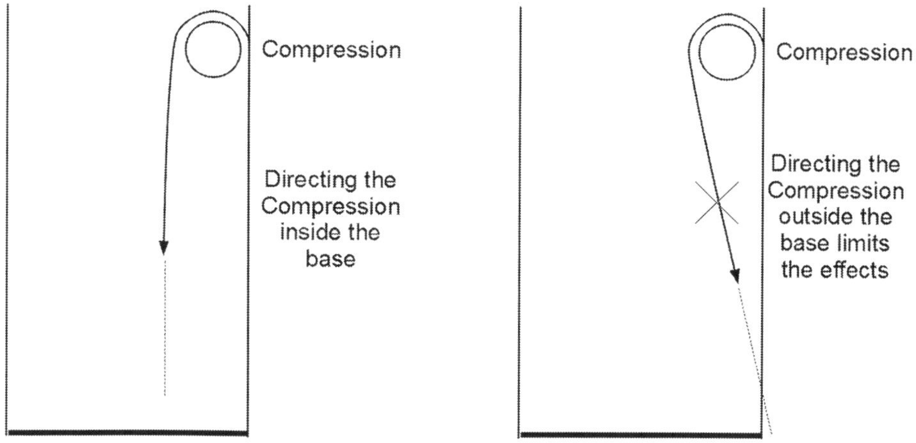

Compression should stay inside the base;
compression directed outside the base lessens the effects

I think you will find that a strict horizontal or vertical spin is great for explanation, but limited in creativity. Find your way into more complex spins by using horizontal and vertical pressures at the same time.

In Conclusion

I recently learned something about math. I used to think of math as a game of numbers. I realize now that math is actually pattern recognition. Mathematicians build upon frameworks of truth to reveal predictability and utility. (For example, 1 +1 = 2, which in itself needed to be proven.)

It struck me that this book is in parallel to that search for reliability or truth in patterns. I feel this book represents the basic "math" of Aiki. Certainly, this book is just the foundational arithmetic of Aiki. The next book (should there be one) is already cooking and looks a bit more like the algebra of the art. I hope to know what it is like to play Aiki on the level of doctorate mathematician. Dare to dream!

I hope that you find these patterns useful.

I hope that you will build upon these patterns to reveal even greater predictability.

I hope that, if you reject these patterns, you take the time to share yours.

In any case, I hope we begin to free ourselves from the suffering that kata brings. May we never rely solely on "just do as I do" as a means to transfer this art. "Just do this" is awkward and, over time, waters down the beauty and effectiveness of Aiki. Get your head in the game, use your words, spiral out, and keep going.

Oh and by the way, I did receive my Shodan rank in May 2009. It took much longer than expected to compile this book. This book only covers the first two and a half years of my recent experience. As predicted, I have already looked back on this training and see areas that have evolved in a major way. There is so much more to share! Let's play some day, and I will let you in on the rest of the secrets.

12763357R00175

Printed in Great Britain
by Amazon.co.uk, Ltd.,
Marston Gate.